BENEDICT ARNOLD The Fighting General

"For the Love of My Country"

By Greg Zoller

Copyright © 2020 by Greg Zoller
Nightwood Design
All rights reserved
First edition
Produced and printed in the United States of America

(Below) Peggy Shippen Arnold with her daughter Sophia, by artist Daniel Gardner, part of collection of Philadelphia History Museum. Loving and devoted wife and mother, Peggy had seven children with Benedict. Five survived to adulthood. Peggy always referred to Benedict as 'her general.'

(Facing page)
General Benedict Arnold
General Arnold was described as "handsome faced, muscular, and well made." A soldier wrote: "There was not a wasted timber on him." Oil painting of Benedict Arnold by Doug Henry, courtesy of the late Bill Stanley, past president of the Norwich Historical Society.

BENEDICT ARNOLD The Fighting General

"For the Love of My Country"

By Greg Zoller

*This book is dedicated to the memory of
Major General Benedict Arnold.*

*Without his efforts and sacrifice, the United States of America
would never have gained its independence.*

CONTENTS

1   What was it like to be an early American colonist?
2   Benedict Arnold: A young boy to a man in a Hell of a hurry
3   The War Begins
4   America's First Victory
5   War Growing Throughout New England & The Entry of "King" George W
6   From Victories in the North to Deep Despair & Heartbreak
7   The Two Bulls: Washington & Arnold Meet
8   Mission Impossible, 1775 Style
9   Fight to Control the St. Lawrence & Quebec: The Two-Prong Attack Begins
10   Storming Quebec: Liberty or Death
11   The Start of 1776 & the Longest Cold Winter
12   The Battle for Canada Ends & The Battle for Survival of the Colonies Begins
13   Commodore Benedict Arnold – Father of the American Navy
14   An Uneasy Winter of '76
15   The Cause of Liberty – Above All Else
16   The Political Arena – 1777
17   The Northern Threat to Crush American Resistance
18   The Dark Eagle
19   General Arnold at Saratoga
20   A Long & Painful Winter for Arnold & America
21   Capital Commander & Introduction to Politics 1778
22   1780 – Arnold Teetering on the Edge & So is America
23   Why He Went to the Other Side Explained
24   The French Alliance Ramping Up – Arnold's Allegiance Winding Down
25   August 1780 – Arnold Takes His West Point Post Seriously
26   Joshua Hett Smith
27   Colonel James Livingston
28   Arnold Getting Bold & Sloppy With His Secret Communications
29   Arnold's First Meeting With The Brits Literally Almost Sunk
30   The Plot Thickens
31   Benjamin Tallmadge: A Man with a Mission & An Ax to Grind

32 A Week of Very High Intrigue
33 Another Plan Begins to Hatch
34 Arnold Wants to Meet With the British Washington Meets the French & Tallmadge Plots Revenge
35 September 20th – The Secret Meeting Date – Oops!
36 Another Missed Meeting – What's Going on?
37 Arnold Gets His Face-to-Face Meeting–
38 All Hell Breaks Loose Andre – Trapped Behind Enemy Lines
39 How to Get Mr. Anderson (Andre') Back?
40 The Famous Capture
41 The Dangerous Parcel of Papers
42 Tallmadge Gets the Capture Under Control – Now the Parcel of Papers
43 Decision Made!
44 Washington Has a Big Mess to Clean Up & It Must Go His Way
45 The Clean-up Continues & Andre's Trial Begins
46 The Trials at Tappan
47 The Aftermath – The War was Far From Over
48 On to London & Canada
49 Very Important Conclusions & Questions
    Bibliography and Sources
    Actual Letters
    Endnotes
    Index

ACKNOWLEDGMENTS

I must acknowledge many historians in my research, especially the very detailed work of historians Russell M. Lea, author of *A Hero and A Spy: The Revolutionary War Correspondence of Benedict Arnold*; Richard J. Koke, author of J.H. Smith: *Accomplice in Treason*, and who is also curator of the New York Historical Society; and James Kirby Martin, scholar of the American Revolution and also author of *Benedict Arnold: Revolutionary Hero*.

Information was gleaned from other great sources, including the Library of Congress, the New York State Archives and numerous others I can't remember over 40 years of research.

Credit goes to my family, especially my patient wife Martha (Marty) Zoller, for putting up with me and my obsessions with history. Thanks go to the many friends who helped with research and encouraged me to write down and produce this historical work, especially Gail Wagner for her research; Paulette Likoudis, editor; Lou Robinson, publisher; and Randolph G. Flood, of the American Revolution Consortium for Civic Education.

I must acknowledge encouragement and help from Kathryn Mapes, PhD; R. Joseph Talbert, document examiner; and Rusty Wise, retired USAF chief who accompanied me on many trips to historical sites and talks.

I must also acknowledge my loving parents, Doug and Dolores Zoller, for their unending support.

Thanks go to all readers who look at history with interest and an open mind. Our early American history was mostly written many years after the actual events happened. The early authors looked for good guys, bad guys and happy endings. I hope my readers will be just as intrigued by truthful and focused accounts with no spin.

INTRODUCTION

I grew up in central New York State, working long, hard hours in the dairy industry. I worked my way up to the position of herdsman and then specialized in herd management records.

Eventually, I saved enough money to put myself through Cornell University's horseshoeing program, then started my own draft horse business. I now employ myself as a full-time farrier and blacksmith.

You could say my life has always been a series of hard work and long hours. As I raised my family and pursued my varied interests, one obsession I have always had was a keen interest in early American history.

I will not pretend to be a skilled writer or historian – I'm an amateur at best. During my studies, I ran across a theory and a story that I felt had never been told.

For centuries, we have been presented with a combination of myths and legends. To me, history needs to be looked at with honesty and integrity. To me, history is just as fun and interesting without any spin and is a valuable insight to how we live today.

My interest in the story of General Benedict Arnold came from links to my family history. My family moved to central New York in 1722. They were Palatine German farmers.

My seven times great grandfather was one of the first settlers in the Mohawk Valley of Central New York. He survived the French & Indian War and was burned out by the Mohawk Indians three times. His sons and other relatives served in the Tryon County militia. Three members of my family fought – and some died – in the Battle of Oriskany. One family member served as a scout and may have briefly served under General Arnold.

I also had a family member who served as a scout during the Revolutionary War. He scouted between Fort Plain in New York and Fort Stanwix – now Rome, New York.

In succeeding generations, one family member even married a Mohawk woman. So, family stories of early American history have always piqued my interest.

The stories I learned of General Benedict Arnold never matched what we were taught in school. As I kept digging for answers, I learned Arnold's defection never made any kind of sense. I'm not sure I would even call it on the level of treason.

So, just for my own satisfaction, I started a hobby of asking questions and looking up answers. What I discovered – I soon felt – needed to be shared. I hope to accomplish that with this book. This book will reveal many things about General Arnold you may have never heard.

General Arnold, it could be said, was the greatest war hero in the history of our nation. Also, you will learn, it's quite obvious that the papers implicating Arnold of treason were most likely planted. The love of his country was the driving force that led him to serve Great Britain.

Benedict's story has to be unfolded very carefully. In this introduction, I would like to help future historians, authors or anyone who else who wants to look into this fascinating story aware that Arnold went from a war hero to our greatest 'villain' in a very short period of time. Any information written about him after September of 1780 has to be taken with a grain of salt.

This book is meant to be a work based on history. Surely, it will be criticized, as any information that deviates from assumed facts of history would be. But I believe my theories of events are quite accurate and I feel they could be vigorously defended as truth.

One must also resist the temptation of putting our forefathers on a pedestal. They were all human beings, just like you and me.

I encourage everyone to look into their own family history. Every family has an amazing and interesting story to tell and share. You never know where your research will lead you.

CHAPTER ONE

WHAT WAS IT LIKE TO BE AN EARLY AMERICAN COLONIST?

In this book, I hope to take you on a far different journey through American history. I will strive to be very honest, unbiased and give you a perspective that deviates from the mixture of folklore we have been given for many generations.

Maybe because of my background, it gives me a far different perspective on the American Revolution. As I research history, I'm not as concerned with how the Washingtons, Franklins and Jeffersons lived, but I always seek to find out how the farmers, blacksmiths, soldiers, servants and plain folks – like myself – lived. How did they see the events unfolding and how did it affect their lives, families and why?

During my studies many years ago, I visited the home of General Philip Schuyler. He was a member of the Continental Congress and he owned very large land parcels in upstate New York. He was appointed commander of the Northern Army. His mansion near Albany, New York is beautifully restored, preserved and well worth a visit. 1

While on a tour there, a very informative guide told me that General George Washington accused Schuyler of treason, but he defended himself and Washington couldn't make the charges stick.

I started to think about that. Was there a flaw in Washington's character we weren't told about? I wondered if the accusation of treason against Benedict Arnold was really justified.

As I dug for answers, I found many perspectives and stories that were never told. The 'spin doctors' have been busy for a very, very long time.

Before I begin this tale, I need to try to put you in the shoes of an early American colonist in the late 1700s. It's almost impossible for us today to even imagine what daily life was like. For most, life in America was simply survival, even in the best of times.

If you were cold, you needed to get near a fire built with wood you gathered or cut by hand with a saw or ax. There was no running water in homes. If you needed to cook or wash, water from a nearby spring, creek or river had to be carried to the house in a handmade bucket.

Any warm water was heated over a fire. Lighting at night was rare and made only by firelight or handmade candles. Wood floors and glass windows were luxuries of the middle and upper classes. For most people, home was a one-room cabin with dirt floors and no windows.

There were no bathrooms. You went to an outhouse, outdoor latrine or into the woods when necessary. Poor sanitation led to rampant disease. This was a major concern and the reason for the rum trade. People knew they could not safely drink the water, so many added rum or made water into beer or whiskey to kill germs.

To eat, you grew, hunted and stored your own food. Most food storage was accomplished by drying or smoking or adding salt if it could be found.

If you owned a horse or an ox, the pastures for them had to be cleared by hand and stumps dug out. Fences were made of rails that you cut and split by hand. All the hay for livestock was cut by hand with a scythe or sickle, raked by hand, dried and gathered for storage away from the elements.

Every small task of daily life was labor intensive. Hand weaving and hand stitching created clothing.

If you got lucky and made it to the middle class, you could afford a frame house. All of the beam work was from timber on the land that was cut with an ax and smoothed with an adz. You would contract with a local blacksmith to make nails or hinges. Even the shingles for the roof were sawed and hand cut. That's why the average citizen settled for dirt floors and no windows.

Unemployment was not a problem or even an option. But lack of employees was a problem. America needed lots of cheap labor and that's why our forefathers wrestled with the sin of slavery. Also, for every slave there were five to seven indentured servants and tenant farmers.

Just consider our third President, Thomas Jefferson. We all know he was a great thinker and inventor, but he was given the luxury of time to accomplish what he did. To run and maintain his farm, Monticello, took a staff of 77 slaves and servants. For Jefferson to travel from Monticello to Washington – about 100 miles as the crow flies – took four days and three nights, with many river crossings. 2

Mount Vernon, President George Washington's home, was not a simple farm. To run his estate took a staff of over 200.

Life in the 1700s was a very, very heavily classed society. God help you if you were in the lower class. The middle class dreamed of high status but was looked down on by the upper class. The upper class clung desperately to their wealth, power and privilege. Almost all Americans previously came from monarchies, so they were used to dealing with aristocracies and accustomed to bowing to it.

Our First Continental Congress was comprised of almost all upper-class members, with only very few middle-class representatives included. 3

I don't want to paint an overly bleak picture of Colonial life. As hard and labor intensive as life was, many saw opportunities. The port cities were booming with trade and if you had a marketable skill or trade you could work with, you were free to start a business. Unlike anywhere else in the world, citizens felt hopeful. If they were free to use their own hands, they could find a way to build a life.

These new Americans had a huge thirst for liberty, it was easy to blame tyrannical taxation on dissatisfaction with Great Britain. But most Americans were busy just trying to survive. Close to 90 percent of colonists paid no taxes at all. Some were upset that during the Proclamation of 1763 and the Quebec Act of 1774, colonists could not lawfully settle lands west of the Appalachian Mountains.

But the Act that upset most average Americans was the prohibition against trade with nations other than Great Britain. The British required all goods to be transported on British ships, and for prices on all commodities to be determined by the brokerage houses in England. This resulted in the formation of a huge and thriving black market. Merchants and sea traders were reduced to smuggling to get the goods and prices they wanted. Large groups of people worked for the black market and/or benefited from it. People wanted the freedom to build their own lives without restrictions from England.

For that reason, many joined militia groups like the Sons of Liberty for the cause of liberty. But these were very high ideals, even for those who had the time and assets to even consider participation.

Most Continental soldiers didn't join the Army for the cause of liberty. Most saw joining as a chance for pay. Food, clothing and a promise of land pensions, if they stuck with it, were to be given in return for their service. When enlistments were up – some as short as three months – most men couldn't wait to get back home.

For all they knew, the government they were fighting for could become just as tyrannical as the one they were fighting off. The British Red Coats weren't the only danger an American soldier faced. At any given time, a third of our Army was out of action with dysentery or smallpox.

As our first Continental Congress met, many wanted to simply state grievances to King George and hopefully reconcile, but the New England states were itching for a fight to establish independence. How could they even consider raising and supplying an army to take on the British Empire? Holding the colonies together for any purpose seemed almost impossible.

There is also another aspect of the American Revolution that is rarely talked about. We had two main groups at war: the Patriots and Americans fighting the British and Loyalists.

There is also a third group especially found in any war zone. I call this group the underground survivalists. If you were a family behind British lines, you risked being labeled a rebel and could have your property, food, fuel and anything else seized. But also, if you were behind American lines you could be labeled a Tory or Loyalist and suffer the same fate.

Many people banded together and formed networks to keep up trade and pass along information. They tried desperately to hang onto their property. They tried to keep their heads low, avoid and survive this 'unfortunate conflict,' as it was called at the time. This group played a very important role in keeping normal life together.

They should be recognized, as they were large in numbers and everywhere throughout the whole war, especially in the war zones. 4

There are some other early American observations that I don't see portrayed very often. For example, prostitution in early America was quite common, but not all looked down on it. It was considered a service that some were able to provide and a basic part of colonial life.
Language was quite a problem, as many spoke German, English, Dutch, French or Spanish. Native Americans also had their own languages.

Many fleeing religious persecution set up their own communities. There were Puritans, Quakers and a variety of Protestant faiths. Many of the Protestant faiths, such as the Puritans, considered the French and French Catholics to be enemies of their faith. That attitude was even enhanced after the French and Indian Wars.

Our Native American communities also tend to be portrayed in an odd light. In the late 1700s, the days of the longhouse were long gone. Longhouses were mainly used for storage and ceremonial purposes.

During the Clinton and Sullivan Campaign, many soldiers were very surprised to find the Iroquois living on well-maintained farms with crops and orchards. They also had towns comprised of square log cabins with glass windows. It made the soldiers quite jealous to see the Indians were living quite better off than they and settlers were. 5

I hope this brief overview of Colonial life helps the understanding of what the average citizen contended with and how it helped to shape the direction of things to come.

CHAPTER TWO

BENEDICT ARNOLD
A young boy to a man in a Hell of a hurry

Benedict V came from a long line of Benedicts. It was a family tradition to name the first-born son Benedict. He had an older brother who died at less than a year old. So, the name Benedict went to him, along with the hopes and dreams of his father.

Benedict was quite proud of his early American heritage. The Arnold family were Puritans fleeing religious persecution in England. They arrived in Massachusetts in 1635. The following year, the family moved to Rhode Island, where they purchased large tracts of land – nearly ten thousand acres.

By the 1640s, the Arnold clan became some of the wealthiest colonists in Rhode Island. Benedict the first – Benedict's namesake – became the colony's governor. He was held in very high regard and had many terms in office. It was recorded that over a thousand fellow colonists attended his funeral in 1678.

As the Arnold clan grew in number, it was their tradition to practice "partible inheritance." Their land was subdivided into smaller and smaller portions among family members. By the time Benedict's father came of age, the Arnold clan – who were mostly farmers – were known as solidly middle class. Benedict's father knew that as the family grew and their parcels of acreage shrank, it made more sense for some of them to take up a trade to survive. 1

Benedict's father made the move to Norwich, Connecticut. It was a new and thriving seaport. He took his youngest brother, Oliver, with him and they set themselves up in the cooper – barrel makers – trade. The elder Benedict had a keen interest in the sea trade and had higher ambitions than simply making barrels.

Fortune smiled on him when he courted and won the hand of Hannah Waterman King. She was recently widowed. Her first husband, Absalom King, was lost at sea. Absalom was a sea trader with valuable trading ties through some very respectable upper-class families in Norwich. Hannah's very large estate, by law, went to Benedict's father when he and Hannah married in fall of 1733. 2

Benedict's father worked very hard in his new trading ventures, eventually even running his own ships to move goods from the West Indies all the way up the coast to Norwich. He held different offices in town and purchased a fine two-story house on five acres, just outside of Norwich.

The Arnolds were very religious and held tightly to their Puritan roots. The business built by Benedict's father thrived. He and Hannah enjoyed a very happy marriage. Benedict's father was affectionately known around town as "Captain Arnold."

Captain Arnold and Hannah had their first male child in 1738 and named him Benedict. He died within the year. The Benedict we know received the family surname when he was born in January of 1741.

In the following years, the Arnold family had four more children – sister Hannah in 1742; sister Mary in 1745; brother Absalom in 1747 and sister Elizabeth in 1749.

Much was expected from young Benedict. Being the firstborn, he was the apple of his father's eye.

The Arnold family not only valued their Protestant religion, but also highly valued a proper gentleman's education. By the age of 12, Benedict was enrolled in a boarding school. The family hope was that he would go on to higher institutions like the newly opened Yale University. 3

Young Benedict studied Latin, writing, mathematics and various other subjects. He seemed to excel in his studies.

There were also many comments about Benedict's athletic abilities. It was often said he was known to be one of the best skaters in New England during the long winter months.

But as Benedict reached his teenage years, his once idyllic childhood began a downward spiral.

Horrible diseases spread through the New England colonies, taking the lives of many. Benedict's younger brother, Absalom, died in 1750. In 1753, diphtheria hit almost everywhere. It was known as throat distemper.

Many children died a painful death, unable to breathe or fight off high fevers. Benedict's two youngest sisters, Mary and Elizabeth, died only 19 days apart.

By the time Benedict reached his 13th birthday, he had only one sibling left, his sister Hannah. They were very close, as they were only a year apart in age.

During these same dark family days, Captain Arnold fell on very hard times. Due to warring superpowers in the Caribbean, sea trading was nearly suspended. The people in Benedict's world put the blame of the loss of sea trade on the Spanish and French, as they considered them enemies of the Protestant religion.

At 15, Benedict heard the tales of the French and Indian War wreaking havoc on settlements in the frontier. It was said he was called up for a short stint in the militia – to help defend Albany – but was called back before he saw any action.

By 1755, Benedict's formal schooling came to an abrupt end. His family fell on very hard financial times due to the downturn in the sea trade. With the loss of his business and his children, Captain Arnold – Benedict's father – suffered deteriorating health and he began drowning his sorrows by drinking heavily.

Hannah, his mother, struggled to keep Benedict in school. He was doing so well, but as times got worse, they could no longer afford tuition. Hannah turned to some well-off relatives – the Lathrops – for help. The Lathrops were upper class graduates of Yale University. They were quite successful in the apothecary and trading businesses.

Benedict was pretty much sold into indentured servitude. He was given an apprentice contract from the Lathrop family. Benedict had more formal schooling than most his age and he readily absorbed instructions from the Lathrops.

Benedict took a keen interest in learning everything he possibly could about the apothecary business. In later years, he even touted his knowledge of apothecary as one of his finest accomplishments, even above his sea trading abilities.

The Lathrops were very impressed with Benedict's work ethics and considered him a model apprentice. They also took notice that he seemed to have a natural talent for business.

But young Benedict had to grow up quickly. Family matters turned even worse. By the time he was 18, his beloved and distressed mother passed away. His father became known for drinking in public, blemishing the once proud family name. His father was looked down upon by the upper-class Norwich community.

Benedict became responsible for caring for his father as his health failed and also for the care of his remaining sister, Hannah. By the time he reached 20, his father had died. Creditors pressed Benedict for debt payments and the family home had to be sold to settle them.

If it weren't for the kindness of the Lathrops, Benedict and his sister would have been destitute or even thrown into debtor's prison.

Benedict threw his troubles into his work. He seemed driven and determined to build back his family's name and he worked tirelessly for the Lathrops.

All Benedict went through gave him an extreme dislike for the class system, although he knew he had to deal with it. After surviving turmoil, he felt a man's deeds and actions should determine his place in society, not his connections or money. He was once known to quote an early unknown poet: "Honor and fame from no condition rise, Act well your part; There all the honor lies!" 4

With Benedict's help, the Lathrops' business continued to grow. They decided to expand the business with a new market and offered to make Benedict a partner. They offered to help set up a new apothecary in New Haven, Connecticut.

New Haven was 50 miles from Benedict's troubled early life in Norwich and he couldn't wait to get started. New Haven, the home of Yale University, was a booming seaport. The deep port hosted sailing ships that traded as far as the West Indies, New York, Boston and England.

Benedict set up his apothecary and became very popular with his customers. He knew how tough times were for many and he gladly extended credit to any in need. He sold books, medicine, rum, sugar and many other items. He advertised for "cash or short credit." 5

His customers were impressed with Benedict's knowledge of apothecary and many referred to him as "Doctor Arnold." Later, as Benedict entered Independence Hall, he was described by a congressman as "hansom in the face, muscular and well made." You might even say Benedict was one of the first 'health nuts.'

It wasn't long before the business grew to the point where he needed help and he soon moved his sister, Hannah, to New Haven to help him out.

Young Benedict was a man of extreme action. He would quickly decide to embrace every available opportunity he could. The old guard families of New Haven became a little nervous about Benedict, as he was quick to criticize the tax policies of England.

Through his need to supply goods and his connections with the Lathrops, Benedict expanded into the lucrative mercantile trading business. He formed a somewhat loose partnership with another young trader by the name of Adam Babcock. It wasn't long before they were operating three ships.

With his sister, Hannah, helping in the apothecary, Benedict's energy and drive knew no bounds. He hired sailing crews and began commanding ships up and down the East Coast. From the West Indies all the way up to Montreal, he traded molasses, horses, rum, pork, grain and timber products. His trading and sea skills grew, and he was soon known as one of the best traders and sea captains in New England.

Men like John Hancock were in the same business as Benedict and they were outraged by the heavy tax burden imposed by Great Britain. The taxes were sucking the freedom and profits from their businesses.

The trading business was not an easy one. Besides having to put deals together, owners had to manage crews of men, staff ships and face dangerous storms while traveling up and down the coast. Giving hard-earned profits to Great Britain was a very bitter pill to swallow.

Benedict was not known as an easygoing person. When he was right, he was quick tempered and if you dared to question his integrity or honor, you'd better be prepared to fight, duel or be publicly humiliated. He was a natural leader of men and they gravitated to him, respecting his strength of character and courage.

The sea trade finely honed his sailing skills and the trade he did in horses turned him into an excellent horseman and expert rider.

By 1765, tensions between the colonies and Great Britain were boiling to the surface. The breaking point was the imposition of the Stamp Act. The British government insisted stamps be placed on some 50 items, including newspapers, pamphlets, wills, land deeds, college diplomas and port clearance papers for all trading vessels. British regulators – Red Coats – were sent to enforce the law and to capture and punish any smugglers.

Groups of resistance such as the well-known "Sons of Liberty" began to organize. These men, such as Boston's Samuel Adams, were considered to be agitators. They organized through intimidation, causing the Stamp Act to be unenforceable and ineffective.

In Connecticut, there was a young lawyer by the name of Jared Ingersoll. Benedict knew him well and employed him as his lawyer. The British government named Ingersoll to be a Stamp Act distributor. 6

One day, on a trip to Hartford, Ingersoll was surrounded by the Sons of Liberty. He was in fear for his life. They made him sign a sworn statement renouncing any intention of administering the Stamp Act. They also forced him to throw his hat in the air and say he would reject Parliament's tax plan in favor of liberty and property, with three cheers. Onlookers shouted "huzzahs." After this incident, no one would step forward to be a Stamp Act distributor.

The Stamp Act and the threat of the act slowed down any significant trading in New England and threw the whole area into a severe depression. Benedict's creditors called him to account, and for a while his debts were a bit higher than his net worth. He made arrangements to settle the terms but came close to bankruptcy and debtor's prison. He had to become much more careful about extending credit to so many. After almost losing his business, Benedict had to hone his business skills.

Men like Arnold and Hancock had to resort to smuggling goods to avoid heavy taxation that was crippling their businesses and destroying profits.

One night, Benedict rocked the political elite in New Haven to its core. He was unloading a ship full of molasses in the dark to avoid paying the three cents per gallon tax imposed by Great Britain. One of the seamen threatened Benedict with blackmail, telling him that if he weren't paid a substantial amount, he would inform the port authorities about what was going on.

Benedict was not going to put up with such behavior, especially from one of his own crew. After the ship was unloaded, Benedict gathered some of his men and found the blackmailer in a tavern. He pulled the man out into the street, had him bound, flogged publicly and then told him to leave

New Haven and never return or he would meet his fate. 7

This action succeeded in keeping the colonists from siding with the British authorities, but greatly upset the upper-class authorities in New Haven. They called Benedict to account and fined him 50 pounds for disrupting order. He gladly paid but felt he had gotten his point across.

The British Loyalists and upper-class old guard of New Haven became very nervous about Benedict. On one occasion, Benedict decided to try his hand at public speaking about the merits of liberty in the town square. He must have been very good at it. The crowd was whipped into frenzy. They made effigies of some of the old guard and burned them.

Although Benedict was considered to be of a lower class, they knew they had better walk lightly around him.

But Benedict wasn't all work and no play. In 1767, he met and courted a beautiful young lady named Margaret (Peggy) Mansfield. She was the daughter of local merchant Samuel Mansfield, who was also acting sheriff of New Haven County.

Benedict won her hand and they were soon married. Over the next five years, Benedict and Peggy had three sons. Benedict VI was born in 1768, Richard in 1769, and Henry in 1772.

It was a very good and stable marriage, but always somewhat strained. Benedict was fiercely determined to make his business successful. He would be gone for months at a time, trading and shipping goods. It made Peggy quite resentful. She worked with Benedict's sister Hannah at the apothecary and was very busy raising her three sons.

By 1770, Benedict had grown his business, trading goods from the West Indies up the coast throughout New England and into Canada. In a very short time, he had become one of the wealthiest sea traders in New England. In 1770, he built a beautiful two-story home for Peggy. It was set on three acres on Water Street in New Haven. There were formal gardens, stables and a coach house. 8

Benedict was very proud of his new home, one of the best in New Haven. It was a wonderful home for his wife, children and his sister, Hannah.

The same year they moved into their new house; the Boston Massacre occurred. British sailors fired on a mob and were arrested for murder. Britain was so oppressive over the issue of taxation mainly because the Seven Years War with Spain and France had doubled her national debt. The mother country was desperate to raise funds to pay creditors. As they saw it, the colonies were acting as ungrateful, unruly children who owed the mother country support for the stability and protection it had provided. 9

By 1773 and 1774, tensions in the colonies – especially in the New England colonies – had reached the boiling point. In December of 1773, Samuel Adams addressed a crowd of some 8,000 – with no microphone – to protest the tax on tea and the crackdown on smuggling. This demonstration brought on the Boston Tea Party. Men dressed as Indians boarded an English ship and dumped her valuable cargo of tea into Boston Harbor.

A very angry king and British Parliament passed the first series of Coercive Acts around March 1774. Essentially, Boston Harbor was shut down until the tax on the dumped tea was paid. By May of 1774, Boston was put under the military rule of General Thomas Gage, commander of British forces in the colonies.

British troops set out to end self-rule by the colonies. By June of 1774, the Quartering Act required all colonists to provide housing and supplies for British troops by allowing them to occupy houses, taverns and any unoccupied buildings. Britain was determined to crush any form of rebellion.

The first Continental Congress met in the fall of 1774. The delegates knew the drums of war were beating. Fifty-six delegates, including George Washington, Samuel Adams, John Hancock, Patrick Henry and others felt forced to take action.

The delegates decided that the Coercive Acts were not to be obeyed. The colonies wanted self-rule, which they believed included life, liberty and property. They also agreed to boycott all English imports.

In late 1774, Benedict was also ready for a fight. He helped form a local militia of about 65 men in New Haven. Some were undoubtedly his crewmembers. They drilled on the green of Yale College University. They were provided with some new uniforms, probably paid for by Benedict.

The local militia voted to make Benedict their captain.

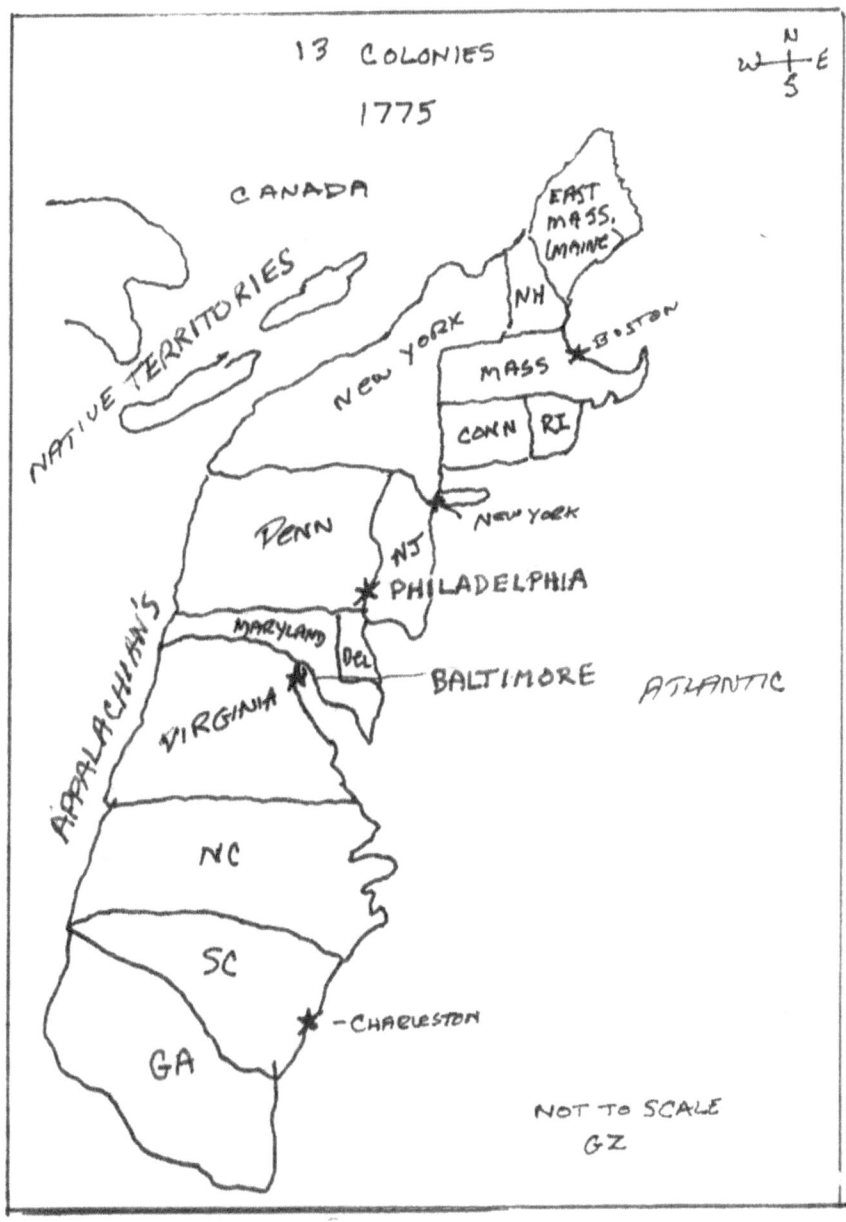

Map 1

CHAPTER THREE

THE WAR BEGINS

In April of 1775, Massachusetts Governor Thomas Gage was secretly ordered by Britain to suppress the open rebellion. He ordered 700 British soldiers to march on Concord to destroy the colonists' weapons depot. His action sparked the Midnight Ride of Paul Revere and others. John Hancock and Samuel Adams were hiding near Lexington. The British wanted them arrested for smuggling and inciting riots. Luckily, they got the message.

At the dawn of April 19, 1775, about 70 brave militiamen went toe to toe with the advance guard of the British force on Lexington Green. The 'shot heard around the world' was fired. The war was on.

The British at Concord suffered the loss of 250 men on their retreat back to Boston. The news spread quickly – for communications at the time – and militia from all over New England were called on to lay siege to British-held Boston.

When the news reached Benedict in New Haven, he quickly assembled his men. They agreed to muster and leave for Boston the next morning. Benedict also accepted a few volunteer students from Yale University to help fill the ranks. 1

The next morning, Benedict's small column received a blessing and prayers from the local reverend. People in town gathered to cheer the group on. All they were lacking were a few more weapons and they needed access to the town powder magazine.

Town authorities and prominent old guard figures were meeting at a tavern. They held the keys to the magazine. They weren't sure they wanted to get involved with this fight and wanted to get more details of what went on in Lexington and Concord. They sent a message to Benedict stating he couldn't have the keys to the powder magazine, nor could he have permission to run to Massachusetts.

Benedict then assembled his men in front of the tavern and demanded the keys, saying, "None but Almighty God shall prevent my marching." Benedict gave the keepers of the magazine five minutes to make their decision. They had no choice but to relent. 2

Once supplied, Benedict's boldness must have inspired the whole town. Most of them turned out to cheer the group of soldiers with a flurry of huzzahs as they tromped toward Boston. Along their march to Boston, Benedict's small force – probably around a nighttime campfire – gathered and wrote a pledge. It provided a good insight of their character and mindset. It was quite unusual for the times.

They wrote: "Driven to our last necessity and obliged to have recourse to arms in defense of our lives and liberties," they promised, "To conduct ourselves decently and inoffensively as we march, both to our countrymen and to one another, renouncing drunkenness, gaming, profaneness and every vice of that nature. Serving in such a great and glorious cause." 3

Also included in their intentions was a curious phrase that showed their Christian and Puritan roots. They wrote that the guidelines would go to "all Christian people believing in and relying on that God, to whom our enemies have at last forced us to appease."

Many other militia groups were covertly planning and marching to a confrontation with the Red Coats at Boston, giving up their families, their wives, their businesses, properties and the safety of their homes. Some were traveling from as far away as Virginia.

Benedict's men arrived in Cambridge by April 29, 1775. But along the march, Benedict had a meeting that would take him in a completely different direction. He met during his journey with a Colonel Samuel Parsons, also a Connecticut patriot. Parsons was returning to Connecticut with orders to recruit more troops.

Parsons informed Benedict of the dire situation around Boston and the extreme need for more ordnance, especially cannons, to drive the British forces out of Boston. In their discussion, Benedict pointed out that there were a large number of cannons that could be seized at Fort Ticonderoga on Lake Champlain. From his trading ventures in the Montreal area, he knew the old fort was lightly manned. 4

Benedict, with his business background, knew things didn't get accomplished by talking about them. He was a vigorous and extreme man of actions. Parsons, excited about Benedict's information, went directly to Hartford and met with the provincial leaders there. They saw the value of launching an immediate strike on Fort Ticonderoga. Funds were withdrawn from their treasury and Captain Edward Mott was appointed to head the strike. Herman Allen was asked to get in touch with his brother, Ethan, to enlist the help of the Green Mountain Boys.

The trek to Fort Ticonderoga was started on April 29, 1775; the same day Benedict's men arrived in Cambridge. Upon his arrival at Cambridge, Benedict provided accommodations for his men, probably supplied by money out of his own pocket. He immediately sought out Dr. Joseph Warren and other members of the Massachusetts Committee of Safety to convince them that he needed to launch a campaign to secure the ordnance at Fort Ticonderoga.

On May 2, 1775, the Committee of Safety named Benedict colonel of a force not to exceed 400 men. They would rely on his "judgment, fidelity and valor" for a secret mission to capture Fort Ticonderoga. They also supplied him with a cash amount of 100 pounds currency, 200 hundred pounds of gunpowder, 1000 flints for muskets, lead musket balls and ten horses. Along with his written orders, Benedict was authorized to draw on the committee's credit for provisions needed by the small army. 5

Benedict knew that time was of the essence since the British would be moving to reinforce the garrisons of the Lake Champlain region. He was not a patient man. Armies moved much too slowly for his liking. As he rode west through Massachusetts, Benedict was probably thinking of the acclaim he would receive if he could capture Fort Ticonderoga and its ordnance. He made the decision to ride ahead of his men. They knew where they were going, but he just couldn't wait any longer. He rode day and night at breakneck speed toward Fort Ticonderoga.

Along the journey, Benedict got word that the Mott and Allen venture was already in progress. He was likely hoping to ask the Green Mountain Boys to join his men. He heard they were meeting at Remington's Tavern in Castleton. Benedict arrived too late for the meeting, but some of the rear guard of the Green Mountain Boys was still at the tavern.

Benedict showed them his orders from the Massachusetts Committee of Safety and informed them he intended to lead the command of the strike force. They probably weren't that impressed, as all Benedict had were some papers and an army, days behind. They told him Allen was their leader, and that they were gathering at Shoreham, the starting point of the attack.

Exhausted from his ride, Benedict spent the night at the tavern and early on the morning of May 9 left for Shoreham, hoping to take command of the Mott and Allen strike.

The Green Mountain Boys were a renegade militia movement based in the mountains of Vermont and New Hampshire. They were a very rugged group of farm settlers who had banded together for their own protection. In today's vernacular, they would be known as mountain warlords. They had no qualms about carrying out raids on Loyalist properties. There was even a reward posted by the Governor of New York for Ethan Allen's head, as a result of raids conducted across the border. The Green Mountain Boys were hoping the capture of Fort Ticonderoga would give them legitimacy as part of the patriot coalition.

Fort Ticonderoga was a large fortress originally positioned by the French in 1755 to fortify the Lake Champlain region. That region, stretching from Canada through the Richelieu River to Lake Champlain to Lake George to the Hudson River to Albany to New York City, was the main travel and supply chain from north to south in the colonies' rough interior. There weren't many roads, but the route would be the equivalent of Route I-95 today. A number of small fortresses protected the Champlain region. Fort Ticonderoga was the oldest and largest fort on the lake.

Benedict caught up with the Mott and Allen contingent about noon that very day, May 9. There was much friction at first, but Benedict claimed command by holding legitimate paperwork issued by the Massachusetts

Committee of Safety. However, the Green Mountain Boys weren't going to be led by anyone but Ethan Allen. When the dust settled, all agreed to a joint command. Benedict's small army was on the way, but days behind. Fort Ticonderoga was still very lightly garrisoned. 6

There were many accounts – favoring one or the other – of how the meeting of Allen and Benedict went down. One report stated that Ethan was in his tent, despondent over how the fort could be attacked, when Benedict burst in and shoved him around, saying, "We're not only going to the fort, but we're going to do it tonight!" 7 As Benedict waved his papers around, it could have been where the phrase 'you and what army' originated. The best guess is that Ethan and Benedict reached a mutual agreement. 8

While all of this was going on, the Second Continental Congress was meeting in Philadelphia. The delegates elected John Hancock as president of the congress and George Washington as commander-in-chief of the new Continental American Army.

But the delegates didn't make any snap decisions. It took them from May 10, 1775 to June 15 to agree on a state of defense, who would lead it, and other details. Benedict and other patriots were already fully engaged in the war. Regardless of how events unfolded at Fort Ticonderoga, it was a surprise attack.

CHAPTER FOUR

AMERICA'S FIRST VICTORY

At approximately four in the morning, under darkness, only one sentry was on duty. Allen and Benedict led the charge through the gates and into the parade ground. The lone sentry rushed to get help, but the whole garrison was caught completely off guard. It turned out to be a bloodless victory. By the time British commander Captain William Delaplace was awakened, the successful attack was nearly over. He surrendered to Allen and Benedict, negotiating prisoner of war rights for his 44 men, 24 women and children.

Much to Benedict's disgust, the Green Mountain Boys found 90 gallons of rum and proceeded to celebrate their victory, getting very drunk and looting the fort. He knew that once they sobered up and had their fill of loot, they would disappear back to the mountains, as they all had crops to attend to.

Two days later, the rebels took a smaller fort to the north, known as Crown Point. It, too, fell easily since only nine British regulars garrisoned it. Within four days, the Green Mountain Boys began slipping home in small groups with what loot they could find and some of Benedict's men began filtering into the area.

By the 14th of May 1775, Benedict no longer had a disputed claim to command. His army had finally caught up with him. With his victories, he secured 201 artillery pieces, with over 100 in good, usable condition. 1

But resting wasn't in Benedict's vocabulary. He was already making plans to secure the whole Champlain region. Opportunity knocked when a good-sized schooner – owned by a wealthy, confirmed Loyalist – was captured in Skenesborough by the Green Mountain Boys on their way to

Fort Ticonderoga. They turned it over to Eleazer Oswald, a good friend of Benedict's. They knew little about sailing, so it was of no use to them.

Benedict couldn't wait to get his sea legs back again. Because of his trading ventures, there wasn't anything about sailing he didn't know.

He had the schooner fitted with two cannons; six swivel guns and renamed the ship *Liberty*. America's first war ship sailed north toward Canada, accompanied by bateaus found in the area. Bateaus were small, flat-bottomed craft similar to rowboats. They could be rowed or pulled along rivers. Sometimes they were improvised with small sails to lessen rowing.

The tiny navy sailed north with an objective. Benedict knew that in the area there was a main supply ship used by the British to transport troops and goods to forts along Lake Champlain. That mission alone should have given Benedict credit as the father of the American Navy.

At the lake's end, Benedict selected 35 of his best, most able men. They rowed all night and made a surprise raid at St. John's, where the British supply sloop was moored. The small British garrison was caught completely off guard. The sloop, more bateaus and two more cannons were secured for America. In addition, 20 Redcoats were captured as prisoners.

They sailed off with their prizes and destroyed any remaining transport the British had stored there before British reinforcements could arrive from Montreal. Now, even if the Brits wanted to attack the southern forts on the lake, they would have to build ships and bateaus first. America's first little navy now controlled the whole lake region.

As Benedict sailed south, he met up with Ethan Allen and about 100 of the Green Mountain Boys. They were rowing hard to try and catch up with Benedict and had dreams of more plunder at St. John's. Benedict gave them some more food, which they were in short supply of. 2

Benedict invited Allen aboard ship and tried to make amends for stepping on toes a few days earlier. They had a drink together and toasted the Second Continental Congress that was meeting in Philadelphia. Allen decided he wanted to go on to St. John's with his boys. Benedict told him there was no point to his mission. They had already captured the ships, and surely, British reinforcements would be coming down from Montreal.

Allen, being quite strong-willed himself, wanted to go on to raid any remaining supplies in the St. John's area. Benedict continued south and was found to be correct. By the time Allen's men got to St. John's, they ran into a column of 200 British regulars coming in to reinforce the area. As Allen's men faced cannon fire and grapeshot, somehow most of them escaped and made their way back down the lake with their tails between their legs. That failure furthered Benedict's reputation as a superior commander and left Ethan Allen a little embarrassed and jealous.

As an experienced ship commander who was very detail oriented, Benedict set about readying his troops at Fort Ticonderoga with regular drills and discipline. He refitted the captured British ship and renamed it *Enterprise*. He also readied the captured cannons for the trip back to Boston.

The loss of the whole Champlain region and the corridor from Canada to the south was a huge embarrassment for Great Britain. British Governor Carlton in Canada wrote to England that some 'horse jockey' named Arnold had led the rout of the area. 3

The Second Continental Congress was made quite upset by Benedict's actions. They supposed themselves to be in a defensive posture in America, but Benedict had made the situation into an offensive war by openly striking British strongholds all the way to Canada. Many moderate congressmen were doing more than just a little hand wringing. Their hope of reconciliation with Great Britain was slipping away. Also, as politics often go, others were trying to suppress Benedict's reputation and take credit for themselves.

Benedict was learning the hard way that merits and actions alone weren't enough to win acclaim. Politics in the early Revolution was a vicious dog-eat-dog business that Benedict wasn't accustomed to. Each state had its own militias and individuals seeking glory for themselves. There was no unified mission or government yet.

By June 10th of 1775, the wrangling reached its boiling point in the field. Benedict was returning from a scouting mission on Champlain to his temporary headquarters at Crown Point. Ethan Allen, James Easton and some of the Green Mountain Boys confronted him. Allen announced himself as legitimate commander of the region. Easton, a tavern keeper with military aspirations, carried out-of-date papers with instructions from the Massachusetts Congress.

Benedict held his temper and said he was willing to give up command when anyone with proper authority appeared to take it. Allen and Easton had to step back because all the soldiers were clearly backing Benedict.

The next morning, all hell broke loose. Allen's party intended to leave the fortifications without "showing their passes" to the sentry. Easton hurled insults at Benedict. He reached his breaking point, which wasn't that high to begin with. Benedict demanded that Easton "draw like a gentleman" and grabbed Easton, who was armed with a cutlass and pistols. He considered Easton a lying, dishonest coward. 4

When Easton declined to fight, Benedict "kicked him very heartily" and threw him out of camp. Thoroughly humiliated, Allen and Easton would prove to be Benedict's enemies in the political ring. Benedict's bravado and strength of character would rub many the wrong way throughout the war, although his men respected and loved him for it.

The political wrangling also reached its peak that summer. The Massachusetts Committee of Safety that had enlisted Benedict was worried they might not be able to continue financial support of his mission to Fort Ticonderoga, even though Benedict was using much of his own funds and credit for paying soldiers and buying supplies. The committee knew he would have to eventually submit an account for reimbursement.

The Committee of Safety sent out a delegation to get information and review the situation. They were under pressure to relieve Benedict of his duties. Many wondered why a second-class merchant from Connecticut was commanding Massachusetts soldiers. Also, others like Easton and Allen were attacking his good name. Benedict was holding on, hoping to hear the intentions of the new Continental Congress, especially what they intended to do about pending British offensives through Canada.

If you think our forefathers acted harmoniously and in one accord, you would be mistaken. Many reconciliation-minded members of the congress were actually nervous and embarrassed about Allen's and Benedict's actions. A majority of the congress voted to withdraw from the Champlain region and give its control back to Britain.

Benedict thought his actions would win him acclaim and couldn't believe the decisions made by the congress. In one letter to the congress, he wrote that their decisions "have thrown the inhabitants into the greatest consternation." At least 500 American families resided in the area and pulling out of the conflict would leave them at the mercy of the Redcoats and hostile Indians. He also wrote about Fort Ticonderoga: "the key of this extensive country, and if abandoned, leaves a very extensive frontier open to the ravages of the enemy and to continual alarms which will probably cost more than the expense of repairing and garrisoning it." 5

Luckily, due to Benedict's assessments, concerns from the Massachusetts congress and the rest of New England states that knew the importance of the Champlain corridor, the congress relented and reversed its decision.

In late June of 1775, Benedict decided to resign his commission, "not being able to hold it longer with honor." On hearing the news of Benedict's resignation, his men panicked for a short time. They needed his leadership desperately and many feared not getting paid for their service, as they had families to feed at home. They went as far as holding Benedict captive aboard the *Liberty*; at least until the Massachusetts Committee of Safety resolved the pay issue. Benedict held no ill will toward the action taken by his men and expressed as much. He knew what they were going through.

Benedict got news of the formation of a Continental Northern Army Department, under the command of Philip Schuyler of Albany, in early

July of 1775. Schuyler was a well-known patriot serving in congress. He was a landowner of vast properties in the area and a member of the elite class. He lived on a large estate near Albany. Benedict resolved to meet with Schuyler to give him intelligence about the Champlain region and maybe even offer his services.

On July 4th of 1775, Benedict left the Champlain region. One of his last statements to the new command at Fort Ticonderoga was that he wanted them to make sure they fortified Mount Defiance, a mountain that loomed over the old fort. He believed the Brits could haul cannons to its summit and force a surrender of Fort Ticonderoga. They should have taken his advice.

As an insight to what kind of leader and commander Benedict was, it must have warmed his heart when in an unprecedented show of affection, local residents gathered at Crown Point to say goodbye and wish him well. They handed him a proclamation of "Gratitude and Thankfulness," for the uncommon vigilance, vigor and spirit he displayed in "providing for our preservation and safety from the threatened and much dreaded incursions of an inveterate enemy."

The residents praised Benedict's "humanity and benevolence in supplying them with provisions in their distress." They also lauded his "polite manner" and "generosity of soul, which nothing less than real magnanimity and innate virtue could inspire." They wished that he would receive rewards "adequate to your merit." 6

Benedict made quite a good impression on the average people and they wanted him to know how much his good service meant to them. In fact, the only time that Benedict can be recalled severely disciplining his men was when two of them were caught looting residents' homes and he had them flogged for the offense. He always insisted that citizens be treated fairly and respectfully. That was surely not the Benedict portrayed throughout history.

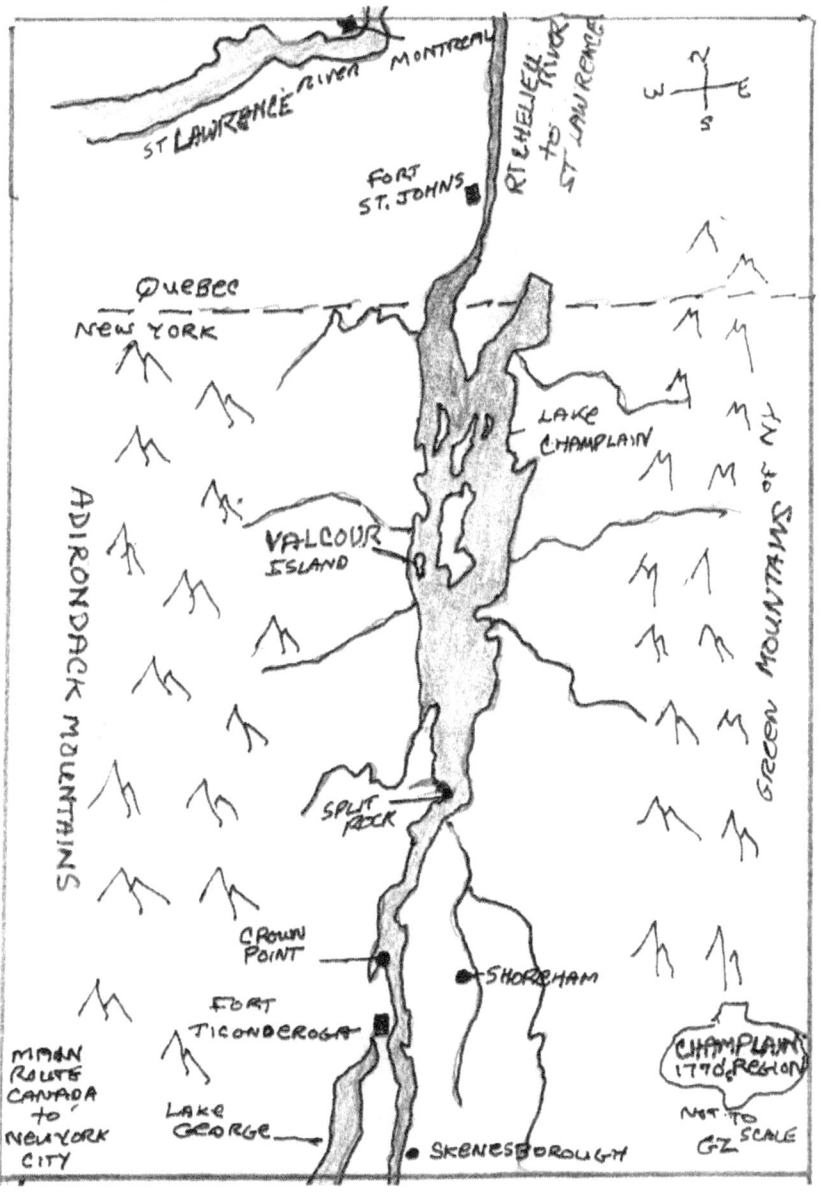

Map 2

CHAPTER FIVE

WAR GROWING THROUGHOUT NEW ENGLAND & THE ENTRY OF "KING" GEORGE

While Benedict was securing the Champlain region, from Canada all the way to Albany, the siege of Boston was growing in strength every day. On June 17, 1775, the Battle of Bunker Hill exploded. Two thousand British regulars tried to assault American forces dug in on Breed's Hill. They succeeded on their third attempt but suffered massive losses. Half – nearly 1000 men – were either killed, wounded, or captured. In comparison, about 400 Americans were lost, including General Joseph Warren of Massachusetts, a rebel friend of Benedict's who had helped him secure his colonel's commission from the Massachusetts Committee of Safety.

While Benedict finally left Lake Champlain for Albany, George Washington was arriving at Cambridge, across the river from Boston. The Continental Congress had just named him commander-in-chief of a new American army and he took charge of nearly 17,000 patriots that had mustered from as far as Virginia to surround Boston.

George Washington served in the Continental Congress as a delegate from Virginia. For a long time, Washington was ranked among the middle class. He worked as a surveyor and served as an officer in the French & Indian War. He rarely distinguished himself during the war, but it gave him credibility as a soldier and an officer.

George had much higher ambitions and he hit the jackpot when he married his wife, Martha Dandridge Curtis. She was a very wealthy widow and sole holder of a huge plantation estate in Virginia. His marriage propelled him into a world of privileged gentry and the very upper class of society.

As Washington attended the First Continental Congress, he knew that if there were to be a war and a new nation, the colonies would need some sort of king or exalted ruler. Most likely, this ruler would come from the military side of events.

Washington wanted this job very badly. At his congressional appearances he dressed in the old military uniform he wore in the French & Indian War. At six feet and one inch tall, he was a very imposing figure, as the average man's height was much shorter. He seemed to want to stay above the political fray and touted his experience in warfare.

The New England delegates preferred the experience put forth by another gentleman named Horatio Gates. He had more experience and had served longer in the British military.

Delegates knew that holding this rough alliance of colonies together for any reason would be difficult, but a commander-in-chief from the southern colonies would help cement feelings of working together.

Washington made himself the obvious choice. His preferred title throughout the war was "His Excellency." He always traveled with one or more of his slaves and was obviously of the elite class. That was what was expected of a military commander in Colonial times.

CHAPTER SIX

FROM VICTORIES IN THE NORTH TO DEEP DESPAIR & HEARTBREAK

As Washington's entourage went to Cambridge, Arnold had already been deep in the fight since Lexington and Concord. He left the Champlain region and made his way south toward Albany, where he hoped to offer his service to General Philip Schuyler. Schuyler was of the upper class of New York. He was a wealthy landowner and skilled politician.

Schuyler had just arrived home after serving in the Continental Congress and he had also just received his appointment as Northern Army commander. Benedict wasn't sure how Schuyler would accept him.

To Benedict's surprise, Schuyler was actually anxious to meet him. The fame earned by Benedict for his Champlain exploits preceded him. He was told he was the talk of many in Congress and Schuyler knew from field reports that Arnold was a man who could get things done. He warmly welcomed Benedict and was hoping to enlist him as a Brigadier general in his division. He had very few leaders he could rely on as men of action.

Benjamin Hinman, the commander appointed by the Massachusetts Committee of Safety to take Arnold's place at Ticonderoga, was already labeled 'king log' by the men for his inability to make command decisions. Schuyler needed to pick Benedict's brain and attain information he needed to hold on to the Champlain region. 1

Benedict suggested that while there was still time in the campaign year, before winter set in they should launch a strike at the Canadian posts before the British could reinforce them. He feared, as Schuyler did, that if the outposts gained in strength a British campaign could go down Lake Champlain and over to the Hudson River. That could split communications and supply lines between New England and the rest of the colonies. 2

His trading ventures to Montreal and farther south gave Benedict insight and he thought maybe the Canadians could be persuaded to join America's cause for liberty.

As Schuyler and Benedict conferred on plans about whether or not they should take an offensive or defensive position, Benedict received shocking news from his Connecticut home. His wife, Peggy, and his father-in-law had both died in June. 3

Benedict's grief was unbearable. He had three children to care for and he started for home. His wife was barely 30 years old and he missed his home and children. Most men would have been crushed by such devastating news. He certainly had done more than his share for the cause of liberty already. Maybe he would quit and say that's enough.

Over the next two and a half months, Benedict was in severe depression as he visited the gravesites of his dear wife Peggy and his father-in-law, Samuel Mansfield. His sister, Hannah, did her utmost to bring Benedict back to his feet. She loved her brother and his children dearly. She agreed to be their surrogate mother and do her best to keep the mercantile business affairs running as smoothly as she could. She told Benedict he could best submerge his sorrows in consideration of the public cause.

Beside all of the business and personal problems Benedict had to face at home, he still needed to make his way back to the Committee of Safety in Massachusetts to settle his expenses for the Ticonderoga battle campaign. He had used a great deal of his own money and knew he wouldn't be fully reimbursed but thought the committee would do their best.

Benedict thought that as long as he was in Cambridge, he would try to present himself to the new Commander-in-Chief, George Washington. Maybe he would offer his service.

What really weighed on Benedict's mind as he prepared for his trip back to Massachusetts was one of his main sources of income, the merchant ship *Peggy*, named for his wife. It had just cleared New Haven's port en route to Quebec. That area was now a potential war zone and he feared the British might seize his ship.

Of Benedict's three sons, the oldest was now only seven years old. He surely protested his father leaving home again.

Riding horseback to the Massachusetts Committee of Safety, now called the Provincial Congress, Benedict arrived there on August 1st of 1775. He presented his documented expenses and accounts of the Ticonderoga mission. As politics often go, there were many disputes over the claims. Only about half of what Benedict submitted was reimbursed. Later on, in the war, the Continental Congress – shamed by the shabby treatment of such a patriot – ponied up funds to cover more of his expenses. 4

CHAPTER SEVEN

THE TWO BULLS: WASHINGTON & ARNOLD MEET

In mid-August, Benedict and Washington finally met in Cambridge. Washington had his hands full after just receiving command of some 17,000 patriot troops on July 3rd. They certainly weren't a cohesive army, but a mix of militia groups and some enlisted regulars. The logistics of defenses, food, supplies, discipline and supply lines must have been overwhelming.

Washington was constantly thirsty for information. He always tried to calculate his moves based on having as much intelligence as he could gather. He was eager to meet this Benedict Arnold, whose reputation had preceded him. While in Champlain, Benedict had sent regular reports to the Continental Congress, where Washington was serving.

In his reports, Benedict had tried to encourage the Congress to back a campaign striking into Canada before the British could reinforce the country. Washington had read the reports while serving in the Congress and was of the same opinion as Benedict. He was also amazed by Benedict's conquests around Lake Champlain. Both men feared the impending doom that was about to come down on America from the northern corridor. 1

If the Brits controlled the St. Lawrence River and fortified Quebec and Montreal, they could easily go south through Champlain to Lake George and onto the Hudson River. That scenario not only would separate the colonies, but also would disrupt all communications and supply lines, probably destroying any hope for independence.

Washington continued to be in awe of Benedict's knowledge and penetrating mind, when it came to military matters. Benedict knew many Canadians well through his merchant trading ventures in the area. He also was familiar with all the waterways going south and had already proved he was the kind of man to accomplish things.

The two men summarized, after much discussion, that a two-pronged attack in Quebec might be the best way to thwart the British before they could reinforce the region in the spring. They needed to move very quickly. Washington and Benedict thought that if a force could travel through Maine and if Schuyler could send a force north from Albany, they could converge on Quebec. If they could gain control of Quebec and the St. Lawrence, they might have a chance at stopping the British.

Washington and Benedict were also counting on many freedom-loving Canadians who were eager to join the rebellion. Some of those even went so far as forming a delegation to go to the Congress as a 14th colony.

The two leaders also knew there would be much resistance from the French-Canadian Catholic population. That group would have to be won over, since many of them had no trust of the New England Protestants. Another factor to be considered was the large contingent of Native Americans in the area. Some were friendly and some were not. Most were indifferent to either side, as they were just trying to survive in such a harsh country. 2

Summer was waning into fall and time was pressing, if the plan was to be launched. Washington wrote an express letter to Schuyler, his northern commander, explaining his intentions and requesting an immediate answer. He also knew Benedict would be the most logical choice to lead the Maine expedition. 3

Schuyler responded favorably to the plan, already confident of Benedict's abilities. He wrote: "how happy" he was "to learn of your intentions and wished the thought had struck you sooner." Washington offered Benedict a colonel's commission and put him in charge of the Maine expedition. They started planning the endeavor feverishly.

Washington knew of a shipbuilder named Reuben Colburn who had come to Cambridge from Maine with some St. Francis Indians – the Indians living in the vicinity of Quebec. They were familiar with the Kennebec River system. Washington needed to put Benedict in touch with Colburn.

Benedict penned a note to Colburn on August 21st, inquiring if he could procure or build 200 bateaus at his shipyard. Each would require four oars, two paddles, and two setting poles and be capable of carrying six or seven men, along with their provisions and baggage. He also asked about the availability of fresh beef and particular information on the wilderness route to Quebec. 4

With Washington's permission, Colburn hurried to his shipyard in Gardinerston, Maine to begin filling the rush order. On September 3rd, Washington sent an express letter to Colburn, formally ordering the construction of 200 bateaus, at the rate of 40 shillings per craft. He additionally asked Colburn to gather food, supplies and up to 20 men who could serve as guides and carpenters qualified to repair the small boats as they traveled through the wilderness.

On September 2nd, a message was sent to Nathaniel Tracy – a wealthy merchant in Newburyport, Massachusetts – asking that he gather enough vessels to transport a body of troops on a secret expedition. Men needed to be moved up the coast from Newburyport to Gardinerston at the headwater of the Kennebec River. 5

With many logistics of their plan coming together, Washington called on September 5th for volunteers, saying he needed experienced woodsmen and men familiar with bateaus. The next morning brought a flood of volunteers for the mission. Many were sick of the boredom and disease of camp life, especially since things were progressing so slowly under the new command around Boston. Some wanted to serve under Benedict because of his growing reputation. 6

The list of volunteers, including Christopher Greene, Henry Dearborn and Aaron Burr, would impress most historians. But by far, the most impressive part of Benedict's force was three groups of Pennsylvania and Virginia frontiersmen. The Virginia force was under the command of Daniel Morgan, who was known as a fierce backwoods fighter. They went to Cambridge, marching 600 miles in three weeks.

The two Pennsylvania forces under William Hendrix and Matt Smith covered some 450 miles in 26 days. They carried tomahawks and scalping knives. They were equipped with long rifles and were renowned as excellent marksmen.

But these men weren't prone to the kind of discipline that Washington expected from his troops. They drank hard, fought hard and had a tendency to start fights in camp, just for fun. Washington was very glad to see these men included in the military effort and was glad to see them leave his command. Benedict knew they were the kind of men he needed for this mission to succeed.

The men chosen were all young, strong men who could move quickly through the wilderness. They would be the equivalent of today's Army Rangers. Benedict's force now numbered 1050. The demand for supplies was a nightmare. Besides the bateaus being built in Maine, there was the list of food, supplies, gunpowder, and transport issues.

Benedict hurried to cover every detail. He enlisted Dr. Isaac Senter, a surgeon from New Hampshire; Reverend Samuel Spring as chaplain; and Eleazer Oswald, a personal secretary who was an old friend from Ticonderoga. The troops were outfitted with new coats, linen frocks and blankets. Benedict also checked and attended to the firearms, flints, gunpowder and tents. 7

Daniel Morgan and Benedict quickly became friends and took command of the three rifle companies within the division. Morgan was a huge man and wasn't afraid to enforce his orders with his fist, if necessary. Curiously, two very brave women accompanied their husbands. Possibly, going to war with a loved one was almost better than trying to survive alone in colonial times.

CHAPTER EIGHT

MISSION IMPOSSIBLE, 1775 STYLE

Benedict had managed to organize and ready the mission in less than one month. The men assembled in Newburyport, Massachusetts for the first leg of the journey by September 17th. Waiting were eleven sloops and schooners ready to make the voyage to Maine. A strong headwind prevented the launch for two days.

Benedict rode among the troops, offering words of encouragement, but the men were anxious to get on with the mission. The wind finally calmed enough, and Benedict had the men loaded onto the ships on September 19th. 1

As they left, there was a celebration of fifes and drums and many huzzahs. Also, shouts of "to Quebec and victory!" It would be the last happy days they would see for a long time. If they knew what was ahead on this mission of legends, none would have gone. 2

They set sail into the Atlantic. The sea was choppy, and fog rolled in. Many men succumbed to seasickness, but they made it over some 100 miles to the coast of Maine in 12 hours. The voyage saved them close to six days of marching. As they picked their way through the many islands near the mouth of the Kennebec River, some of the ships went off course and that held them up another day. They finally arrived at Colburn's shipyard on September 22nd. 3

Colburn's men had worked day and night to finish the rush order of 200 bateaus. Many were hastily put together with green lumber and they were smaller than requested. To accommodate all the men and supplies, another 20 bateaus were needed. Colburn managed to put together more boats in three days. The carpenters who were asked to go along on the trek would certainly be needed, as these crafts would need repairs.

As Benedict waited for Colburn and his men to get ready for the next leg of the journey, he studied his scouting reports. They were truly going into an unknown wilderness. The Kennebec River is a fast flowing, deep river, filled with rapids and waterfalls. It runs quickly from the high Maine Mountains to the Atlantic, with tremendous force. Most would not want to cross many places with a small boat, let alone pulling loaded boats upstream. 4

Benedict had crude maps and scouting reports he had requested prior to the mission. What he didn't know was how inaccurate the reports were. The journey was estimated to be 180 miles, but clearly it was close to 350 miles. The scouts were troubled by the thought of encountering bands of Mohawk Indians, especially since they would have to cross the lands belonging to the warrior, Chief Natanis. They weren't sure how this army's intrusion would be received. 5

Sending his men upriver in waves, Benedict's first group was Daniel Morgan's riflemen. They were to scout out the route and make pathways for portages around the raging rapids and waterfalls. The rest followed with the food stores and supplies. The first group set out on September 25th. Over the next four days, Benedict sent three more divisions into the wilderness. Benedict set out on September 29th, following from the rear.

One event took time from the many details Benedict had to oversee.

A young soldier, James McCormick, got terribly drunk just before embarking and shot another soldier dead. His division held a court martial and sentenced him to death by hanging. The accused man broke down at the gallows. Benedict took pity on him and described McCormick as very simple and ignorant and normally a peaceable fellow and a proper object of mercy. 6

I don't think Benedict approved of capital punishment. He never once allowed it. He made arrangements to send the disgraced soldier back to Cambridge for trial.

As Benedict entered the mighty Kennebec River, he was glad to finally have his whole force in motion. He hoped to advance from the rear to the lead of the column within four or five days. He traveled on a dugout canoe with his friend, Eleazer Oswald, and some Indian guides.

As he made his way past groups of his soldiers, Benedict offered praise and encouragement. But he was becoming very concerned as he made his way onward. Many of the bateaus were falling apart. In a letter to Washington, Benedict wrote: "When you consider the badness and weight of the bateaus and large quantity of provisions, etc. we have been obliged to force up against a very rapid stream. You would have taken the men for amphibious animals, as they were a great part of time, underwater." 7

One of the first huge obstacles was Skowhegan Falls, a 100-foot drop in the river that Benedict described as dangerous and difficult to pass. For those who have seen Skowhegan Falls, that would truly be an understatement. There, the river boils over enormous boulders.

Benedict managed to traverse some 50 miles in three days to catch up with Morgan's riflemen. They were trying to breach the next obstacle, Norridgewock Falls, a 90-foot drop of fast, flowing rapids. It took the columns nearly a week to get up and around it. To this point, they had help from some of the local settlers, but the region farther west was pretty much wild and uncharted territory. Most of the columns, although exhausted, had made it past Norridgewock Falls by October 8, 1775.

As Benedict made the journey upriver from this point, he described how mountains began to appear on each side of the river, high with snow on tops. He had sent Morgan's riflemen on to the next obstacle, called the Great Carrying Place. This was a 12-mile stretch of bogs, ponds, fallen trees and impassable brush. The weather also turned badly for the army. Snow and bitter cold temperatures followed torrential rains. 8

Slogging through, the men lost boats, cut their feet and hands while enduring rough, soggy terrain, cold and exhaustion. Some continued to drag bateaus along with them. Many became ill not only from hypothermia and fatigue, but also from drinking brackish water near the ponds. Benedict set up a makeshift hospital along the way. It was filled to capacity as soon as it was built. Supplies were running dangerously low because of so many losses in the river. Rations were supplemented with fish, the occasional moose and other wild game.

It took each of the four divisions a week to cross the Great Carrying Place and it took a huge toll, with so many sick and exhausted. There was much thought of turning back.

The Great Carrying Place took them to the Dead River, with miles more of streams and rapids. Their supplies were dwindling, and Benedict reluctantly ordered half rations, hoping they could supplement with fish and wild game. Conditions worsened. Torrential rains fell from the 19th through the 22nd of October. The river rose some eight feet, forcing the men to look for higher ground. Everywhere they looked there was rushing, freezing cold water, to the point where it was impossible to make out any directions or trails.

The columns were now stretched out nearly 20 miles and much of their provisions were lost in the flood. Benedict had the men make a camp and called for a counsel of war with the officers in the area. They now realized they weren't in a race to win Quebec, but now a race to survive, with winter not far behind.

At the war counsel, Benedict gave his assessment first, but agreed to abide by the counsel's decision. He surmised there was no point in trying to retreat, as the danger of going back looked almost as difficult as pushing toward Canada and the nearest French settlement where provisions could be obtained. He also thought the men would soon reach Lake Megantic, where they wouldn't have to fight the currents. Benedict had no idea of the other prong of attack, as they were so isolated. He thought that if he could put together some fast teams, they could get to the French settlements and return with some supplies to stave off starvation.

Officers at the war counsel agreed to Benedict's plan, but everyone was definitely on edge. At this point, winter was setting in. Game and fish were almost impossible to find. They were facing starvation.

Unknown to Benedict, another counsel was convening at the far end of the column. Roger Enos, the head of the rear column, was truly suffering from what Dr. Senter called faint heartedness. He took some of the sick and turned back to the Maine settlements with almost 300 troops, but without Benedict's permission. When news of the defection spread throughout the columns, many were disheartened, but pushed on. Enos also left with more than his share of the remaining provisions. 9

Enos and his division made it back to Cambridge. It was of note that Washington had him arrested and tried by court-martial. He was found not guilty, mainly because no one was there to speak against him. Benedict never showed any ill will or malice toward Enos because he knew what the men were enduring.

On October 25th, heavy snow and high winds hit the columns. Their next objective was Lake Megantic, but before they could get there, they had to cross the 'Terrible Carrying Place.' It was a steep two-mile march over the mountains dividing Maine and Canada. Some had to abandon what was left of their bateaus as they struggled through the snow and rocks. After successfully reaching the peak of the divide, they had another seven miles of log and rock-filled streams to descend before finally reaching the lake. 10

Benedict received a scouting report as they entered the seven-mile stream. Some scouts he had sent ahead reached a French settlement and said they appear very friendly and rejoiced to hear of our approach. There were also no British forces to contend with in that area. It was the first good news in a very long time.

The column and divisions were now stretched out more than 20 miles. Provisions were all but gone. Many men were sick and delirious. They stumbled up and over the mountain pass, some dropping any unnecessary weight like tents and bateaus. Some even lost their weapons.

Jemima Warner, one of the women who had made the journey, lost her husband to exposure. No one had the strength or tools to bury him. She lingered with him for a bit before covering him with leaves. The grieving wife picked up her lost husband's rifle and caught up with the column. This brave, young American woman – probably only 19 to 21 – was the first female to serve in American combat, proudly under the command of Benedict. She would later meet her end while manning an artillery battery during the Battle of Quebec. Surely, the daring Jemima qualified for induction to the Women's Hall of Fame at Seneca Falls, New York.

Mrs. Grier, wife of Sergeant Joseph Grier, was another woman accompanying the troops into battle. She was mentioned respectfully in letters written by some of the soldiers. Her fate is not known.

Desperate for any kind of food, men boiled candles and made gruel from hides or leather to be used for moccasins or boot repair. The starving soldiers ate lip salve and shaving soap. Captain Dearborn's Labrador dog – traveling with the troops – was eaten by the starving men. Dr. Senter wrote that "assassins" and "was instantly devoured, without leaving any vestige of the sacrifice" took the Labrador. Other dogs also accompanied the march, but none lived to see the month of November. 11

Benedict knew the desperate situation his army was in and headed a fast team to reach the French settlements and bring back provisions for his men. While paddling up Lake Megantic, they found "a very considerable wigwam." It gave the men a place to dry out quickly and rest briefly from the harsh weather. The respite also gave Benedict a few moments to write a quick report for Washington. He penned: "I have been much deceived on every account of our route, which is longer and has been attended by a thousand difficulties I never apprehended. But if crowned with success, and conducive to the public good, I shall think it trifling." 12

Benedict pushed himself to the limit and soon reached the French settlement at Sartigan. The people there welcomed him warmly. They referred to his men as "Les Bostonnais." He bought whatever provisions the French could spare for his troops. He paid far more than the normal value, in the hope of bonding with the local population.

On the morning of November 2nd, the men couldn't believe their eyes. They saw cattle being headed toward them, followed by birch bark canoes loaded with grain, mutton and tobacco. One soldier wrote, "We were blessed with the finest sight my eyes ever beheld." Another wrote that they "shed tears of joy in our happy delivery from the grasping hand of death." 13

Buoyed by nourishment, Benedict's men began moving the provisions toward the rear of the column as quickly as they could. It was too late for some. They looked for stragglers they could help, but some 40 or 50 brave young men had died of exposure and starvation.

Curiously, while the column traveled along the Dead River and toward Lake Megantic, they were passing through the Indian territory overseen by Chief Natanis. The Indians watched from a distance. Natanis was very impressed by Benedict, a leader who went to and from, encouraging and helping his men. He even sent some of the braves out to dangerous places on the trail, to assist the soldiers. Natanis had never seen a leader of soldiers who showed so much compassion for his men. He was so impressed by Benedict that he would later follow him into the battle at the walls of Quebec.

The soldiers sifted in toward Sartigan. Benedict took a few good men – including Dr. Senter – and forged ahead, buying provisions and setting up food stations along the way to the St. Lawrence River. He got quite a few days ahead of the column and decided to go to a nearby settlement called the Village of Gilbert, where there was a large Native American community. Dr. Senter wrote that the tribe addressed the colonel with great pomp.

Benedict parlayed with the tribe and must have made a persuasive argument as to why they should join and help the American army, and drive out the king's soldiers. He must have made quite an impression, as Chief Natanis also spoke on his behalf. Forty of his warriors accepted a short-term enlistment in the army and agreed to help Benedict's comrades. 14

As Benedict's men regrouped and benefited from nourishment, morale began to rise again. Beside the bravery it took for Benedict to just walk in and parlay with Native Americans, there was an interesting side story that attests to Benedict's character.

There was a Private Henry who was severely ill and sitting by the trail. Henry wrote: "The commander knew my name and character and good-naturedly inquired after my health." When Benedict saw how sick Henry was, he ran down to the riverside and hailed the owner of the house which stood opposite across the water.

Benedict made arrangements for Henry's care, then handed the private two silver dollars so he could pay a French family for food and lodging while recovering there. It was one of many acts like this that endeared Benedict's men to him. Not exactly the self-serving interest portrayed in many history books. 15

It was early November 1775 when most of the forces reached the banks of the mighty St. Lawrence River. The number of men ready to attack Quebec was now down to 650. The weather had turned unusually cold and wet. Some officers obtained the use of horses, but one wrote that the horses were sinking nearly to their bellies on what were called roads.

Unfortunately, Benedict had lost the element of surprise. News had reached Quebec that a force was marching through Maine and the British forces in Quebec were preparing for an invasion.

On Sunday, November 5th, Benedict went to the local Roman Catholic Church and presented it with Washington's proclamation of friendship. Benedict was hoping to enlist any assistance he could, but received none, as many were in fear of reprisal from British Governor Carlton.

The governor had issued a message prior to Benedict's visit that they were determined to burn and destroy all the inhabitants in the vicinity of Quebec unless they came in and took up arms in defense of the garrison. Benedict also learned that the British forces in Canada were already engaging the American forces driving north from Albany. 16

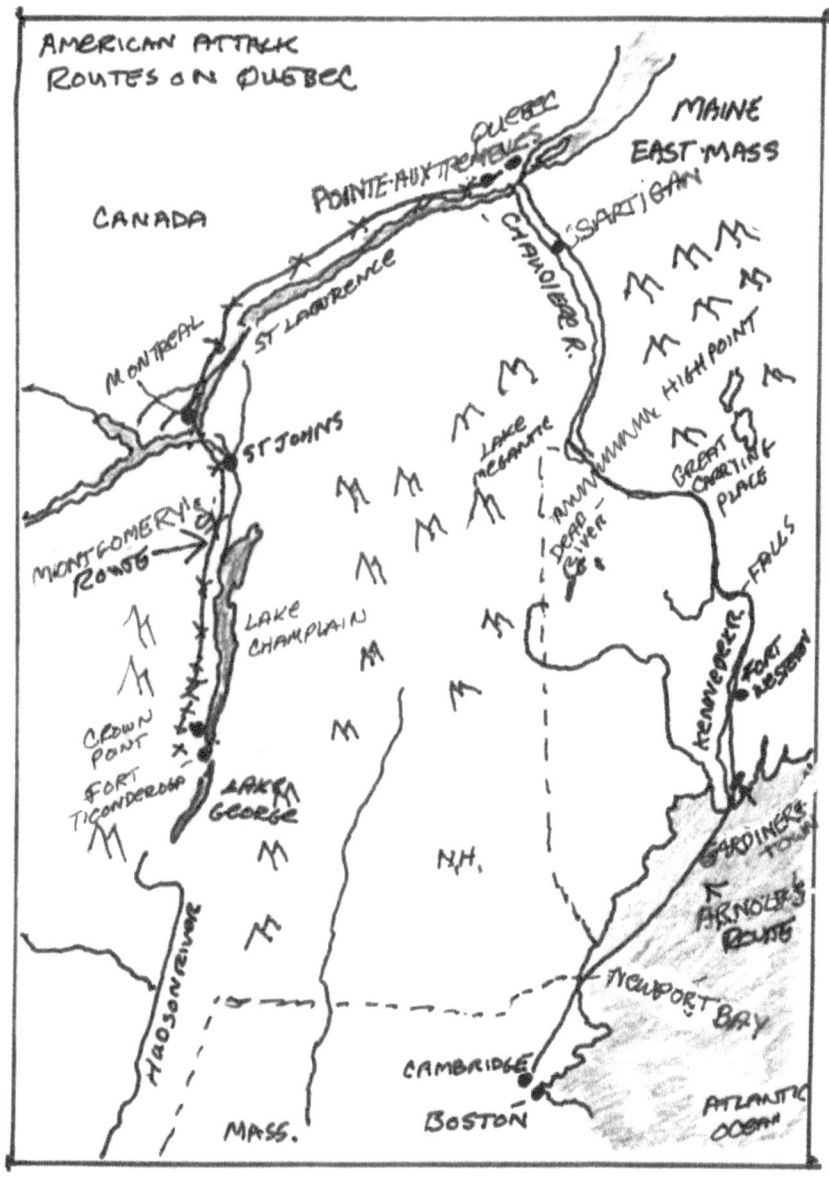

Map 3

CHAPTER NINE

FIGHT TO CONTROL THE ST. LAWRENCE & QUEBEC: THE TWO-PRONG ATTACK BEGINS

The second prong of the American offensive into Canada – under the command of General Schuyler – traveled up Lake Champlain, where the general fell gravely ill. He was forced to retreat back to Albany. While recuperating there, he took charge of sending supplies north toward Canada. He also became sidetracked by negotiations with the Six Nations of the Iroquois Confederacy. Schuyler was attempting to keep the combined force of Native Americans neutral or to have them side with the Americans.

When Schuyler left the Champlain region, he left a very adept and experienced General Richard Montgomery in charge of the expedition. Montgomery was a former British officer and very experienced in warfare. He was hoping to position himself for glory in the American army. When he reached the north end of Lake Champlain, he first had to deal with the now reinforced fort of St. John's. He spent 45 days laying siege. It took until November 2nd of 1775, but he brought about the surrender of 700 British regulars and Canadian defenders.

It is interesting to note that one of the captured prisoners of war who survived the siege at St. John's was a young British officer named John Andre'. More was to be heard about him.

Governor and Commander Guy Carlton – in charge of the British forces in Canada – was in a bit of a pickle. Losing the Champlain region to this Benedict Arnold had already embarrassed him. Now, he had a threat reaching toward the St. Lawrence and Quebec. He heard rumors and had intelligence about Benedict's forces coming through Maine, but he had to deal with Montgomery's siege of St. John's.

Carlton left Quebec quite lightly defended and put out desperate calls to England for reinforcements to hold the region. He sailed down river to Montreal, to try and bolster support for defense of the city but was largely unsuccessful in gaining Canadian assistance. Carlton had some highly trained, veteran troops with him, under the command of Colonel Allen Maclean. A division of about 170 Royal Highland Emigrants was commanded by Maclean.

Maclean was ordered by Carlton to sail back to Quebec to help defend the city. As Maclean faced a strong headwind and wasn't making much progress downriver, he captured two Indians who were acting as couriers for Benedict. They carried information of Benedict's force near Quebec. Maclean knew he had to get back quickly to defend Quebec City. He abandoned the ship and his men marched overland back to the walled city, arriving there on November 12th.

It was the same day Benedict was holding a council of war to discuss with his men the taking of Quebec. Had Maclean not intercepted Benedict's couriers, the Americans might have taken the largely undefended City of Quebec and controlled the St. Lawrence.

Benedict's men could see their goal, the walled City of Quebec, on the far side of the St. Lawrence River. The high, ten-feet thick stone walls that encircled most of city loomed over the river. Two British warships were anchored near her port. Benedict constantly sent out reconnaissance to ascertain the city's defensive strength and to find out where Montgomery was.

During the November 12th council of war, it was decided that if the wind subsided, a night crossing would be attempted and be, hopefully, undetected. If all went well, maybe even a preemptive strike would be tried. The British had already destroyed most of the boats in the area, just to thwart such an attempt. But Benedict's men had gathered a small armada of bateaus and canoes in preparation. 1

Later the following night, the winds faded away and the crossing was launched. It took four waves of men to get most of the force across. By 4 a.m. of the next morning, 500 men had crossed the great river silently and undetected. During the night crossing, one of the canoes capsized, throwing its men into the freezing waters of the St. Lawrence. With the help of their comrades, the men were fished out of the water and taken to the shore. There, they found a small hut and started a fire to keep from freezing to death.

A group of British seamen saw the glow of the fire in the hut and rowed a small boat to the site to investigate. Shots rang out and three of the British seamen were hit with musket fire. Benedict's men then knew the element of surprise was slipping away. They decided an assault on the city was out of the question. Some houses outside the walls were seized and Benedict had the chance to rest his men under the watch of guards he posted there. 2

As the next few days passed, Benedict and Maclean were busy gathering intelligence about the strength of arms held by each. Some civilians were fleeing the city, while others were going to the city for protection. To obtain information, both armies questioned those coming and going.

On November 14th of 1775, Benedict decided to try a show of force. He spread his men out in the fields in front of the city, known as the "Plains of Abraham." They offered huzzahs and rifle fire in the name of liberty. The British responded with cannon fire. It was all pretty much for show because of the distance involved. 3

Benedict then sent some of his men under a white flag with demands and terms of surrender, but they were fired on and that infuriated Benedict. His little army had only five rounds of ammunition per soldier and certainly not enough men to storm such a well-fortified city by themselves. They decided reluctantly to pull back and wait for reinforcements from Montgomery.

In colonial times, the only form of communication was letters and couriers were constantly moving under orders to relay messages. There were also many trying to intercept these brave messengers to gain their treasured information. It was a very dangerous job. One of the couriers used in Canada was well known – the feisty little Aaron Burr.

Benedict was not the type to take retreating or waiting very well. He penned a letter to Washington, saying, "If only I had been ten days sooner, Quebec would have fallen into our hands." He added that he was waiting with great anxiety for General Montgomery's help. In his letters, Benedict seemed a little unsure of himself, wanting an experienced general to take charge. 4

The curious and odd thing that Benedict didn't know was that Carlton, the governor and commander of Canada and Quebec, was trapped between Montgomery and Benedict. He had tried to get back quickly to Quebec, but the winds held him on the river and his fleet was under fire from American cannons on the shore.

The Americans demanded surrender of the British ship with Carlton on board. He refused to be captured and disguised himself as an inhabitant of Canada, complete with a wool cap. He was lowered off the warship and into a whaling boat in the middle of the night. The men in the whaling boat paddled silently with their hands and slipped through the American blockade of the river. By dawn, they had passed the blockade and were picked up by a British boat. Carlton made it safely past Benedict, who had seen the ship, but had no idea Carlton was on board.

By November 19th, Carlton made it back to the walls of Quebec. It was the same day Benedict was setting up camp in a small French village called Pointe-Aux-Trembles. Its citizens greeted Benedict warmly and gladly provided the troops with what they needed, including leather to make boots, as most had been eaten or destroyed by the terrain during the march through Maine.

It was said that men were driven to grateful tears when they saw a load of cowhides that Benedict had purchased for them. After November in

Quebec and the trip through Maine, many men had nothing or just rags to keep their feet warm. They got busy making boots.

Benedict paid dearly out of his own funds to meet his troops' needs and extended his credit with local merchants. Some of the merchants were trading partners with Benedict before the war.

Montgomery also had his hands full. He had just taken Montreal on November 13th and was overseeing security there. Benedict penned a letter to him, stating his need for more supplies, provisions and hard cash, as his were nearly exhausted. He knew merchants he had traded with in Montreal who might be able to help or lend credit. He related that too much had already been borne by his Kennebec column. 5

Montgomery gathered troops and supplies in the hope of reinforcing Benedict. He left his second-in-command, General David Wooster of Connecticut, in charge of garrisoning Montreal with about 500 troops. Wooster was an older member of the elite class and he was upset with the Continental Congress for only giving him a brigadier's commission. He also resented serving under Montgomery.

General Montgomery finally came into view of Benedict's position on December 1st, 1775. He traveled up the St. Lawrence River with a contingent of 1,325 soldiers, most from New York. The number was almost 700 short of what Benedict had requested and believed would be necessary to storm Quebec.

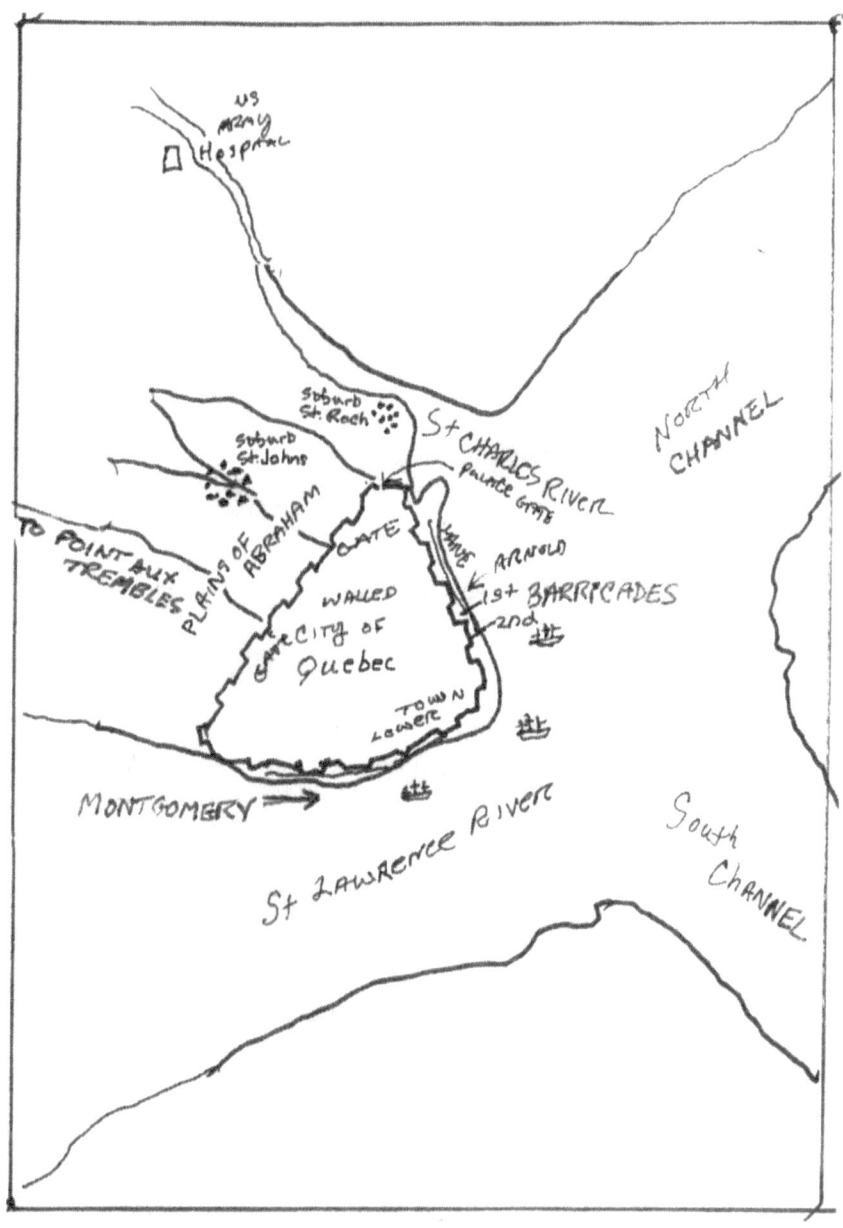

Map 4

CHAPTER TEN

STORMING QUEBEC: LIBERTY OR DEATH

Montgomery and Benedict began planning together on the first day of December 1775. Montgomery had a wealth of military experience and was well schooled in British tactics. He suggested they had three options: "siege, investment or storm". Time and weather ruled out siege or investment. They knew the British would be sending reinforcements as soon as they could. If Quebec didn't fall before their arrival, all efforts would be in vain.

Quebec was also growing in strength daily. In November, some 150 more Royal Highland Emigrants arrived from Newfoundland, along with a supply ship from England. Carlton would also draft the inhabitants of the city to take up arms.

Storming the city was the only viable option. It was decided they would start by harassing and wearing down the defenders from the outside. The plan was to not let them rest and keep them guessing when an assault would come.

Benedict pointed out that any assault needed to be launched by the first day of January, since many of the soldiers' enlistments would be ended by then. He knew the men were eager to go home, and considering what they had been through, he couldn't blame them.

In a letter Montgomery penned back to General Schuyler, there was telling information about Benedict and his column. He wrote of Colonel Arnold's detachment: That they were an exceedingly fine one, certainly injured by fatigue. But there is a "style of discipline" among his troops, "much superior to what I have been used to seeing in this campaign." Regarding Benedict, he said he was "active, intelligent and enterprising." Montgomery said he was paying "particular attention to Colonel Arnold's recommendations." 1

Montgomery brought with him cannons he had seized from Fort St. Johns. A campaign of harassment was begun through the month of December. Artillery batteries were formed out of ice, since digging in the frozen ground was impossible. This was where the first woman killed in American combat met her fate. Jemima Warner's artillery position was hit by cannon fire from the wall around Quebec.

Daniel Morgan's riflemen were put to good use as snipers. Under the cover of homes outside the city, these excellent marksmen picked sentries off the city's protective walls. By passing letters into the city, attempts were made to persuade the civilian population to put pressure on or resort to mutiny against the British rulers.

At night, they moved artillery batteries closer to the walled city in order to be more effective, but they were so outgunned by the heavier artillery of the British that they received much more damage than they delivered. One soldier wrote that his artillery was like peas hitting a plank. 2

On December 15th, Benedict, one of the captains and a drummer marched up to the city gates under a flag of truce and demanded to speak with Governor Carlton. Benedict carried a letter offering safe passage to England for the British officers, if they should choose the wise course of surrender.

In the frigid air, Carlton made them wait for a reply then sent the message that he would never negotiate with rebel scum. As Benedict left, he shouted, "Then let the general be answerable for all consequences." 3

Carlton knew if he could hold his position behind the heavily fortified city, relief would come from England when the weather broke. He also knew the extreme cold and heavy snow had to be wearing down the rebel force. And he was correct. Many suffered frostbite. There were desertions and numerous Americans were reaching the end of their enlistments and they dreamed of going home.

The plan of harassment was largely ineffective. The men were instructed to build scaling ladders to mount the walls when the opportunity presented itself. The officers formed a plan of attack from two different directions, to confuse the enemy and, hopefully, force surrender. The signal for the attack to begin would be rocket fire and the appointed time would be under the cover of darkness at 4:30 a.m.

Benedict's troops were instructed to wear sprigs of hemlock and a piece of paper on their hats so they could tell friend from foe, once inside the city walls. All of the hat papers were marked with the same three words: Liberty or Death.

In a howling snowstorm on December 31st of 1775, all men were positioned by 4 a.m. It was the last day of their enlistment period and many felt it would be their last day on earth. Most commanders of the era thought it more prudent to direct their forces from a distance, but Benedict had a working-class mindset. He never asked anyone to do something he wasn't willing to do himself.

When the rocket signal went off, Benedict led his column along the narrow pathway toward the first barricade of the city. Heavy snow was biting his face and he could hear the city's warning bells ringing. He was the first man to confront British musket fire.

Benedict sustained a horrible shot to his lower left leg. He fell into the snow but urged the force forward and on to victory as he lay on the ground.

As Daniel Morgan caught up with his friend and commander, he could see that Benedict was bleeding from his boot. He directed that Benedict be carried to a general hospital set up for the wounded. The hospital was located in a home about a mile from the city.

Morgan then pressed his men forward. Besides Benedict, Morgan was probably the hardiest and fiercest fighter most have ever read about. Morgan and his men made it past the first barrier but lost many to wounds and death. He yelled for the scaling ladders to be positioned for going over the huge wall surrounding Quebec.

As Morgan led the charge over the wall, a volley of enemy musket fire threw him backward and he landed in the snow. Men began to panic in the fear that their leader, Daniel Morgan, was dead. But he was just knocked out, with his face blackened and bleeding from gunpowder burns.

When Morgan regained consciousness, he shouted to his men to follow him and he charged back up the ladder. He vaulted over the wall, landing on a platform that held two cannons. Somehow, he managed to land between the barrels of the cannons. His men quickly followed, and the surprised British forces retreated in panic.

Before assaulting the next barrier, Morgan was hoping to hear Montgomery's division charging from the other side, but it was all too quiet. A British captain swung open the barricade and demanded that Morgan's men lay down their arms. Morgan shot the man dead on the spot and his troops surged forward and into a horrible volley of musket fire that stopped their advance.

Carlton sent men from different directions, ferociously firing on the patriot army. Shots were also raining down on them from the top of the wall. Some took cover in shops along the street, but the attack was ending by 10 a.m.

Morgan was one of the last to surrender. He was cornered against a wall and surrounded but said he would not give up his sword to a tyrannical British government. He slashed his sword at anyone daring to get close. Finally, a priest appeared and offered to accept his sword so Morgan could surrender with honor.

Montgomery's prong of attack from the upper part of the city made it past the first barrier. General Montgomery raised his sword to direct the men toward the second barrier, where unknown to them, were mounted cannons and musket men hidden in a log structure at point blank range.

When Montgomery raised his sword to lead the charge, the British opened fire, and he died instantly. His men offered some resistance at the fortified structure, but because of the snow and wind, many muskets wouldn't fire. The troops panicked and fled back to the Plains of Abraham. Benedict, not being able to put weight on his leg, was carried to the field hospital, which was under the command of Dr. Isaac Senter, his friend who marched with him through Maine. Dr. Senter later wrote of Benedict's wounds: "The ball had entered the outside of the leg, midway between the knee and ankle, then took an oblique course downward and lodged in the rise of the Achilles." 4

Dr. Senter probed for the ball and easily extracted it. Once the bleeding was under control, the doctor bandaged the wound and informed Benedict that amputation wouldn't be needed unless infection set in.

As more wounded poured into the hospital, Benedict kept gathering the sad news of how the attack was progressing. His heart sank when he learned of Montgomery's death, and worse, the surrender of his Kennebec warriors and Daniel Morgan.

In his zeal of overcoming the patriot attack, Carlton sent a division toward the hospital to crush the remaining rebels. Suddenly, a breathless artillery Captain, Isaiah Wool, burst into the hospital and told Benedict about an advancing force. Benedict asked him to offer resistance if he could. Wool called on anyone who could still fight, wounded or not, to join him in the street. 5

Two cannons were dragged toward Quebec and hidden among the trees. When the British division was in range, a mighty round of fire was aimed at them. The surprised soldiers retreated. The hospital and remaining soldiers were spared.

Dr. Senter pleaded with Benedict, for his own safety, that he be carried back farther into the countryside so the enemy would not find him. Benedict steadfastly refused. He ordered that his pistols be loaded, and his sword placed on his bed. He also ordered a loaded weapon for every wounded soldier. Benedict said he was determined to kill as many as possible if they came into the room. 6

As he lay there in agonizing pain, Benedict penned a letter to the remaining forces in Montreal, informing them of their critical situation and the urgent need for reinforcement. As he sent the courier to Montreal, he made it clear that there would be no notion of retreat until he knew the fate of his men. The following day, Carlton sent an envoy with one of his prisoners, Major Return Jonathan Meigs, asking for any personal effects and baggage for the care of his prisoners of war.

With a heavy heart, Benedict now knew the fate of his men. Patriot losses stood at 51 killed, 36 wounded and nearly two thirds of his column captured as prisoners. Benedict had as many personal effects gathered as he could to send back with the envoy and Major Meigs. He also gave money from his own pocket to help provide good care for his comrades. 7

It was not a happy beginning for the year of 1776.

CHAPTER ELEVEN

THE START OF 1776 & THE LONGEST COLD WINTER

Benedict steadfastly refused to retreat, and he eventually had himself moved to larger quarters, bedridden with his leg wound. Due to the intense pain, he decided to turn over his outside duties to one of his captains. Although he couldn't get outside, he could write letters and send couriers to try and improve a very bad situation.

Many of the remaining men reached the end of their enlistments and some left camp to go home. Benedict, being confined to bed rest, could do nothing to bolster their support or get them to re-enlist.

To make matters worse, all of his supplies were running dangerously low and Benedict also needed cash to pay for Canadian assistance. Many of the Canadians were on the side of American liberty, but Benedict feared that if money ran out, so would much of their support.

The winter outside was howling. It was one of worst winters in Canadian history. Benedict had a siege he wanted desperately to maintain, and he hoped that if he could get reinforcements, he would launch a second assault to try and free his comrades. He was also short of gunpowder and due to the winter conditions, only two of every ten muskets could fire properly.

Luckily, British Governor Guy Carleton remained in his defensive position inside the walls of Quebec. Had he decided to attack, the small American army would have easily been overrun. But Benedict and Carleton knew as winter ended and the ice on the mighty St. Lawrence began to break up, Great Britain would be bearing down with force to retake what the Americans had gained.

From his bed, Benedict sent couriers out into the icy, windy winter landscape at a blinding pace. Letters went out in every direction. He wrote first to General David Wooster, an older aristocratic general from Connecticut, who Montgomery left in charge of Montreal after his departure. With General Montgomery's death in battle, General Wooster became the main commander in the region.

Wooster immediately sent out 150 men and supplies to relieve Benedict, but he made no serious effort to leave Montreal himself. Benedict then wrote to General Schuyler, Washington and Congress about his grave situation. He pleaded for more troops and supplies. He also had feelings of inadequacy. One January 11th letter asked the delegates of Congress to send an experienced general as early as possible. 1

Unknown to Benedict was his growing hero status in the colonies. Thomas Jefferson was comparing him to Hannibal going over the Alps or Xenophon's retreat in classic warfare. He also suggested that Benedict should receive the fallen Montgomery's major generalship. Samuel Adams was one of his biggest supporters, referring to Benedict as a genius. Adams did all he could to try and revive the campaign before Britain could reinforce Quebec. 2

General Schuyler also sang Benedict's praises and called for many efforts to reinforce him. Benedict Arnold, in the 1775 campaign season – with a handful of men – accomplished more than Washington had with thousands. Washington was more than a little jealous and fearful of Benedict's growing popularity. All this time, he was still encamped around Boston. Congress petitioned him to release some of his men for a relief effort.

But Washington wrote, "I have not a man to spare," although he boasted about Benedict's efforts in the northern campaign, since he was under Washington's command. He may have started seeing the second-class colonel as a threat to his glory. 3

In March of 1776, Washington finally captured Dorchester Heights, placing fortifications and cannons that threatened the harbored British fleet. The cannon placement, being in range of British ships, forced the British fleet to leave Boston. But as much glory as George Washington received from chasing the Redcoats out of Boston, everyone knew the cannons used to accomplish it came from Benedict's adventures in the Champlain region.

Benedict's name was spreading as far as London. It was beyond belief that this horse trader from Connecticut – lacking proper breeding – was becoming a force to be reckoned with.

By the end of January 1776, as winter howled in Quebec, Benedict's leg began to slowly heal. He felt like a caged animal. He began hobbling around, against Dr. Senter's orders, and he decided to resume his full duties. His distress calls were slowly being answered. Benedict was welcoming troops, as they slowly poured into camp through blinding blizzard conditions.

Benedict's hope of a second assault began to rise, as his troop numbers were up to 2,505 by the end of March. Now, one of the biggest threats to his small army was an outbreak of smallpox. Up to a third of the men were unfit for duty. Many were horribly sick, with some at death's door. A makeshift hospital was set up to quarantine the cases as they appeared, but by the end of March, Dr. Senter was out of medicine. Smallpox ran rampantly through the camp and also within the walls of Quebec.

Benedict forbade the practice of self-inoculation, but many soldiers went through with it. They sliced themselves open – usually in the thigh area – then took active, infectious pustules from a smallpox victim and placed them in the wound. The disease would still be contracted, but it wouldn't be as severe. This practice would render a man useless for nearly three or four weeks.

Also suffered were colds, pneumonia and frostbite that caused the loss of fingers and toes. Just surviving the winter of early '76 was a battle within itself. Benedict made note at the end of March of nearly five feet of remaining snow sufficiently hard to bear a man and horse. 4

Smallpox was raging within the walls of Quebec. Although there were ample food stores, there was a desperate need for firewood. A British military detachment was sent out to gather wood, and on one occasion, they left the city in force. They brought with them rolling brass cannons to protect the men while they gathered every bit of wood they could find, including boards from houses and fences. In a short time, they rushed back to the city with nearly 40 cords of wood, before the rebel army could react.

By March, Benedict began planning a second assault on the city. He also started a harsh campaign of harassment. He was hoping to get the civilian population to revolt or at least force Carleton's troops into open combat. He slowly burned down most of the city's surrounding suburbs, trying to force Carleton's hand, but to no effect. Carleton stubbornly stayed behind the high wall defenses.

Benedict also wanted to destroy British warships moored in Quebec's harbor. As part of his battle plan, he decided to make use of his own merchant ship, the *Peggy*. She was moored in the area with a cargo of rum. The *Peggy*, who was named for Benedict's wife, represented a third of Benedict's personal source of income. It must have pained him terribly, but he felt the sacrifice was justified in the cause of liberty.

The cargo of rum was unloaded, which the men appreciated, and the ship's hull was filled with explosives. Benedict's idea was to sail her into the British warships and blow her up to cause their destruction. This surely wasn't the act of a self-serving patriot, as many history books have reported.

Benedict received a message informing him he had been promoted to brigadier general by Congress. This lifted his spirits as he hurried to make preparations for a second assault on Quebec. But with such little military experience, he still felt inadequate for the mission and kept requesting a ranking general for the area. Everyone knew time was running out for any attempt to take the city. By late March, the ice on the St. Lawrence was beginning to break up and reinforcements from Britain were surely on their way. 5

On April 1st of 1776, David Wooster, the commanding general in the area, finally moved from his comfortable quarters in Montreal to Quebec. The next morning, Benedict gave him a tour by horseback of all the patriot positions he had been working on and details of his preparations. Wooster grumbled about everything he saw and after the tour he dismissed any advice or recommendations Benedict had offered.

Benedict was trying very hard to suppress his anger and frustration with Wooster, especially with all they had endured over the past three months. That very day, sudden word came that Carleton was planning a foray out of the city. Benedict, ready for action, ran to his horse. The mount suddenly spooked and reared, causing Benedict to lose his balance. His horse crashed to the ground, pinning Benedict's wounded leg.

Carried back into his headquarters, Benedict was again bedridden for another ten days. It was like darkness had fallen over him and the camp. Carleton's move turned out to be a false alarm. Benedict knew he probably couldn't hold back his anger with Wooster much longer. He requested permission to retire back to Montreal. Wooster considered Benedict a second-class, inexperienced, overzealous soldier and easily granted his request.

On April 12th of 1776, a very dejected Benedict rode out of Quebec to Montreal. He was very slowly learning a new reality. In the business world, as long as he had the freedom – which he was willing to fight for – he could always set his own destiny. All he needed was his own strength, merit and skills in order to succeed or fail. 6

But in colonial America, there was a new world of rank, politics and class for Benedict to adjust to and his perseverance was not always enough. He found others could undermine his efforts, actions and honor. This, to Benedict, was a very bitter pill to swallow.

As Benedict rode into Montreal, he was in search of General Wooster's former headquarters. He learned that Wooster spent a very comfortable winter at a chateau on the river. Benedict assumed command of the city and began receiving meetings with prominent residents. Some of them were old trading acquaintances of Benedict's.

Benedict heard many complaints of Wooster's high-handedness throughout the winter. He assured the residents he would do his best to make amends. He had little time to rest or reflect on his quest in Quebec and the harsh winter of 1775. There were rumors of preparation in progress for an assault on Montreal, from the west. The British in the outposts of the wilderness regions along Lake Ontario had aligned with some Native Americans and were hoping to attack rebel forces around Montreal.

Available troops under Benedict's command had to prepare for a possible assault, and if Wooster failed in Quebec, he needed to prepare for an orderly retreat toward the Champlain corridor. Washington was busy moving his main army toward New York City, as he felt Britain's next move would be targeted there. Apprehension and fear were beginning to build in the Montreal area, knowing that Great Britain's ships and reinforcements could arrive any day to retake the region.

Benedict received a surprise visit at headquarters on April 26th, 1776. Congress had sent a new commander, Major General John Thomas, to the Quebec region. Thomas was a doctor by trade, but he had much military experience in the Seven Years War in Canada. He was 51 and described as very tall.

Thomas was anxious to meet Benedict Arnold, who was growing in fame. Thomas had heard much about Benedict. He told Benedict he was being referred to as 'America's Hannibal' in the halls of Congress and brought warm greetings from Washington. He also needed to get Benedict's opinions on the Canadian affairs.

Benedict relayed the sad state the Canadian campaign was in, not pulling any punches. They talked for hours of possible ways to re-invigorate efforts before the British arrived. Thomas told Benedict he had close to 1,500 patriot soldiers at Fort Ticonderoga and Crown Point, waiting for the ice-clogged waterways to open so they could move north to help. Thomas also informed Benedict that a small envoy of congressional commissioners from Philadelphia would be along in a few days to see him and assess the situation. 7

He was hoping they were bringing some hard money, said Benedict, to reimburse the Canadians who had sacrificed so many goods to maintain the army. Thomas told him maybe they could help with the politics, but he thought all they would be bringing was good will.

General Thomas moved on to Quebec to see how Wooster was handling affairs there. On April 29, 1776, the Philadelphia commissioners arrived. Benedict received them with great pomp and a salute of cannons. The citizens of Montreal turned out to see what all the fuss was about. The head of the delegation was none other than Ben Franklin. At 70 years of age, the journey from Pennsylvania to Canada must have been arduous for him.

Franklin's mission was three-fold. He wanted to assess conditions in the northern theater for himself and he also wanted to meet and bolster support from the Canadian population, hoping to get them to join in the struggle, as a 14th colony. Not the least, Franklin was curious to meet Benedict Arnold, who had accomplished so much, given so little. Franklin was very much impressed by Benedict. He remained a friend and strong supporter of him throughout the war.

The other men in the delegation were Samuel Chase and Charles Carroll of Maryland. Both were delegates to the First and Second Continental Congresses. Carroll spoke fluent French and brought along Father John Carroll, a cousin who was a Jesuit priest. They would prove to be a great asset in dealing with the French-Canadian Catholic population and leadership.

Benedict assessed the situation for the delegates and impressed on them the need for currency, to maintain Canadian support and to settle accounts owed. If they were to continue the Canadian campaign, he stated, he wanted to do it with honor. The delegation wrote back to Congress for the need of close to 20,000£ of currency, to regain the affections of the people, and if funds weren't available it would be better immediately to withdraw. 8

By the end of May, all the decisions in the region were made for the patriot force. They received news of a sizable British relief force that had crossed the Atlantic and was bearing down on them. Benedict asked the Canadian Commission for permission to head back to Quebec to do everything in his power to keep possession of this country. The commission – Franklin, Carol and Chase – agreed, but cautioned Benedict not to make too bold a stand, if forces were too great to repel. They might need to fall back to save patriot soldiers and fight another day.

Ben Franklin started making his way back to Philadelphia, but Carroll and Chase stayed behind to bolster Canadian support. Congress instructed Washington to dispatch troops, and he finally sent 2,000 men, but it was too little, too late. By the time the troops made it to the Richelieu River – at the northern part of the Champlain corridor – the American army was already in full retreat.

Benedict met with General Thomas, who was already retreating from Quebec. He updated Benedict on the situation there. Thomas tried to implement some of Benedict's battle plans but was to meet with much resistance from Wooster and other officers. He told Benedict that they did sail his merchant ship, the *Peggy*, into the harbor with her now deadly cargo. But the British warships blew her up before she could do the intended damage.

The generous sacrifice of Benedict's ship and cargo was for naught. His men were on reduced rations and close to half had contracted smallpox. Orderly retreat was their only option left.

On his way back toward Montreal, Benedict was met with more bad news. British Commander George Forster had made allies with the Conasauga Indians and was making a move from the southwest toward Montreal. Forster engaged Benedict's troops at Fort Anne, a small fort to the west. He managed to capture 500 patriots, killing 28 of them. The Indians stripped the men of all their possessions, even some of their clothes.

Benedict was infuriated and began preparing to attack this force. He had no intention of leaving more prisoners behind in Canada. Benedict gathered as many men fit for duty as he could find – about 450 – and made a rush toward Forster's position.

Forster had received false reports that Benedict was advancing toward him with more men than Benedict actually had, and heard others were joining him. He decided to retreat west with his prisoners in tow.

Benedict reached Fort Anne, where the men were overrun and captured. He could see the retreating force in the distance. He sent a party of Caughnawaga – Indians allied with the patriots – ahead with a message. He wrote that should his men not be freed, or if any of them were murdered, he intended to sacrifice every Indian who fell into his hands and would follow them to their towns and destroy them by fire and sword.

Forster wrote back a reply, saying, if Arnold followed, he would kill every prisoner and give no quarter to any who fell into his hands. Benedict was furious at his reply and loaded 300 men into bateaus they found still intact at Fort Anne. They gave chase and received enemy fire at dusk, then silently rowed past the enemy position to cut off their escape route. 9

As night fell, Benedict called a council of war among his junior officers. The officers in his team were very much against attacking the British and Indian positions since they were so outnumbered. Quite an argument ensued, but the men could not sway Arnold's intentions. He had no intention of losing 500 soldiers to certain death at the hands of the Indians.

That very early morning – at about 2 a.m. – Forster sent two prisoners with a truce flag to suggest a future prisoner exchange. Benedict decided, on his own, to try and bluff Forster. He knew Forster didn't know how many men Arnold had with him. He wrote back to Forster to say he was ready to launch an attack, adding that if his prisoners were murdered, his force would sacrifice every soul who fell in his hands. 10

Forster took the bait since he had his own problems and wasn't sure whether he could control the actions of the Indians who were with him. The Indians were eager to kill and scalp the prisoners.

Arnold's actions that night saved 500 men from certain death. The next day, Forster began to ferry the prisoners back to Fort Anne.

After securing the men back, Benedict left his officers in charge of moving them south toward Lake Champlain. He gave orders to burn Fort Anne and the Conasauga Indian village – Indians who supported Forster – along the way. He then hurried back to Montreal to help with the evacuation. Benedict's men decided not to burn the Indian village, due to rumors and scouting reports of strong Indian resistance. 11

Chase and Carroll were still in Montreal and were much relieved to hear the soldiers captured at Fort Anne were safe. The commissioners now knew of the impending, looming threat traveling down the St. Lawrence.

They also knew of the bad condition of the retreating army and judged the Canadian campaign to be beyond repair. Before they left for Philadelphia, they wrote a letter to Congress, stating that General Thomas was dying of smallpox and they wrote of Wooster's actions in the theater, saying he was totally unfit for command, thus he should be recalled immediately.

Benedict was asked by Chase and Carroll to assume overall command until another senior officer could take over. They begged for a load of supplies from the good citizens of Montreal, pledging payment at a later date, on the faith of the united colonies. 12

On May 31st of 1776, Benedict wrote a letter to General Horatio Gates, informing him of the mission. He was very downhearted, especially not wanting to leave his troops who were imprisoned in Quebec. But he knew, for now, there was no choice. He wrote that the group was neglected by Congress and had never received envoys and timely support. Benedict would use all his strength, making every possible preparation to secure and retreat, which he was hoping to do with honor. 13

Benedict also wrote with frustration, "I wish with all my heart we were out of the country. We had much better begin anew and set out right and methodically." 14

The very day that letter was sent, a new commanding general was sent to the area by Washington for relief efforts and hopes of somehow turning events around. His name was General John Sullivan, a lawyer from New Hampshire and a delegate to the Continental Congress. He – like Benedict – had lots of zeal, but little military experience.

Sullivan ignored Benedict's advice and gathered any troops who were still in condition to fight. He decided to make a stand and engage the now-reinforced British troops between Montreal and Quebec. Sullivan was badly routed out, with 400 patriot losses, half of them imprisoned.

Benedict galloped at a feverish pace between Montreal and St. Johns, attending to evacuation details. He had a makeshift hospital set up on Isle Au Noix, an island 12 miles up the Richelieu River toward Lake Champlain. Benedict needed a place to safely care for the very sick and disease-ridden troops, as they made their way south.

On June 13th, he wrote to General Schuyler for the need of any kind of watercraft available to move men back down Lake Champlain. He stated, "You may expect soon to hear of evacuating Canada or being prisoners." 15

General Sullivan arrived at St. Johns with what was left of his rear guard on June 17th. His troops had set fire to any forts they passed along the way. They gathered as many boats and canoes as they could find and destroyed as many bridges as they could, to slow the advance of the British troops who were not far behind.

    On June 18th, Benedict ordered his remaining men into the boats and told them to go. He and an aide rode by horseback north to see how far behind them the British troops were. They rode hard north until they met up with General John Burgoyne's advance columns. He needed to know how much time they had.

    Then, they rode quickly back to the shoreline, where they hurriedly unsaddled and unbridled their horses. Benedict pulled his pistol and shot his horse, telling his aide to do the same. They could leave nothing for the enemy to find and use against them. Benedict pushed the last boat from the Canadian shores by himself.

    They arrived at the makeshift hospital on Isle Au Noix that very evening. The island was a horrible site of unspeakable distress. The sick – some of who could not see, speak or walk – were enduring maggots that crawled over their smallpox ravaged bodies. Those healthy enough to continue were dragging their dead comrades into shallow burial pits.

    A very heavyhearted Benedict had to turn his attention to the thousands of British troops poised to march on northern New York. Intelligence reports said there were well over 8,000 well-trained and well-supplied British troops preparing to advance. He found General Sullivan, who was also on the island.

    Sullivan asked Benedict to take a letter describing the situation to General Schuyler, who was probably between Fort Ticonderoga and Albany. Benedict was more than happy to comply with Sullivan's request, just to get off the island of misery. He set off with Sullivan's letter immediately and finally got some rest as he sailed down Lake Champlain. It was the first rest he had gotten in many days.

Schuyler wasn't at Fort Ticonderoga, so Benedict went south to Albany, where he caught up with Schuyler on June 24th of 1776. Benedict was anxious to discuss defending the Champlain corridor. Both armies were now locked in a race to build offensive and defensive capabilities, in order to travel the length of Champlain.

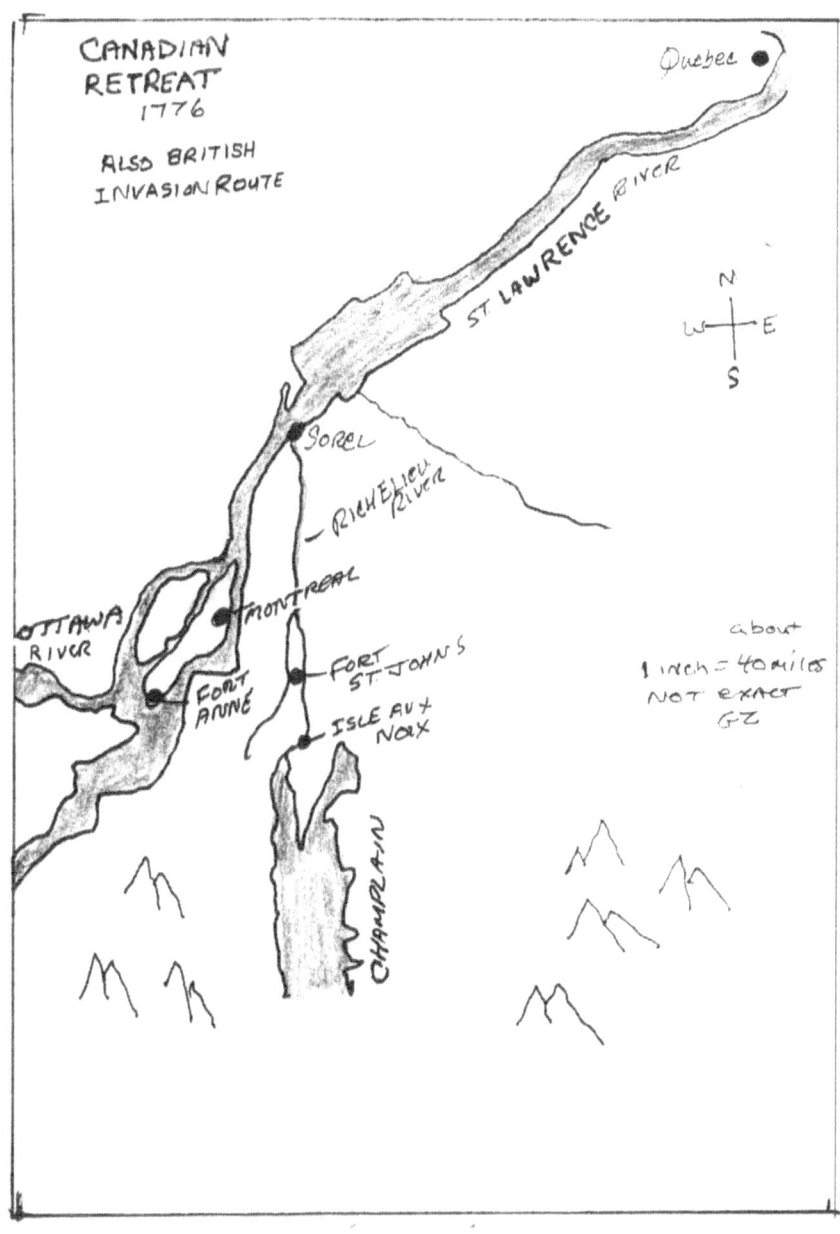

Map 5

Arnold was proud of his new home in New Haven Connecticut on Water Street. The home had formal gardens and a carriage house. Photo by Henry R. Hallett. *Courtesy Library of Congress.*

Depiction of busy New York Harbor, 1756-1761. Oil painting of East River Waterfront by unidentified artist. *Courtesy of the New York Historical Society.*

Fort Ticonderoga, site of America's first victory and first offensive strike by Arnold and Allen. *Public domain.*

Fort Ticonderoga from the top of Mount Defiance. British hauled cannons to the summit rendering the fort indefensible. *Public domain.*

Portrait of Daniel Morgan by Alonzo Chappel. *Courtesy Library of Congress.*

Morgan was a huge man who ruled his band of Virginia riflemen with his fists. He fought with Arnold through Maine and the battle of Quebec, and also at Saratoga.

Image of Ben Franklin, who traveled to Quebec to try to enlist Canada as a 14th colony, and to meet the new General Arnold. He was a great supporter of Arnold until September 1780. Maybe Arnold's picture should be here?

"Carrying the Bateaux at Skowhegan Falls," drawn by Sydney Adamson and engraved by Charles Wesley Chadwick. This image shows the difficulty of moving Bateaux up the raging Kennebec River. *Courtesy Library of Congress.*

Portage of the Great Carrying Place drawn by Denman Fink, halftone plate engraved by H. Davidson. *Courtesy Library of Congress.*

A view of the City of Quebec. This etching was published by Robert Sayer in London in 1768. *Historic Urban Plans, Inc.*

A painting by F.C. Yohn depicts the storming of Quebec in blinding snow. Benedict was the first man in, and the first man shot. For many, it was their last day of enlistment, and their last day on earth. *Courtesy, Library of Congress.*

The death of General Montgomery in the attack on Quebec, Dec. 31, 1775. Artist John Trumbull. Public domain, *courtesy of Yale University Art Gallery.*

"View of Quebec from the East," by Joseph F. W. Des Barres, ca. 1781. *Library and Archives Canada / C-080270*

CHAPTER TWELVE

THE BATTLE FOR CANADA ENDS & THE BATTLE FOR SURVIVAL OF THE COLONIES BEGINS

For those who think our forefathers were all gentlemen working in harmony, that was not the case. The political wrangling, backbiting and debauchery were outrageous, and in 1776 were reaching a feverish pace. It seems when there was a victory of any kind, there were many ready and willing to claim credit, even discrediting others in order to do so.

But when word of the lost Canadian campaign hit Congress, the blame game hit an all-time high. There were courts of inquiry, accusations from junior officers who felt compelled to testify and many character assassinations. Benedict considered them small-minded, self-serving patriots and many of them were.

General Schuyler was hit with many accusations, even to the level of treason. Sullivan, Arnold, Wooster and Thomas all came under fire. Washington made sure he didn't catch any blame and suggested sending General Horatio Gates to take control of the northern theater. Schuyler saw this move as a threat to his command and leadership. But he managed to defend himself quite well in Congress and cleared his name.

Schuyler now had Gates to deal with. Benedict, for his part, was just busy trying to get the job done. He thought it best to let his actions speak for themselves. Men like Schuyler, Washington and Gates – of the upper class – knew this political maneuvering would be more important later on and paid more particular attention to it.

When Gates arrived in Albany, he, Benedict and Schuyler left together to get back to the Champlain region. They arrived at Crown Point on July 5th of 1776. The northern army, what was left of it, had to regroup. The long Canadian campaign had taken a terrible toll. A total of 5,000 men went north. Many were wounded and recovering. Many with smallpox were too sick to fight, some were missing in action and a good number were prisoners of war.

At the north end of Lake Champlain was the huge reinforced British army preparing to bear down on the patriots. General Sullivan became very upset over being replaced with Gates and felt he had to go to Philadelphia to defend his honor. There was also much tension between Gates and Schuyler, as now there were two commanding generals in the same theater.

On July 7th of 1776, Schuyler called for a council of war. He agreed to leave the main command in Gates' hands when he wasn't in the theater. The main points of defense on the lake were Fort Crown Point and Old Fort Ticonderoga. It was clear that there weren't enough resources to defend both forts. Fort Ticonderoga was chosen, but Benedict pointed out that the old fort was nearby Mount Defiance. If the British maneuvered cannons to her summit, they could easily rain artillery into the fort. Many at the council scoffed, saying cannons could never be hauled up such steep and wooded terrain. 1

After the war council, Sullivan left for Philadelphia to offer his resignation and defend his honor. General Schuyler also left the area, as he had an urgent matter to attend to. He was in the middle of negotiations with the Iroquois Nation. He was hoping to gain their neutrality. The Iroquois could easily upset any supply lines and communications if they took the side of Great Britain.

Schuyler was largely successful with all the tribes, except the fiercest – the Mohawks and Senecas. Most of the other tribes agreed to stay neutral or side with the Americans.

By late July, the American troops received the news that Congress had issued the formal Declaration of Independence. It gave the men a more definite idea of what they were fighting for and morale started to lift in the camp.

But storm clouds were surely forming on the horizon. In June and July, a massive British war fleet arrived at New York's harbor. It must have been an intimidating and awesome sight. Several hundred warships and auxiliary ships sailed into the harbor, carrying 24,000 British and 5,000 Hessian soldiers, and 10,000 sailors of the Royal Navy. Estimates vary from 2 to 3 hundred vessels. The British fleet was under the command of General William Howe and his brother, Admiral Lord Richard Howe.

The new, young America was about to be crushed and the rebellion put down.

With the incredible British force in New York City under Howe and another huge force in Canada under Governor Carleton and General Burgoyne, the situation for the small American army looked quite bleak. The campaign season was running toward fall and the American army needed to find a way to slow the British advance or face a crushing defeat before winter. 2

CHAPTER THIRTEEN

COMMODORE BENEDICT ARNOLD – FATHER OF THE AMERICAN NAVY

At Fort Ticonderoga, General Gates began formulating his defensive battle plans. The obvious way for Carleton and Burgoyne to attack south was to go down Lake Champlain. Gates needed a way to slow the British before winter. The Americans needed a navy to engage the enemy on the lake.

This huge and impossible task was handed to Benedict on July 7th, 1776. He had vast sea experience and the tenacity to accomplish it, if it were at all possible. Benedict left quickly for the small port town of Skenesboro, where the new American shipyard was already in motion. Carpenters and ship builders converged there by the hundreds. Many skilled craftsmen from Pennsylvania, Massachusetts and Connecticut began the task of building the first American navy.

Supplies were short, but Benedict was good at managing details. He secured sailcloth, anchors, tar, brushes, cannons, ammunition and gunpowder. He also supervised all construction details: to build and equip ships. Work in the shipyard went on day and night. It was hoped that a respectable navy could be formed in just three to four months.

Benedict did have one distraction from his duties when Gates summoned him to Fort Ticonderoga for hearings on the earlier campaign season. Some of the junior officers Benedict had rubbed the wrong way wanted satisfaction. Benedict was prepared to settle these petty arguments by duel, if that was what they wanted.

Sometimes, Benedict's abrupt, no-nonsense manner got him into trouble and made bitter enemies with other officers. He would have been smarter to pay more attention to political matters, as these small-minded officers did what they could to damage his reputation. Some of the officers cleared themselves of charges, and Benedict was also cleared, so Gates dissolved the court.

Benedict didn't let the distraction keep him from his duties, as he hurried back to Skenesboro to ready the fleet. Though the proceedings made him a bit resentful and angry, he threw himself back into his work – even harder – for the cause of liberty. 1

By late August of 1776, most of the fleet was ready for battle. The fleet consisted of nine gundalows – flat-bottomed, single-masted craft with fixed, square sails. They could only move with the wind. Other movement depended on men rowing with oars. The boats were about 50 feet in length and held a crew of 45 men. Each gundalow was equipped with three to five cannons and up to eight swivel guns. They were christened *Boston, Connecticut, Jersey, New Haven, New York, Philadelphia, Providence, Spitfire* and *Success*. 2

Also ready for service were three row galleys. These were more maneuverable craft. They were 70 to 80 feet in length, with two short masts that had swiveling triangular sails. The row galleys could tact with the wind, but also had oars for calm conditions.

The row galleys had quarterdecks and cabins. They were equipped with eight to ten cannons and up to 16 swivel guns. The craft were christened *Congress, Trumbull* and *Washington*. Another part of the fleet were the sloops *Enterprise* and *Liberty*. They had been seized during the prior campaign season, when Benedict first entered the region.

Two more ships, the cutters *Lee* and *Royal Savage*, were ships seized by General Montgomery at St. John's during the start of the Canadian campaign. These schooners accommodated up to 60 men, three to four cannons and up to ten swivel guns. By late August, Benedict had a fleet of 16 warships ready for battle. He wanted twice that number, but he knew that time and the enemy would soon be pressing upon his troops.

To add to the fleet's problems were the lack of experienced sailors. Many men were available, but they didn't want to face the storms or the enemy on the water. The army drew lots to see who would serve in the navy.

Although Benedict had extensive maritime experience, most of his crews had little to none. He also lacked experienced artillery fighters. Before he could set sail, he had to find a ship's surgeon. To make matters worse, there was an extreme shortage of gunpowder.

The fleet they were about to face had much larger artillery and ships, navigated by professional, experienced sailors.

As the patriot fleet was frantically preparing, the British were at the north end of the lake, doing the same. They dismantled warships on the St. Lawrence and moved them to St. John's for re-assembly. They were also building more ships and bateaus at their shipyard.

Benedict pushed on, night and day, getting ships ready while drilling and training his men how to sail and use artillery. As preparations got closer to completion, General Gates set up a meeting with his commodore, Benedict. He informed Benedict that the fleet was to be used as a defensive action only, which certainly wasn't in Benedict's nature. If he engaged the enemy, he was to inflict as much damage as possible to slow them down, then retreat to help defend Fort Ticonderoga, hopefully with minimal loss of life or arms.

Battle preparations to face Carleton and Burgoyne were underway. The American mission was to try and halt any progress south by the British until the next campaign season. The Americans' hope was to re-group and try to fight the British off the next spring or summer. Victory against the overwhelming force was not a reasonable expectation.

Benedict's fleet set sail in late August of 1776. Halfway up the lake, progress was going quite well when a fierce storm with gale force winds crashed into the fleet. Benedict gave orders for a southward retreat. The gundalow ship, *Spitfire*, didn't react in time to fend off the strong winds. Surging waves pushed the ship toward shore and certain destruction.

Realizing the ship was in serious trouble, Benedict jumped into a small boat and directed his very frightened oarsmen to row him toward Spitfire. Through a speaking horn, he screamed orders to the ship's captain, giving him instructions of how to trim the sails properly. The ship soon swung about and avoided any damage. His men commented on Benedict's fearless behavior. They knew they had a leader they could look up to and respect.

The fleet made it to a bay and relative safety from the storm. At least, they had passed their first test as seamen. A grateful Benedict called his men together and they went to shore to celebrate. They enjoyed a good meal and drank toasts to the health of Congress and Benedict. They proclaimed the spot they stood on as Arnold's Point, in honor of their commodore. 3

As the weather cleared and the lake calmed down, they set sail north again, toward the enemy. Benedict surveyed the islands and coves along the way, looking for any structures in the lake that could give them some advantage in battle.

By September 3rd of 1776, they reached their northern destination and had yet to encounter any sign of their enemies. Benedict sent out scouting craft and put the fleet in battle formation across the lake. He wanted the British to know they wouldn't sail down Lake Champlain without a fight. At least, they had won the race to enter the lake, but knew the invading force would be preparing to engage.

The British and Indian allies formed a raiding party and attacked one of Benedict's ships that were closest to the shore. The brave crew drove them off but lost three men and sustained six wounded. Sentries posted along the shore noticed enemy activity. Benedict realized the British were planning to attack the fleet with land artillery and ships, simultaneously. He then ordered the fleet a few miles south to ruin their plan.

Benedict received intelligence of the enemy's strength. They had one ship alone capable of carrying 18 cannons. He needed some kind of advantage and found it in a bay by Valcour Island. He thought, as the British fleet sailed down the main channel, he could ambush them from the bay. By the time the Brits could make a turn into the wind and react to his fleet, he could do much damage to their rear guard, maybe even sinking row galleys that would be carrying thousands of their soldiers.

If Benedict's idea worked and they survived the battle, they could still swing south toward Ticonderoga. They anchored the small fleet in Valcour Bay in a half-moon battle formation and Benedict continued training his men. In a sense, they had already accomplished part of their mission – slowing the British – as they now knew they couldn't sail the whole Champlain corridor without resistance. 4

Benedict, while nervously waiting for the enemy onslaught, sent messages to General Gates. He requested more experienced seamen and more gunpowder. Gates replied, saying the supplies requested just weren't available, and also informed him that Washington was engaging the enemy near New York City. Benedict knew he would have his hands full at any minute.

The minutes turned into weeks. The British were taking their time in preparations, as they wanted to be sure they had all capability to destroy any resistance. September passed and the leaves were beginning to show their bright fall colors. The temperature dropped and Benedict had to request more clothing for his men. Food stores were also getting low. It had to be torture, knowing that 850 cold, wet sailors were about to face nearly 7,000 well-supplied troops. 5

On October 10th of 1776, Benedict called for a council of war. He called his officers together to go back over the battle plans. One of the officers suggested, on seeing Carleton's fleet, that they retreat toward Fort Ticonderoga and engage the enemy along the way. Benedict knew that was what the British expected them to do. He also knew they would easily out sail the smaller patriot ships and blow them out of the water.

Benedict's plan was quite unconventional. He said he would let some of the British fleet pass by the island's bay. He would keep his ships in a tight, crescent-shaped formation and attack from the side and rear. The British would have to make long turns into the wind to engage the American fleet.

With the hope of divine providence, he thought his seamen could inflict enough damage to escape or drive the British back toward Canada for repairs. He told his men he would be giving orders and directions from the middle of the crescent and he assigned the officers he wanted on his left and right flanks.

As the council of war broke up, Benedict gave his most chilling instructions. He told his men to make sure to cover the powder magazines with wet blankets to keep hot lead and sparks from exploding them, and also to spread sand on the ships' decks so the men would keep their footing in any pools of blood.

Benedict's plan did have some serious flaws. He was counting on the overconfidence of the British navy and assumed they wouldn't send any scouting craft to search for enemy vessels. Also, if the wind was in their favor, they could turn quickly into the bay, trapping his fleet or drop anchor and foil any attempt of escape. He had to make sure the British would engage in battle on his terms.

At the moment Arnold was light one ship. The *Liberty* was at Ticonderoga getting provisions. On October 11th of 1776, Benedict's assumption of British overconfidence proved correct. He could see their lead ships in the channel, moving south without any scouting vessels. He waited patiently until part of the fleet sailed past the island and when the wind was right, he gave orders to drop sails and quickly sailed toward the enemy, offering volleys of cannon fire. The Battle of Valcour Island had begun.

Benedict's plans went perfectly. With the wind in his favor, the little American fleet inflicted major damage to the Royal Navy. Gun smoke filled the air and wood splinters covered the cold waters of Lake Champlain. The battle roared on, with both sides delivering damaging strikes from about 11 a.m. to dusk. Benedict kept himself highly visible to encourage his men, shouting orders and directing fire, even aiming by himself many of the cannons on his ship. His face was blackened with burnt gunpowder.

By nightfall, the battle had ended pretty much in a draw. Both sides caused extensive loss to the other, but neither was overpowered. There were about 60 casualties on each side, with many wounded. The British couldn't believe they could not sweep this little navy aside, nor could they believe how much tenacity Benedict and his men had showed in battle.

While the battle raged, many Redcoats and Indian allies worked themselves over to Valcour Island, lining the shoreline and hoping to catch the Americans in crossfire. Benedict managed to keep his fleet just out of their range. The only part of Benedict's plan that went awry was when the sun set, and the battle ended. His fleet was hopelessly trapped in Valcour Bay.

The enemy controlled the shorelines and the British fleet was controlling the end of the bay in battle formation. The British and Benedict knew that by sunup, the American fleet would have to surrender or face annihilation. But that evening, divine providence stepped in.

It was a dark, cold fall night and heavy fog rolled into the Champlain Valley. Benedict decided to try a breakout. He ordered the wounded be put into cabins to muffle their groans. A lantern was mounted on the stern of each ship, with the side toward the British fleet covered. Benedict ordered the oarsmen to row as silently as possible.

Single file, with each ship following the lantern of the other, they rowed silently between the British fleet and the New York shoreline. As the sun rose, the British were about to savor their victory. But when the fog lifted from the lake, the whole American fleet was gone! Carleton was furious.

The crippled – but still alive – American fleet sailed quickly toward Crown Point and Fort Ticonderoga all night. The very embarrassed British fleet set sail in pursuit. Benedict had a good head start, but the wind was favoring the British ships. In order to preserve what was left of his fleet, Benedict decided to turn back to the north and engage the enemy. He had one other warship and three gundalows with him. He knew a narrow spot in the lake called Split Rock and decided to make a stand there.

The captain of Benedict's other warship was soon surrounded by three British vessels and took some nasty broadside shots. Many of his men were wounded, so he struck his colors and surrendered.

The British then concentrated on Benedict's ship. The royal fleet had five times the firepower Benedict had, as they paid no attention to the smaller gundalows. Cannons trained on Benedict's men. The angry British would have their prize and revenge.

Benedict proved he was an expert at maneuvering ships, relying on his experiences of sailing from the West Indies to Canada. Somehow, he managed to engage the British fleet for a full two hours. He knew the British would be overconfident and as the battle raged, he studied his position and the shoreline, waiting for the right moment.

The British commander could not believe that Benedict refused to strike his colors and surrender. His ship was pinned broadside, with two warships and another at his stern, firing relentless grapeshot and cannon balls. Benedict later wrote that his men fought back "briskly." 6

At the perfect moment of position, Benedict shouted to his men to quickly take their places on the oars. He passed between two of the very surprised British warships. They were at a point where they couldn't turn and catch the wind. Benedict called to the gundalows to do the same and follow him. They rowed quickly into a cove and grounded the ships.

Surprised, the British tried desperately to maneuver and catch them with cannon fire. Benedict had the men and wounded quickly unloaded and used what was left of the gunpowder to blow up the ships and keep them from the enemy. They made their way by land toward Fort Ticonderoga, skirting around Indian raiding parties.

Benedict finally arrived at Fort Ticonderoga at 4 a.m. on October 14th of 1776. It would be the first sleep his Champlain veterans had in three days.

At Fort Ticonderoga, which was now better reinforced, Benedict's navy prepared for a massive British onslaught, which never materialized. The fledgling American navy had completely accomplished its mission. By now, it was so late in the campaign season that the Brits decided to fall back to Canada and regroup. They would have to put off their assault at least until the next spring.

If Arnold's naval campaign didn't go as well as it did and the British weren't stopped on Lake Champlain, the British would have intercepted the retreating divisions of Washington's army in the area around New York. It would have crushed the entire rebellion.

Benedict should have gone down in history as Father of the American Navy.

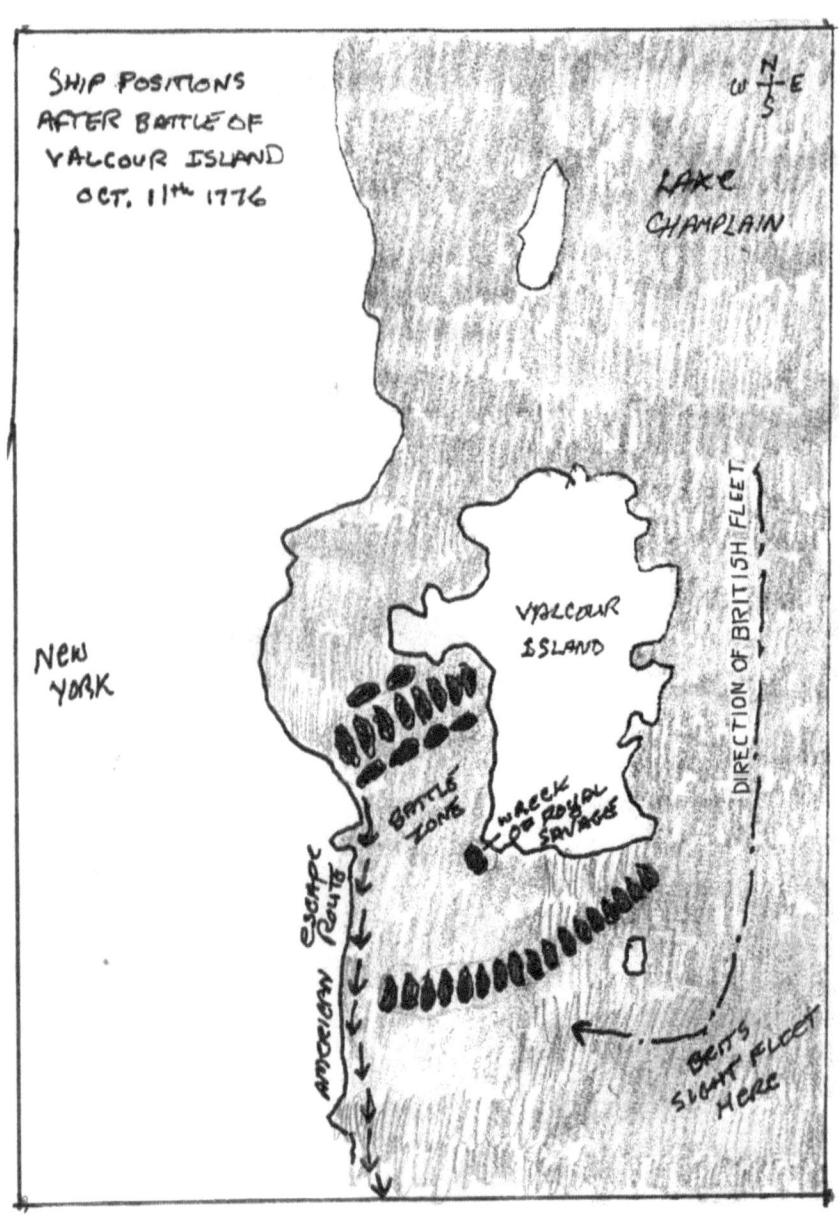

Map 6

CHAPTER FOURTEEN

AN UNEASY WINTER OF '76

Benedict's reputation was spreading throughout the colonies and even back to England. The tenacity of this 'horse jockey' from Connecticut was unbelievable.

Governor Carleton, out of respect for such bravery and also as a means to conserve rations and spread dissent among the American troops, sent British warships under a flag of truce to Fort Ticonderoga. He turned over his captured prisoners of war. 1

By mid-November of 1776, the Americans knew the Champlain region and Fort Ticonderoga would be safe, at least until spring. The generals released the militia who came to help defend the old fort. The generals then traveled to Albany to confer with General Schuyler, and on November 21st of 1776, they granted the regular army troops furloughs to go home, at least for a while. 2

October and November of 1776 weren't going well at all for George Washington. He retreated from Manhattan and his army suffered heavy casualties. They fought hard against General Howe's forces in the Battle of White Plains, but to no avail. Washington had to retreat farther west. The enemy had captured over 100 cannons in Manhattan, along with thousands of muskets and other weaponry. They also lost Fort Lee in New Jersey to General Cornwallis.

Washington suffered 3,000 casualties in the two defeats. In late November, he abandoned the New York area and moved his forces west toward the Delaware River.

In a desperate situation, Washington was in full retreat across New Jersey. He wrote to the northern army for reinforcements. Schuyler and Gates held back furloughs on eight regiments, since their enlistment times were still good until January 1st. Gates marched south to help relieve Washington.

Benedict wanted desperately to go home and see his boys, who he hadn't seen in 16 months. He wanted to see how his sister, Hannah, was managing with the boys and attend to the business affairs she was also helping with. He mentioned to Gates and Schuyler that he needed to settle some public accounts and that he wished to go home, at least for a while.

But Benedict's sense of duty and honor steered him in another direction. Knowing of Washington's dire situation, he sailed down the Hudson River, secured a horse and rode hard to reach Washington's camp.

He arrived at Washington's headquarters before Gates and the Ticonderoga divisions. While on his journey, he received a letter from Washington. It was almost a week old. George had given him orders to hurry toward New England, as he had heard the British invaded Rhode Island. By the time he got the letter, he was almost at Washington's camp, so he went there first. 3

On or about December 21st of 1776, Benedict discussed the military situation with Washington, and being offensive-minded, he suggested to his Excellency that he should make use of his troops before January 1st – when their enlistments would run out – just as he and Montgomery had been forced to do in Quebec.

The following day, Benedict made haste toward New England. The journey would at least allow him to return home to New Haven, if only for a brief visit. Around New Year's Day, Benedict arrived home to see his boys and sister Hannah. He couldn't believe how much his sons had grown. They wanted to hear his tales of adventures. 4

Hannah gave him the bad news that his accounts were dwindling due to the war, besides his own purse, which he was draining constantly in the war effort. The British navy had curtailed shipping. Merchants like John Hancock and Benedict were reduced to smuggling to avoid bankruptcy.

As news that Benedict was in New Haven traveled through town, many neighbors and citizens turned out to give him a warm welcome. His newfound hero status was heralded throughout New England. Benedict appreciated the warm welcome and rejoiced at some more great news. He had been petitioning Washington and Congress to put his Kennebec warriors, especially Daniel Morgan and his riflemen, on the earliest prisoner exchange lists. He finally got the good news that they had been released from the Quebec prison. 5

Morgan received a colonel's commission and went on to revive his band of Virginia riflemen. Another officer under Benedict's command, John Lamb, was also given a colonel's commission and was assigned by Congress the task of forming a second continental artillery regiment. But Congress wouldn't or couldn't appropriate the funds necessary. Out of his own funds, Benedict gave Lamb the money he needed. Lamb was a friend of Benedict's, who had suffered a bad facial wound during the Battle of Quebec.

Such affection and appreciation for troops was a rare commodity, but not with Benedict. He was a very different sort of general. He had to keep his visit at home short. By January 12th of 1777, he arrived in Providence, Rhode Island to assess the situation. 6

While in Rhode Island, Benedict received some more happy news. He found out Washington used his advice to begin offensive operations before enlistments ran out. Washington launched a Christmas night raid on British outposts in Trenton and was victorious. He also captured Princeton a week later. Finally, George had accomplished something positive in the war effort. 7

Gates had advised Washington to retreat to the Pennsylvania Mountains and take until spring to regroup. He didn't think it was wise to initiate these offensive operations. He especially didn't like Washington taking advice or influence from Benedict.

Horatio Gates faked an illness and left his men with Washington. He then traveled to Congress and began a nasty smear campaign, not only against Benedict, but also Washington. He hoped to use his upper-class status to possibly even replace Washington with himself. If it weren't for Washington's victories at Trenton and Princeton, it may have worked. Had Washington not taken Benedict's advice, he probably would have been replaced as commander-in-chief.

While in Rhode Island, Benedict found the British were entrenched in Newport and had full control of the port there. But being in the middle of a New England winter, they were showing no signs of moving offensive operations toward Providence, nor toward any rebel positions.

Benedict wanted to spring an attack and try to drive the enemy out of Newport and back to New York City, or even Great Britain. But many enlistments had run out and he had not nearly the troop strength necessary to do anything other than hold his position in Providence. Since the British weren't doing anything offensively, Benedict decided he would ride to Boston to see if he could bolster enlistments to get volunteers and find financial support for a campaign.

In Boston, he was surprised to be received as quite a celebrity, as news of his exploits had preceded him. His new stature went a little bit to his head. He thought he should update his uniform, so he made a visit to Paul Revere's shop. He ordered new epaulets, along with a sword knot, a sash, a two-belt apparatus and one dozen silk hose. He thought if he was going to mingle with New England's elite, he should look the part. 8

Benedict attended social gatherings and gala balls, trying to build support for the cause. He became quite infatuated with a Boston debutante named Elizabeth DeBlois. She was an attractive daughter of a wealthy Boston merchant. He hoped to court and possibly even marry her. He sent gifts and did what he could to gain her affection. 9

Now an infamous military leader, Benedict was dreaming of a new America, one where ability, achievement and virtuous service would be a measure of a citizen's worth. He hoped for an aristocracy of talent, rather than one based on class and money. He would prove to be quite naïve and idealistic in his thinking. Benedict lingered in Boston until nearly March, in his efforts to win Miss DeBlois and raise support for the revolution.

Benedict then made his way back to Providence. He resolved that a defensive strategy was his only option, at least until late spring. While there, he received information that Congress, and Washington were making preparations to gear up for the coming campaign season. He wondered where he would be asked to serve.

As he prepared his troops and defenses around Providence, Benedict received some devastating news. He normally ignored all the political wrangling of Congress, but he didn't know that others – like Gates – were stabbing him in the back politically. The elites in Congress gave out assignments and promotions to many, except Benedict.

Benedict expected and deserved to receive a command position. He hoped it would be in the northern department. But Congress completely passed him over. Washington even wrote to him, saying Congress must have made a mistake. Benedict thought his virtuous service and battle wounds would be enough, but Congress deeply wounded him worse than the bullet had. 10, 11

Congress had given out their promotions based mainly on political connections and class status. Arnold was considered second-class to most of Congress.

Benedict not only had seniority – serving since day one in 1774 – he also believed a man's actions are what should determine elevation or rank assignments, not small-minded politics or class.

The five generals who were promoted over Arnold were Arthur St. Clair, Adam Stephen, Thomas Mifflin, William "Lord" Sterling, and Benjamin Lincoln—none of whom had distinguished careers in the military. St. Clair gave up Fort Ticonderoga without a fight in 1776; Adam Stephen was drunk during the battle of Brandywine and eventually cashiered out of the Army; Thomas Mifflin was involved in the "Conway Cabal" to remove Washington as Commander and replace him with Horatio Gates; Lord Sterling took a beating during the battles of Long Island and Brandywine, but really didn't do anything spectacular; and Benjamin Lincoln lost Charleston during the Siege of March-May 1780. None of these individuals ever came close to Arnold's heroics in the field. 12

When Congress by-passed Arnold, it caused him to consider the matter a major affront to his honor. His honor and reputation meant everything to him.

The concept of honor, today, is rarely addressed or talked about. I'll let Arnold do the talking.

In a letter dated March 11th of 1777, Benedict wrote to Washington to give an assessment of the Rhode Island situation. He wrote that Congress was promoting junior officers to the rank of Major General.

"I view it as a very civil way of requesting my resignation as unqualified for the office I hold. My commission was conferred unsolicited and received with pleasure only as a means of serving my country. With equal pleasure, I resign it when I can no longer serve my country with honor." 13

He angrily decided he would ride to Congress, resign his commission and defend his honor. He left General Joseph Spencer in charge of the defensive operations in Providence and rode back home to New Haven.

On his arrival home, Benedict told his sister Hannah, that he would soon be a civilian and he intended to be back soon to help her rebuild the business. His decision to resign from the army gave him some calm, as he could – at least – spend more time with his sons.

While in New Haven, Benedict diligently put together his public accounts of the past campaign season, as he funded a great deal of his efforts from his own pocket. He was looking forward to reviving his business and he was quite bitter toward the elites in Congress. As he readied to go to Philadelphia to resign and regain his honor, he got some sad news. His courtship proposals to Miss DeBlois had been rejected.

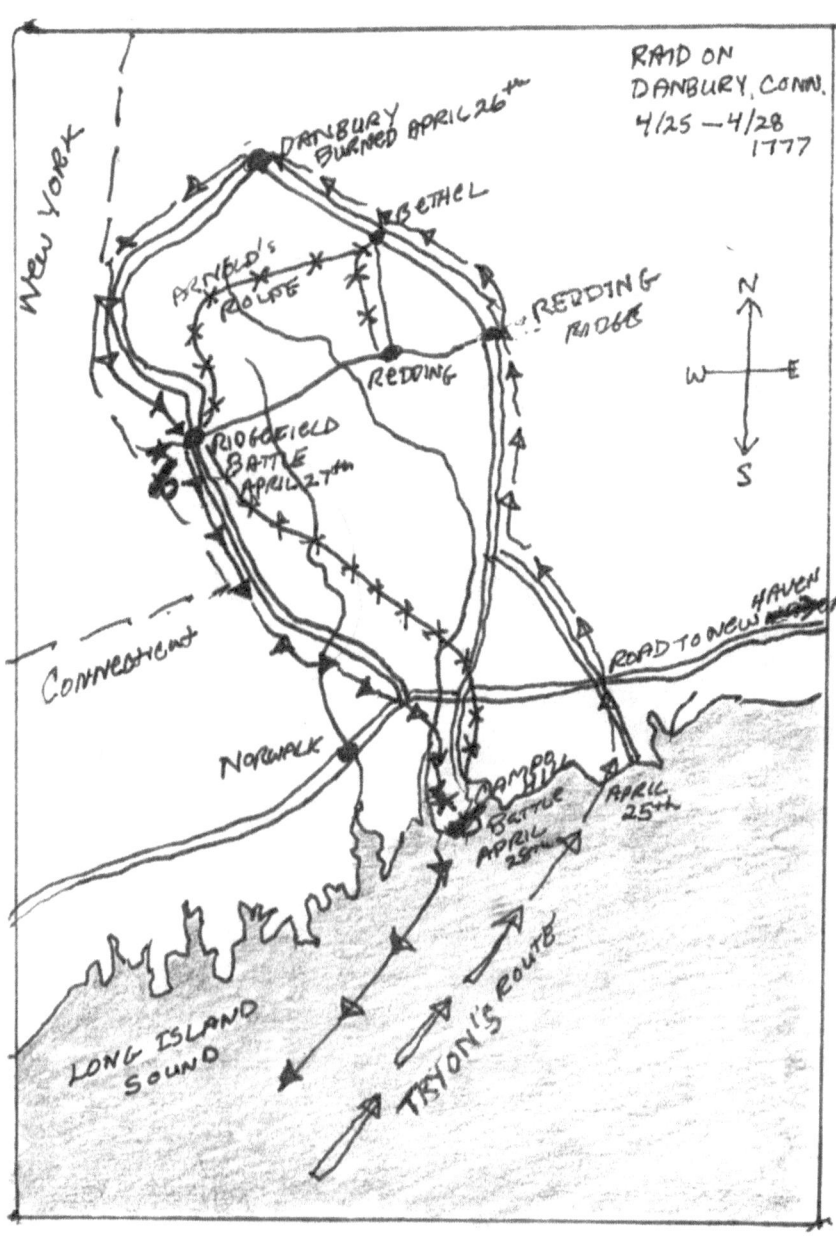

Map 7

CHAPTER FIFTEEN

THE CAUSE OF LIBERTY – ABOVE ALL ELSE

Winter faded and the first signs of spring were beginning to show in April of 1777. A sad and bitter Benedict rode his horse toward Philadelphia. So much was going through his mind – how he was going to present his resignation, how to revive his merchant business and how much his family needed him at home.

Suddenly, a courier galloped toward him with shocking news. A large British detachment had landed in Norwalk, Connecticut – some 30 miles from Benedict's home – and was marching toward Danbury, the site of a major patriot supply depot. His sense of duty and value of liberty's cause overrode his personal problems. Benedict yet again prepared for combat. 1

Just a little side story: When the British launched their raid, many riders, like the one that informed Benedict, were riding to warn the countryside. That very dark and rainy night, a young sixteen-year-old girl named Sybil Ludington, sprang into action. Though her story is not well documented, enough historians accept the account as related by her family. A statue was erected in her honor.

Sybil left that night to help her father, who was a local militia commander. She mounted her horse about 9pm and rode through the rain until dawn, a ride of nearly 40 miles. She rode to alarm and assemble militia, and to warn all the residents of the British Raid.

Sybil's ride was more than twice the distance and more successful than that of Paul Revere. She is known as the Female Paul Revere and a heroine of the American Revolution. It is said she raised nearly four-hundred militia members that Benedict would surely need.

Benedict rode hard toward Danbury. As he passed the homes of residents, he put out a call to muster any available militia to Danbury immediately. He arrived late in the evening of a cold, rainy April night.

Connecticut militia General Gold S. Silliman and the local militia were found at nearby Redding, Connecticut. Silliman provided the details of the day's events for General Arnold. Also showing up was old General David Wooster, who Benedict had to contend with in Quebec. Silliman explained what he knew. That day British commander William Tryon, the Royal Governor of New York (who was given the rank of Major General of the Provincials) had landed in Norwalk with twelve ships, a hospital ship, and several transport vessels., and a huge British raiding party. Mostly British infantry and a battalion of Loyalists, numbering 2,000 strong, were marching straight inland toward Danbury.

The continental troops stationed to protect the supply depot numbered only about 150 men. They found out about the advancing force, hid what supplies they could, and were forced to retreat into the countryside.

Tryon ordered his troops to destroy everything in their path. They destroyed all the supplies they found, and then proceeded to burn some 40 homes and buildings. By day's end, all of Danbury was burning. The British hoped also to crush the rebels' will to fight, but their actions only filled the rebels with resolve and hatred. 2

The rebel generals agreed on that very cold and rainy night to move in closer to the raiding party with their militias, who were now numbering nearly 600 men, with hopefully more on the way. They could see the glowing embers of what was left of Danbury. At about 2 am, Benedict told the men to dry their gunpowder and be prepared to see action at dawn.

Benedict thought he was outnumbered nearly three to one. He planned on cutting the raiding party off before they could reach the sea. He assumed they would be heading back to their ships in Norwalk or possibly to Tarrytown on the coast, causing more destruction. The small village of Ridgefield would be a possible interception point. An emergency war council was held.

It was agreed there would be a plan to have General Wooster and his son attack the rear guard of the British column with about 200 of the men. Benedict would take the remaining 400 and make a line at Ridgefield, directly challenging the enemy. As Benedict quickly marched toward Ridgefield, he picked up another 100 militia. 3

At 11 a.m. on that very morning, Wooster attacked the rear guard of the British column with about 200 of the men. The British turned and charged at Wooster's American force. Wooster was suddenly hit in the groin by a musket ball as he ordered a retreat. His son tried to help him up, but a bayonet impaled him. Wooster died painfully five days later, giving up his and his son's lives for the cause of liberty.

Wooster's actions gave Benedict's men valuable time to ready their positions. The British column came into view at about 3 pm. Benedict's men waited nervously in Ridgefield, taking cover behind wagons and stone walls. The British made a frontal attack, but the rebel lines held steady with Benedict's encouragement. Frustrated that they couldn't break the rebel position, the Brits sent out flanking parties, seeing they had superior numbers. The flanking maneuvers were working, causing the rebel lines to break up and flee.

Benedict brandished his sword and rode desperately back and forth, trying to form a rear guard to protect the fleeing troops. His horse suddenly dropped to the ground, thrashing in pain. Benedict's mount was hit with nine musket balls and the commander was pinned beneath. As Benedict was trying to free himself from the throws of the dying animal, a British soldier rushed toward him, ordering him to surrender, screaming, "You are my prisoner!" Benedict was heard to reply, "Not yet." He pulled his pistol and killed the soldier with one shot. He struggled free from under the horse and limped away toward a nearby swamp. Shots were raining all around him and he barely got away. 4,5

Tryon never thought he would meet so much resistance. He decided to stop the attack and regroup. That night, he made camp in Ridgefield, to tend to the dead and wounded. There were still 15 miles to get back to the coast.

Benedict found another horse, and never sleeping, he worked all night assembling his men and going through the countryside to try and rally more help. He was still hopelessly outnumbered. He knew there were only two roads Tryon could take to get back to his ships. Unfortunately, some Loyalists warned Tryon where they saw the American force assembling. Early the next morning, Tryon moved his men farther north to skirt around Benedict's force.

With such low numbers of soldiers, Benedict decided to try and hit the side and rear of the British column, using hit and run tactics. Benedict constantly exposed himself to enemy fire to encourage his men. The British made it to a point called Campo Hill near the coast, which gave them an advantage against the attack. They also gained reinforcements from the ships, including some artillery.

When Benedict formed lines of aggression, one witness later wrote about the event, saying, Arnold continually exposed himself, almost to a fault, and reportedly, exhibited the greatest marks of bravery, coolness and fortitude under fire. Benedict rode up the front of the lines, ignoring the heavy musket fire and grapeshot. He was heard to shout, "By the love of themselves, posterity and all things sacred, do not desert me!" He hoped to keep his rebel lines from breaking.

The rebel line finally broke, as the British charged down the hill. A musket ball ripped through the collar of Benedict's coat. Then, his horse took a hit to the neck and it went down. Somehow, Benedict survived with only bruises. Tryon's force easily escaped to the waiting ships.

The Americans had made quite an impressive stand, for their numbers. Benedict's old Kennebec friend, John Lamb, whose artillery unit he had funded, managed to get some artillery pieces into the battle, but Lamb himself was wounded with grapeshot. It was the second time Lamb was hurt while fighting under Benedict. He had already lost an eye in Quebec. Benedict wrote of the engagement, never speaking of his own actions. He related how many of the officers and men had behaved well. 6

The news of Tryon's raid and Benedict's heroism quickly reached Congress. Many of the congressmen felt quite embarrassed that this American hero had just been passed over for promotion. On May 2nd of 1777, they quickly promoted Benedict to Major General. John Hancock sent word of the promotion on to Washington with a message that Benedict's behavior was highly approved by Congress. 7

John Adams went much further. In those desperate times, America needed a hero. The army's enlistment quotas were falling far short of what was needed.

Adams requested that a medal be struck in Benedict's honor. He went into great detail. On one side, he wanted a platoon firing at General Arnold on horseback, his horse falling dead under him and Arnold deliberately disentangling his feet from the stirrups and taking his pistols out of his holsters before the retreat. On the other side of the medal, he wrote that he wanted Arnold to be mounted on a fresh horse, receiving another discharge of musketry with a wound in the horse's neck. 8

Congress felt Benedict would be satisfied with a Major Generalship, but they fell short of giving him seniority over the others they had promoted. So, Benedict would have to serve under other soldiers he had commanded just months ago. Even Washington commented there must be something amiss in their thinking.

Benedict still felt quite frustrated and betrayed by politics and politically minded officers. He knew that while he had been giving his all in the field, others in Congress were busy slandering his name and his honor. He was determined to have full satisfaction, to the point of drawing pistols if necessary. He also had public accounts owed to him and he hoped for at least partial restitution.

As Benedict again set out for Philadelphia, he fully intended to resign his commission. He wasted no time in his quest to be heard by Congress. A very surprised George Washington received Benedict at his headquarters in Morristown, New Jersey on May 12th of 1777. Benedict requested permission to travel to Philadelphia, since no major actions were going on at the moment.

Washington wanted to keep his fighting general in the field and did his best to calm down Benedict's manner. He was in need of someone to command a supply depot in Peekskill, but Benedict would hear none of it.

At that point, Washington knew he – nor his army – could stop Benedict from going to Philadelphia. Washington penned a letter to John Hancock for Benedict to take to Congress. The letter addressed the seniority issue of Benedict's promotion and he wrote that it was universally known how Benedict had always distinguished himself as a judicious, brave officer of good activity, enterprise and perseverance. 9

He again counseled Benedict to remain composed.

CHAPTER SIXTEEN

THE POLITICAL ARENA - 1777

Benedict arrived in Philadelphia on May 16th of 1777 and found lodging with the Maryland delegation and Representative Carroll, who had gone north to work with him in Montreal. He spent the weekend mingling with delegates to Congress. On Monday, May 19th, he entered the Pennsylvania State House, which some were now calling Independence Hall.

He presented Washington's letter and his own complaints. The next day, Benedict insisted on a court of inquiry to clear any charges against his name, and he requested his public accounts be settled. 1

The delegates actually caught Benedict off guard when they acted the very same day, offering him hearty thanks for his acts of heroism. His case was turned over to the Board of War for satisfaction. He was surprisingly honored with the gift of a horse, to replace the two shot from beneath him in Connecticut. They wrote that the horse was from a grateful nation, for his gallant conduct. One of the delegates wrote of Benedict's appearance: "His face handsome" and his muscular stature as a man low in height, "but well made." 2

On May 22nd, the Board of War met with Benedict and poured over documentation relating to his public accounts. The next day, the board expressed entire satisfaction concerning the General's character and conduct. They ordered that their findings be published.

Though his spirits were buoyed by the actions of Congress, Benedict still had much anguish over the matter of seniority of rank. He continued trying to change the thinking of the delegates. Unfortunately, Congress

– being mostly upper class – decided it best to dole out the rank of general based on class and influence, rather than merit or accomplishment. 3

Benedict wasn't the only general with issues for Congress. General Schuyler had many grievances to address, as did General Gates.

The political wrangling over the next month was nearly unbearable. John Adams wrote to his wife Abigail: "I am wearied to death with the wrangles between military officers, high and low. They quarrel like cats and dogs. They worry one another like Mastiffs, scrambling for rank and pay, like apes for nuts." But he wouldn't admit that Congress was the cause of most of the wrangling. 4

Benedict was getting a belly full of colonial politics. He felt the aristocracy was out of touch with the general population and the military. He also thought they were far too indecisive and slow to act. He especially didn't care for the courting of the French. He let it be known that he didn't want to fight off one monarchy to get in bed with another.

Tension was building. It was well known that two extraordinarily large British armies were making plans to pounce on America from New York City and Canada. Everyone was speculating about when they would force their campaigns.

Washington kept busy developing a wide spy ring to see if he could glean information about British General Howe's intentions for attack. Washington also moved his men 20 miles south to Middlebrook Heights, a well-defensible mountainous region. Howe tried a luring tactic to get Washington's army onto flatter ground for a decisive battle.

Benedict rode determinedly toward Princeton, under orders to engage the enemy if necessary. It was to Benedict's liking, as he was always offensively minded. But Washington didn't take the bait and stayed entrenched in the mountains. 5

Howe, realizing the American army couldn't be taunted into the open, retreated back to New York City. With the threat over, Benedict returned to Philadelphia. He entered Independence Hall on July 11th of 1777 and handed over his letter of resignation. He felt dishonored because he wasn't granted seniority and intended to go home to his family and business. Benedict said he would return at a later date to settle his public accounts.

Unknown to Benedict, Congress had just received an urgent communication from Washington. He wanted Benedict Arnold sent to him as soon as possible. Washington had received news that British General John Burgoyne – who was labeled by Americans as 'Gentleman Johnny' – had moved down Lake Champlain and captured Fort Ticonderoga. The looming force to the north was on the move. 6

The congressional delegates couldn't believe Washington didn't request General Gates. They didn't want to second-guess his thinking, since they needed immediate action.

Congress decided to disregard Benedict's resignation. John Hancock gave Benedict orders to immediately repair to Washington's headquarters and take all of Washington's directions. 7

Benedict said he would gladly go and fight as a private citizen. But Congress wouldn't hear of it. They were in urgent need of a fighting general and the seniority issue would have to wait. Benedict was in Washington's camp by July 17th of 1777. Reports were received that Burgoyne's army was on the move and Benedict prepared to go to the northern theater. Over the following month, Benedict seemed to be almost everywhere.

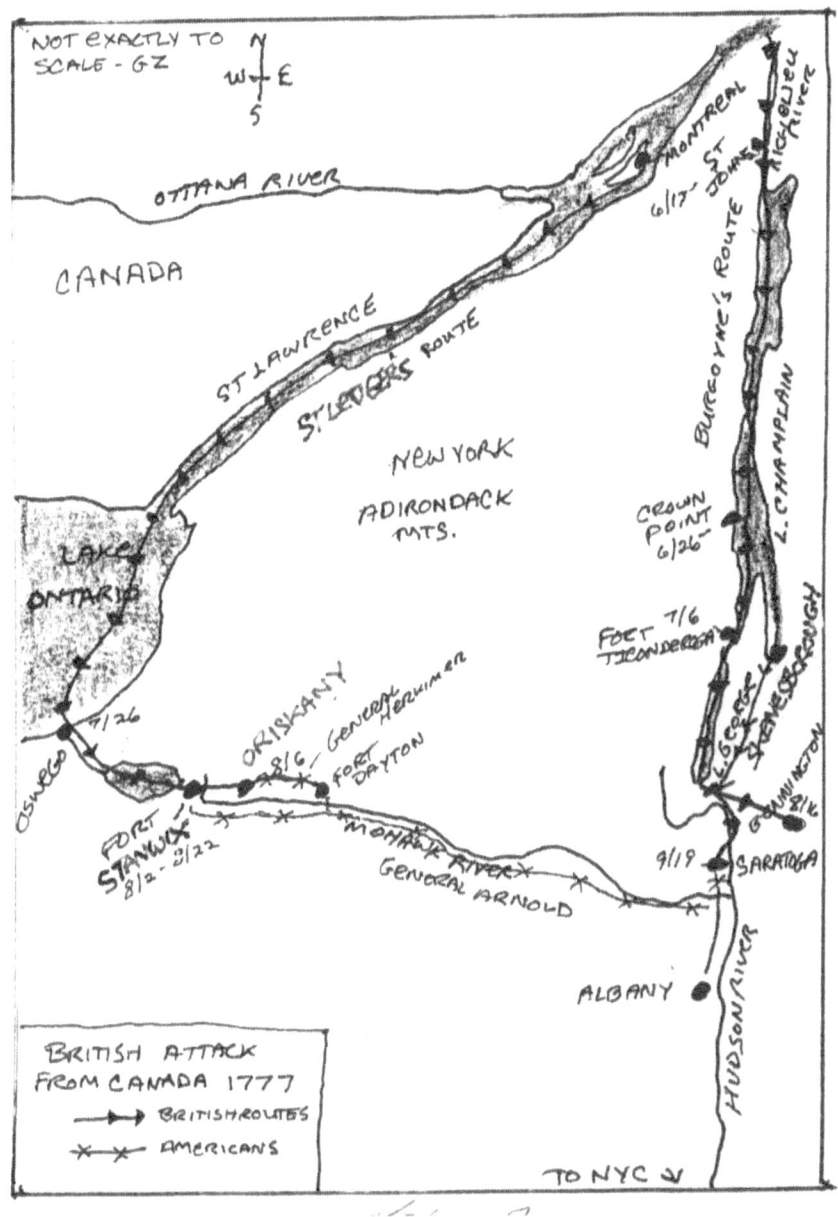

Map 8

CHAPTER SEVENTEEN

THE NORTHERN THREAT TO CRUSH AMERICAN RESISTANCE

General Burgoyne moved down from Canada with an intimidating force of nearly 10,000 troops. The huge army consisted of British regulars, Hessian allies and Indian war parties. The Canadians weren't so supportive of the British, registering only 150 men.

Burgoyne traveled in the style becoming to a British major general of aristocracy. He drank champagne and traveled with his mistress and other lady cohorts. He was quite confident he would sweep away any resistance in the Champlain corridor. His plan was to march to Albany and wait in comfort for Howe to send more reinforcements from New York City. Burgoyne sent a second force under Lt. Colonel Barry St. Leger through the western regions from Lake Ontario.

St. Leger was to travel through the Mohawk Valley and link with Howe in Albany. He anticipated, after crushing any American resistance and meeting with General Howe's army, America would be split, overpowered and the upstart rebellion would be over.

As Burgoyne made his move down Lake Champlain, Benedict's previous warning about reinforcing Mount Defiance came to pass. The commander left in charge of Fort Ticonderoga, Major General Arthur St. Clair, thought no army could possibly haul artillery up the steep, wooded slopes of Mount Defiance. But that's exactly what they did. The British artillery commander had a saying: "Where a goat can go, a man can go, where a man can go, we can drag a cannon." 1

When the rebels saw the cannons easily trained down on their positions and the massive flotilla in the lake, they had no choice but to abandon the indefensible fort and flee into the countryside. The Americans did everything they could to slow Burgoyne's progress south. They dropped trees on the roadway and destroyed any usable bridges.

Burgoyne's tactics were totally ruthless. He sent Indian war parties ahead of his regular army. They burned homes and people. They also scalped and tortured local residents. Burgoyne thought the terrorism would weaken the resolve of the colonists, but it did the opposite. All local and state militias were spurred to take up arms.

General Schuyler asked Benedict to do whatever he could to slow the British army's progress. As they were totally overwhelmed and outnumbered, the only option for the patriots was to hit and run, then hope for more recruits and the reinforcements that would help them make some kind of stand. 2

The rough terrain of what is now called the Adirondacks did the most to slow the British down. Between Lake Champlain and Lake George, they had to haul their supplies, artillery and men through a challenging three-mile portage, as Lake George is nearly 200 feet higher in elevation than Lake Champlain. By the time they reached the end of Lake George, it had taken them close to three weeks.

Benedict and his men seemed to be in skirmishes almost everywhere in the lower Champlain region, on nearly a daily basis. On July 27th of 1777, one of Benedict's reports may have helped turn the tide of the war. He had encountered a horrible scene. He wrote a report about a beautiful, blond American girl named Jane McCrea. He reported that she was found scalped, stripped and butchered by Burgoyne's Indian raiding parties. His description of that find became a rallying cry throughout the colonies and was one of the most talked about atrocities of the war. 3

The story spread like wildfire – surely embellished along the way – but it caused militia and regular enlistments in the army to increase substantially. As the rebel forces grew, Benedict became more hopeful at the prospect that they could actually find a way to stop or even defeat Burgoyne.

Benedict was hoping his friend, Daniel Morgan, would arrive with his riflemen. He thought that with Morgan's help, they would make a remarkable stand.

Luckily, Burgoyne's progress was painfully slow, with such a large army to keep supplied, in addition to such wild and treacherous terrain. His pace was minimal. But Burgoyne wrote that he was having a jolly time. Besides the staggering numbers of men, he also had 50 teams of oxen to haul artillery and supplies, along with some 500 horses. He had contracted to bring another thousand horses from Canada, but they still had not arrived. Heavy rain also impeded his movement. His supply lines were being stretched farther and farther without any contact from his southern reinforcements. 4

Burgoyne made a decision to launch a large raid into the nearby Vermont countryside, in an attempt to plunder much-needed supplies, horses and oxen. He sent Hessian Lieutenant Colonel Friedrich Baum with 900 soldiers he considered to be lesser troops, compared to his British regulars. They consisted of mostly Hessian infantry, Canadians, a few Loyalists and Indians. He thought this raid would accomplish two purposes. They would easily gain much-needed supplies and he was hoping to trick the American forces into thinking he was turning his army southeast toward New England.

The diversionary force, led by Baum, met a band of 1,500 New Hampshire militiamen. Some of them were Green Mountain Boys and militia General John Stark led them.

Congress passed over John Stark, like Benedict, for promotion. Feeling dishonored, he resigned his commission. He said he would serve the people, not Congress. But he did get a commission to head the New Hampshire militia and he gathered troops to hinder the progress of Burgoyne's army.

On August 16th of 1777, near Bennington, General Stark's militia crushed Burgoyne's diversion. Stark's forces only sustained 60 killed and wounded. The Hessian force lost some 207 soldiers, including Colonel Baum himself. Countless more were wounded and over 700 were taken as prisoners. In this one daring action, Burgoyne's army was reduced by nearly 15 percent. 5

Burgoyne confidently pushed slowly forward toward Albany. He was hoping to be reinforced by St. Leger or Howe when he arrived there. He still felt he had more than enough of an army to sweep away any rebel resistance.

General Schuyler's plan of putting Benedict in charge of hit and run, coupled with the supply line disruption by the New Hampshire militia under Stark, was seriously slowing the progress of the British army. Schuyler held a council of war on August 12th of 1777. Information concerning Barry St. Leger's force, advancing from the west, became known.

St. Leger had moved through Lake Ontario and planned on marching through the Mohawk Valley toward a rendezvous with Burgoyne in Albany. The only substantial fort in his way was Fort Stanwix, which he could have bypassed, but he decided to lay siege to the fort and its inhabitants.

The militia force in the area, known as the Tryon County Militia, was under the command of General Nicholas Herkimer. He gathered a column of men to try and break the siege of Fort Stanwix. Herkimer sent out orders to muster all patriots in the area and have them gather at Fort Dayton. Most of the militiamen were Palatine German farmers who had settled in the area.

Herkimer managed to gather about 800 men and was supported by a number of Oneida and Tuscarora Indians. On August 6th of 1777, near Oriskany, the militia was working their way up a steep ravine on the route to Fort Stanwix, when they were ambushed in the ravine by some of St. Leger's army and a fierce band of Mohawk and Seneca Indians. 6

Joseph Brant, a famous Indian chief and orator, led the Indians. Brant was educated by Sir William Johnson and had even spent time in England. He tried to convince the entire Iroquois Nation to fight as one with the British. He managed to get only the Senecas and Mohawks to take his side. Brant and the Mohawks led many raids in their effort to burn out the German settlers in the Mohawk Valley.

During the battle, Herkimer was wounded badly in the leg, but he still managed to direct the battle from beneath a tree, while smoking his pipe. The fighting was some of the most terrible in the war and it went on for nearly two hours. About 150 of the militia fell, many sustained wounds and some 50 were taken as prisoners. It was known to be one of the bloodiest battles of the Revolution. Men fought in pairs, with one shooting and the other reloading. Much of the fighting was hand-to-hand with knives and tomahawks. The Senecas and Mohawks tortured many of the prisoners to death.

The tortured bodies of the soldiers were left displayed near the battlefield to discourage any other attempts to attack.

The Herkimer militia had to withdraw back to Fort Dayton. General Herkimer's leg was amputated, and he died shortly afterward.

General Schuyler received the news of the bloody August 6th Battle of Oriskany. He related the sad information during his August 12th war council. If Fort Stanwix fell to St. Leger, nothing could stop his march through the Mohawk Valley to Albany. The officers present at the emergency war council pressed Schuyler not to reduce their numbers, with Burgoyne's army looming just to the east.

Visibly angry, General Schuyler said he would lead a detachment, by himself, to relieve the settlers at Fort Stanwix. The ever-offensive Benedict piped up and volunteered to take on St. Leger. 7,8

Schuyler felt relieved when Benedict spoke up and volunteered for the mission. He knew if anyone could accomplish the task, Benedict would find a way. Schuyler also knew that if Burgoyne made a thrust toward Albany, he would need Benedict's talents in the field to stop him. Schuyler decided to pull his army back 12 miles toward the Mohawk Valley, to a more defensible position. He sent Benedict to relieve Stanwix and, hopefully, stop St. Leger.

CHAPTER EIGHTEEN

THE DARK EAGLE

Benedict was given a brigade of 900 men and quickly proceeded west. He hoped to augment his forces with what remained of Herkimer's militia and the Indian allies of the Oneida and Tuscarora tribes. Keeping his army moving swiftly was essential, as they would be badly needed if Burgoyne launched an offensive.

Pushing his way rapidly toward Fort Dayton, Benedict planned on assembling there, in preparation for his offensive strike.

From German Flats, Arnold wrote a note to General Gates. He said: "You will hear of my being victorious or no more and as soon as the safety of this part of the country will permit, I will fly to your assistance." 1

On August 21st of 1777, Benedict's officers requested a council of war. They had just received reliable intelligence about the size of St. Leger's army. And, as usual, they were to be outnumbered two to one. The men wanted to wait for additional troops to arrive, especially after getting the details of the bloody battle at Oriskany. 2

Benedict knew there wasn't time to reinforce his men. Something had to be done before Burgoyne made another move. This was when one of the strangest events of the Revolution unfolded.

Benedict's reputation served him well on this occasion. He was known throughout the colonies, and especially in this region, as a formidable warrior general.

Indian tribes in the region, mainly the Iroquois – and others – had named Benedict 'The Dark Eagle.' His odd fighting style was one the Indians had never witnessed before. This general fought in front of his troops, swooping down on the enemy on horseback, with his sword drawn. They were reminded of an eagle zeroing in on its prey.

The Indians were accustomed to seeing generals directing battles from behind the lines and Benedict's aggressive fighting style struck fear in their hearts.

That very night, as the war council broke up, the mother and brother of a local Loyalist, Hon Yost Schuyler, approached Benedict. They pleaded with Benedict and begged him to spare Hon Yost's life. Hon Yost was under an order of execution by Tryon County officials.

Hon Yost had been caught recruiting Tory soldiers for St. Leger's army. Benedict told Hon Yost's mother and brother there was nothing he could do. In anguish, the mother pleaded with Benedict to at least speak with her son, who was in the prison at Fort Dayton.

Benedict went to the man's jail cell. He found Hon Yost to be a very strange and animated fellow. Some reports described him as half-witted. Today, there would probably be a psychological diagnosis for his condition, possibly acute bipolar disorder. But the Native American tribes respected his unusual behavior. They considered him 'touched' by the 'Great Spirit,' and possibly even a prophet.

Hon Yost offered Benedict a plan, in exchange for his life. He said he would charge into St. Leger's Indian camp and spread fear of General Arnold's mission to destroy them and St. Leger's army, possibly even driving them off. 3

Strangely, Benedict approved of Hon Yost's plan, but to make sure he followed through with the ruse, he incarcerated Hon Yost's brother in his place. He also sent with Hon Yost a trusted Oneida scout to help with the deception and keep an eye on Hon Yost, in case he betrayed the plan.

A very thankful Hon Yost seemed to relish his role excitedly. He even shot holes in his clothing, so he looked like he had just escaped Benedict's clutches.

On August 22nd of 1777, Hon Yost ran breathlessly into the Indian camp near Fort Stanwix and wildly related his tale. He said the Dark Eagle would soon be there to crush them all. They asked how many men he had. Hon Yost replied, "As many men as there are leaves on the trees!" The tribes panicked. They refused to face down the Dark Eagle, if he had that many men.

St. Leger tried his best to calm the situation and called on the chiefs of the tribes to have a war council. But within a few hours, with Hon Yost's help, the story had grown throughout the native camp. Some were saying Benedict had cut Burgoyne's army to pieces and was marching toward them with over 3,000 men.

When he wrote about the episode later, St. Leger said the chiefs grew furious and seized upon the officers' liquor and clothes. The Indians decamped, fleeing west into the Niagara frontier and leaving St. Leger to fend for himself. Now, with half his force deserted, he made the decision to end the siege and fall back to Canada. 4

Benedict marched into Fort Stanwix, arriving on August 24th of 1777. The siege concluded without a shot. Benedict gave the fort's commander great applause for their spirited conduct and vigorous defense.

Within four days, Benedict was back at Fort Dayton, preparing to move his now 1,200-man army down the Mohawk River to battle with Burgoyne.

CHAPTER NINETEEN

GENERAL ARNOLD AT SARATOGA
"If the day is long enough, we'll have them all in Hell before night!"

During the campaign season of 1777, Congress was in a tither. The capital was moved to Baltimore because of fears that Howe was going to make a move on Philadelphia. When Fort Ticonderoga fell in July, the leaders in Congress were incensed. Washington was almost always on the defensive and a scapegoat was needed to blame for the loss of Fort Ticonderoga.

Congress was as much to blame as anyone, as they never sent needed resources – requested many times – to supply the northern army. The ax fell on General Schuyler. He was made to take the blame for the devastating loss, to the point of accusations of treason. Nothing could have been further from the truth. Schuyler had accomplished even more than he possibly could, given the resources available to him. 1

Between the activity of Benedict and Schuyler's work with the Native Americans, there was still a fighting chance in the north.

Congress called forth their darling, General Horatio Gates, to take command of the northern army. Gates was a well-established aristocrat like themselves, even though he had done little in the war effort except for fighting to advance himself. Congress was delighted with what they perceived to be a great decision. 2

Washington, even though he was an aristocrat himself, didn't trust Gates' constant quest for power. Schuyler handed over command to Gates on August 19th of 1777. Benedict made it back from Fort Stanwix to headquarters on August 30th of 1777. Gates needed Benedict to help formulate future action against Burgoyne's army.

Trying to stop this huge British army coming toward Albany was foremost in Arnold's mind on August 30th of 1777. With his division, he finally got to the intersection of the Mohawk and Hudson Rivers and ran into troops already posted there. He inquired about where headquarters was set up. Gates had set up preliminary headquarters on Van Schaick's Island, at the Van Schaick mansion.

The Van Schaicks were a very prominent, long-established Dutch family who established a very successful trading business and farm prior even to the French and Indian Wars. They were very involved with the Patriot cause. Benedict had just met their son-in-law, Colonel Peter Gansevoort. He was the man in charge of the defenses during the St. Leger siege at Fort Stanwix.

Years earlier, General Philip Schuyler was asked by Congress to form a northern army. Schuyler needed funds to make it happen. He approached the Van Schaick family for help and received from them a loan of ten thousand dollars in gold – a huge sum at that time.

Later on in the war, Schuyler petitioned Congress for funds to pay the Van Schaicks back for their help. Congress cited some political excuses, saying Schuyler wasn't authorized to make the loan and the Van Schaick family was never repaid.

But, on August 30th of 1777, the family allowed its home and lands to be used as a staging area and headquarters to plan the upcoming battle with Burgoyne. The Van Schaick mansion still stands today and is well worth a visit. 3

With the weakening of British forces in Bennington and St. Leger's retreat to Canada, the Americans knew Burgoyne would have to make a move toward Albany. Gates wrote to Congress to tell of the relief of Fort Stanwix and the driving off of St. Leger's army. But not surprisingly, he never mentioned Benedict's role. The glory and success of the mission belonged to him and a few minor officers.

Benedict wasn't too happy his friend General Schuyler was replaced, especially with the likes of Gates. He also learned that Congress took up his seniority issue again and he was denied. But Benedict held his tongue. He had bigger fish to fry. He intended to prove his worth on the battlefield, in a decisive meeting with Burgoyne. He was starting to realize not all of his enemies were Redcoats.

'Gentleman Johnny' Burgoyne was in a bit of a pickle. The New Hampshire militia, too, had cut off his supply lines. 4

Fifteen percent of his army was lost in his diversion, and now the Indian allies he was relying on had reached the end of their agreed enlistments. Those Native Americans began to filter back to their homes.

Burgoyne still had a huge army of well-trained British regulars and a large group of Hessian allies. He was considering either a full-scale retreat to Canada, or whether to cross the Hudson River and make a push toward Albany. He thought if he made it to Albany he could – realistically – get reinforced by Howe's army in New York City.

The very thought of retreat, with a rebel army nipping at his heels, was totally unappealing. Burgoyne also had no respect for the rebel army and thought they would only fight defensively against such large numbers of battle-hardened and well-trained troops. His opinion of the rebel army was that they were a bunch of undisciplined bumpkins and no match for him.

Burgoyne made his push across the Hudson River on September 12th of 1777. It took two days to get his artillery and supplies across. He actually landed on property owned by General Schuyler. The British army plundered the ripe grain and food they found there to feed the men and their horses. One officer wrote that the general's holdings were reduced to a scene of distress and poverty. 5

Meanwhile, the American army was busy preparing to do battle. Tension grew between Benedict and Gates. Benedict pushed to have one large offensive strike and a decisive battle with Burgoyne. Gates, holding the command position, thought the only chance to defeat Burgoyne would be to entrench his lines from a better position and let Burgoyne dictate his own movements. It was exactly what Burgoyne hoped the rebels would do.

Benedict, not holding the higher rank, had to quell his feelings. Gates sent him on a mission to look for the best defensive grounds. He was sent with a Polish engineer, Thaddeus Kosciuszko. His expertise was used to determine strategic elevation and range for artillery. Thaddeus and

Benedict agreed on the best site, four miles north of their present position, at a place known as Bemis Heights. 6

The Heights were an expanse of high, rolling hills rising out of the plain near the Hudson River. From the Heights, they could reach the British with artillery. Heavy woods and ravines to the west also protected them. For any type of frontal assault, the enemy would have to forge uphill.

On the very same day that Burgoyne made his move across the Hudson, the American army was setting up its new position at Bemis Heights.

Benedict was given command of the left wing, with many divisions of close to 3,000 men. The right wing was given to General John Glover. Gates set up headquarters in a small farmhouse at the center of the staging area. Trenches were dug and breastworks for artillery were constructed.

As Benedict prepared his wing for battle, his friend Daniel Morgan arrived the same day Benedict returned from Fort Stanwix. He brought with him 331 of his riflemen. Benedict was also glad to have many of his Kennebec warriors with him again. He was grateful to have so many battle-savvy men at his side. They knew what they were about to face.

Benedict, not knowing most of the Indians fighting for the British had gone back to their homes, assigned Morgan to be farthest to the west in the woods and open areas. The Americans knew Morgan and Benedict would be first to engage any enemy attack from their respective positions.

The American army was growing in strength daily. More and more men from New York, New England and elsewhere were filtering into the different divisions. From scouting reports, Burgoyne knew that. He realized he had to make a push toward Albany as soon as possible. On September 15th of 1777, the British army advanced south toward Albany, but they were slowed because of bridges destroyed weeks before by General Schuyler. 7

By September 17th, the British reached a place called Sword's Farm, about four miles north of Bemis Heights. General Gates called for another war council that day. Benedict begged for orders to let his wing go out and assess the enemy's strength. Gates relented, since he needed the intelligence, but ordered Benedict not to press full engagement.

At the dawn of a foggy, fall morning, Benedict led his men – close to 3,000 – in a northeasterly sweep toward the encamped British force. There were some small, bloody encounters, but Benedict did not press a battle. 8

Burgoyne reported that the enemy appeared in considerable force. He believed it was to obstruct bridge repair and draw him into a wooded area where he couldn't use his artillery. Late that afternoon, Benedict pulled his troops back to Bemis Heights and reported the day's events to Gates. Benedict's assessment was that the enemy would assault Bemis Heights within 48 hours, most likely by trying to flank his position in the left wing.

Gates shrugged off Benedict's assessment. He was sure Burgoyne would concentrate his movements along the road by the river. Burgoyne formulated his attack plan. He decided he would split his army into three battle groups.

One group, under General Simon Fraser, would split out toward the ridge line angling southward, taking with him light infantry (fast moving troops), sharpshooters and light artillery. Burgoyne would send a lighter group along the river road with his supplies, so the Americans would think he was going to push them along the river. The third and largest group, consisting mainly of British regulars, would turn into the American position on Bemis Heights.

Burgoyne assumed American troops would not risk any kind of offensive attack and would hold to their entrenched defensive positions. If they remained entrenched, he would soon have them in a deadly crossfire and rout them out. He also assumed that if they did try an offensive strike, they would come up against his main thrust of British regulars. 9

What Burgoyne didn't know was that his plan was leading him into the most battle-hardened American troops fighting under Benedict. Also, his field general Fraser, would come into direct contact with Daniel Morgan's riflemen. Burgoyne's main advance was aimed directly into Benedict's left wing.

On the morning of September 19th, a very cool, heavy fog settled into the Hudson River Valley. It was perfect cover for Burgoyne to launch his full charge into action. A rumble of cannon fire would be the signal for the three columns to begin their advance.

Benedict begged Gates for permission to send out Morgan's riflemen to probe the enemy and assess their attack plan. He kept pushing Gates, warning him that if the enemy weren't faced, Burgoyne could get artillery close enough to reach Bemis Heights. Gates, who the men had nicknamed 'Granny Gates,' was plagued with indecision. He finally relented to Benedict's pleading.

After getting Gates to make a decision, Benedict rushed to his horse and rode into action. He rode first to Daniel Morgan's position and sent his riflemen northwest to find the enemy's position. British General Fraser – with his division – was pushing hard to get around the top of a deep ravine. He was trying to get his men and artillery ready to advance along the ridgeline to Bemis Heights.

Burgoyne's regulars had to skirt around the bottom of the same ravine. They had agreed that when each division was ready for the full assault, they would signal each other with cannon fire. Their respective maneuvers took them until nearly noon, and the morning fog was no longer hiding their actions. 10

The main push of the British army was converging on some open ground known as Freeman's Farm. The farm was about 20 cleared acres that still had numerous stumps and a log home surrounded by heavy woods. The farm was about a mile from Bemis Heights.

Burgoyne never dreamed the American army would dare to launch an offensive battle. But Benedict had already decided he had no intention of letting Burgoyne dictate his movements. He would use his wing to disrupt Burgoyne's battle plans. Just past noon, Benedict could hear Morgan's riflemen firing on Fraser's column. He quickly sent two divisions to reinforce Morgan's men.

Benedict noticed a gap at Freeman's Farm, between the two British columns. He now knew he had his battlefield. Around 2 o'clock, Benedict led his first charge into Fraser's flank. He was repelled but gave them considerable damage. He then wheeled to the right against the other British column. For the next three hours, the American army forced up to six charges into the British positions and also fended off counter charges. 11

It was one of the hardest fought battles of the American Revolution. Reports of Benedict's part in the battle showed he was almost everywhere, leading the front of the charges. Some soldiers wrote of the battle that he acted like a madman. Some wrote that his voice rang clear as a trumpet. He called on his men to follow him and he hurled them like a tornado into the British lines.

Another man wrote of Benedict's actions that nothing could exceed the bravery of Benedict on that day. There seemed to shoot out of him a magnetic force that electrified his men and made heroes of all within his influence, said the writer. 12

As smoke from the cannon fire and muskets filled the valley that day, Benedict had deployed his whole wing of 3,000 men in the two British columns by late afternoon. By sunset, Benedict could smell victory and he was sure one more aggressive charge would finish off the British columns. He rode furiously to Bemis Heights to get more reinforcements from Gates.

Burgoyne realized the same thing Benedict did. He was in serious trouble. He was forced to call on his third river column to send reinforcements. They would have to abandon their supply lines along the river. Burgoyne knew that if Benedict led one more thrust at him, he would be finished.

When Benedict reached headquarters, he was breathless and eager to request more men to finish off Burgoyne. Gates resisted, still wringing his hands and indecisive. He had already told Benedict, that morning, not to expect reinforcement. Intimidated by a very agitated Benedict, Gates consented to release a small division.

Benedict, not wanting to lose the momentum of the battle, ran to his horse and was heard shouting, "By God, I will soon put an end to it!" Gates could not stand the thought of Burgoyne surrendering his sword to the likes of Benedict Arnold. Gates sent out an express rider with orders for Benedict to return to headquarters. 13

With the delay caused by Gates, Burgoyne had time to get his third column ready to reinforce his lines. He made a quick surge into the American force. Without Benedict and with darkness falling, the Americans retreated back to Bemis Heights.

If only Gates had quickly reinforced Benedict, or if he even made his own move on the British river column, Burgoyne would have been finished that very day. The British army had paid a high price, with 556 killed, wounded or missing. Patriot losses were more modest – 63 killed, 210 wounded and 38 missing.

Burgoyne regrouped his men and began digging entrenchments and setting up redoubts on the north side of Freeman's Farm. Not knowing what the next American move would be, the British hastily buried some of the dead in shallow graves and gathered their wounded. Some wrote that in the middle of the night, large groups of wolves could be heard feasting and howling over the carnage.

There were many accolades written about the American performance on September 19th of 1777. One of the most telling was written by a British officer who reported the courage and obstinacy with which the Americans fought were the astonishment of everyone. They had shown they were not the contemptible enemy incapable of standing a regular engagement, as imagined before. 14

But the battle was not over. Burgoyne still had a considerable force, although somewhat crippled and its supplies almost totally cut off. He could dig in and wait for possible reinforcements, inflicting major damage to American forces, or he also could possibly try to punch through American lines on his way to Albany.

Burgoyne's army was now like a wounded beast, at just a mile from Bemis Heights. The next real phase of the battle would be behind the American lines. Gates and Benedict were about to lock horns.

Benedict implored Gates to attack the British next morning, before Burgoyne could erect any strong defenses. He knew that many brave American soldiers would have to spill their blood to try and breach the entrenchments. Gates and his adjutants completely ignored Benedict's pleas and he had to fight to keep his composure. Day after day, Gates sat in headquarters, refusing to make any strikes on the weakened British army. 15

Gates' favorite adjutant, James Wilkinson, who he affectionately called 'Wilkie,' wrote of the September 19th events to Congress, saying he wasn't even sure General Arnold was in the field, giving all the credit of any action to the 'brave' General Gates. He also belittled Daniel Morgan's actions.

Of course, Gates and Wilkie didn't know who was in the battlefield that day. The only knowledge they had of September 19th was the sounds of the battle from a mile away. Gates was feeling very threatened by and jealous of Benedict's growing reputation among the troops.

One officer wrote about Benedict: "He alone is due the honor of our late victory. He has earned the life and soul of the troops, enjoying the confidence and affection of his officers and soldiers. They would, to a person, follow him to conquest or death." Another officer wrote that Arnold was not only the hero of the field on September 19th, but he had won the admiration of the whole army. 16

Benedict endured insults from Gates and his faithful adjutants in his headquarters. Benedict was feeling that his honor was threatened. He was becoming furious at being ignored.

The whole matter peaked on the night of September 22nd of 1777. Benedict charged into Gates' small headquarters and a shouting match broke out. One officer wrote of the generals that they were using high words and gross language.

Gates relieved Benedict of the command of his wing. Before he left, Benedict demanded a general pass, to go to Washington's division and possibly have it in his power to serve his country. Benedict stormed back to his tent to try and calm down. Now, the clash between the generals was out of headquarters and out in the open. 17

The officers, on hearing of the confrontation, began to panic and they tried to reconcile the men – but to no avail. The field officers held a separate meeting and composed a letter from general officers and colonels, thanking Benedict for his service and conduct, but requesting him to stay in camp. 18

A groundswell of support from his men caused Benedict to relent and he said that he would at least stay in camp. He was completely dejected, very angry and determined to formulate his own plan of action.

Gates became upset by the lack of support from the men and officers but continued to ignore Benedict. He threatened to arrest him for insubordination if he tried to take command. Granny Gates sat on his hands for almost two weeks, hoping Burgoyne and Benedict would just go away. 19

During a war council, Burgoyne's officers suggested retreating to Canada. Gentleman Johnny wouldn't hear of it. He simply couldn't accept the humiliation he would receive if he left a numerous army in the field with the ability to travel south to attack General Howe in New York City. Burgoyne's supplies were running dangerously low and he decided to advance, again, toward the American army's left wing. He sent a large reconnaissance force along the ridgeline toward Bemis Heights.

Even after hearing reports of enemy movement, Gates continued to be unresponsive. Daniel Morgan decided he would take the initiative. With the help of two other divisions, he encircled the British reconnaissance force and drove them back to Freeman's Farm.

Around three o'clock in the afternoon, Benedict heard the roar of cannon and musket fire from his camp. He knew Burgoyne was making a move. Benedict had decided he was prepared to die for his men and his country. He strapped on his sword, put his pistols in their holsters and rode his horse madly toward the engagement.

On that brightly-colored fall afternoon, Benedict appeared from nowhere in the field at Freeman's Farm, under no orders but his own. Some wrote that he had a fierce look of determination on his face.

Benedict first encountered a unit from his old home state of Connecticut. He asked the men, "Whose regiment is this?" They responded, "Colonel Latimore's, sir." Benedict shouted to the men, "God bless you, boys. If the day is long enough, we'll have them all in Hell before night." 20

A rousing shout of huzzahs went up as Benedict entered the field on his powerful, brown horse. He quickly located Latimore, who gladly granted Benedict's request to take command. Benedict rode back and forth in front of his troops with his sword drawn, quickly aligning forces to make a charge.

The British, seeing the general they had to face before and hearing the roar of huzzahs across the field, knew they were about to be in a fight for their lives.

Benedict spun his horse to the left toward Daniel Morgan's riflemen, who were engaged in a fierce firefight with General Fraser's light infantry. He could see Fraser on a gray horse, riding behind his lines and giving instructions. Benedict shouted to Morgan to have his sharpshooters cut Fraser down. Daniel Morgan understood Benedict's thinking, even above the echo of musket fire. The story goes that Morgan sent his best sharpshooter, Timothy Murphy, up a tree to take out Fraser. On his third attempt, Murphy's musket ball hit his mark.

The British lines panicked on seeing their commander fall from his gray horse and quickly retreated toward Freeman's Farm. In the mass confusion of Fraser's retreating column, Burgoyne directed fire to cover the retreating troops.

Benedict quickly seized the opportunity and led a massive charge into the other British flank. Some later wrote of Benedict's actions as he rode between the warring armies, that he must have gone mad or was drunk with too much rum. Men had never seen a commanding general charging in front of his troops. 21

Spurring his mount on, Benedict rode between the two armies as they fired intensely at each other. As the British cannons blasted grapeshot, many American soldiers fell during the charge. Whatever the men were facing, Benedict was impressive and inspiring.

Astride his horse, Benedict was so close to the British lines that his view from horseback gave him the advantage of being able to peer over the British entrenchments. He realized the charge was aimed directly at the strongest part of the British defensive fortifications. He quickly turned his horse to the left, looking for a weak spot in the British defenses.

With lead flying at him from all directions, he spotted a weakness between the major British redoubts – about 120 yards wide – that was lightly defended. Benedict shouted to his men to follow him and pointed his sword toward the weak spot in the enemy lines. He then spurred his horse and charged through the British lines himself, with his men pouring in behind him.

In the heat of battle, Benedict was slashing his sword wildly at the enemy. He even accidentally wounded the head of an American soldier, which he apologized for later. He said that because of the intensity of the fight, he wasn't aware it had happened.

Now, the Americans held the fleeing, panicked British troops in a deadly crossfire. But one retreating regiment of Hessian soldiers quickly reformed a line and fired a volley of musket fire. All aimed directly at Benedict. One musket ball shattered the bones in Benedict's left leg. The others hit his horse. The animal reared into the air and fell directly onto Benedict's wounded leg, pinning him to the ground as it thrashed till death. From his position beneath the horse, Benedict commanded his men to pursue. 22

In an act of revenge for the shooting of his general, one young American soldier was ready to bayonet a wounded Hessian. From under his horse, Benedict called him off. He said to the young man that the Hessian was only doing his duty.

As the men poured through, they were able to extricate Benedict from under his bold, but lifeless mount. Colonel Henry Dearborn asked Benedict if he was badly wounded. Benedict replied that the wound was in the same leg and that he "wished the ball had passed his heart." Shortly after, he passed out from the pain. 23

Darkness fell on the battlefield as what was left of the fleeing British army retreated for the cover of trees along the Hudson River. Benedict had his complete victory, but at a high price. However, Benedict would have said that many others paid even more.

Benedict was loaded onto a makeshift stretcher and then a medical cart, enduring a slow, bumpy ride to an army medical hospital set up in Albany. Soldiers along the way thanked and encouraged him as he tried to focus, despite the pain.

Burgoyne formally surrendered his sword to Horatio Gates near the village of Saratoga, on October 17th of 1777. Gates, who never once left headquarters or showed himself anywhere near the battlefield, audaciously ignored Benedict and proclaimed himself as the hero of Saratoga.

Benedict's only consolation was that the officers and men in the struggle knew the truth of the battle, and even Burgoyne himself credited only General Benedict Arnold for his defeat.

The Philadelphia II, replica of the 1776 gunboat.
Courtesy, Lake Champlain Maritime Museum

General Philip Schuyler, Commander of the Northern Army, supporter of Arnold and negotiator with the Iroquois and Arnold supporter. Schuyler was accused of treason by Washington. Painting by J. Trumbull, engraved by T. Kelly. *Courtesy Library of Congress.*

Painting of General Horatio Gates, by Gilbert Stuart, 1794, Metropolitan Museum of Art. Gates betrayed Arnold at Saratoga and attempted to betray Washington. Gates showed his true colors at Camden.

Remains of fortress at Crown Point, a narrow spot on Lake Champlain. Arnold thought Crown Point was the best offensive position on the lake. *Public domain.*

At Ridgefield, Arnold's fighting style had won the hearts of the Army and his countrymen. He had two horses shot from under him. His fame had now spread as far as London. This print of "Arnold's Intrepidy was published by James Sharpe of London in April 1780. You can see Danbury on fire in the background.

Daniel Morgan and his riflemen at Saratoga. October 7, 1777. Painting by Hugh Charles McBarron Jr. *Source : US Army Center of Military History.*

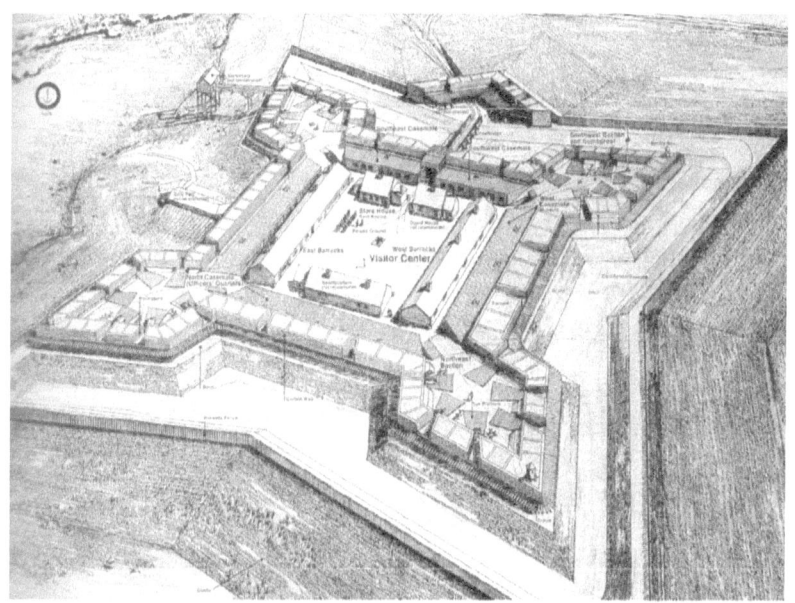

Artist's rendering of Fort Stanwix in Rome, New York. *Courtesy National Park Service.*

John Adams, a huge supporter of Arnold until September 1780. Painting by John Singleton Copley 1797, engraved by James Smither. *Courtesy Library of Congress.*

Oneida Chief Warrior Hanyery receives his reloaded weapon from his wife, Tyonajanegen. His son is in the background. The Oneida's were Americas first allies and fought with the Tryon County Militia at Oriskany. *www.historicalimagebank.com*. (Image continues next page.)

Battle of Oriskany. General Herkimer, wounded in the leg, directs the battle. One of the bloodiest hand-to-hand battles of the Revolution. Painting by Frederick C. Yohn. *Courtesy Library of Congress.*

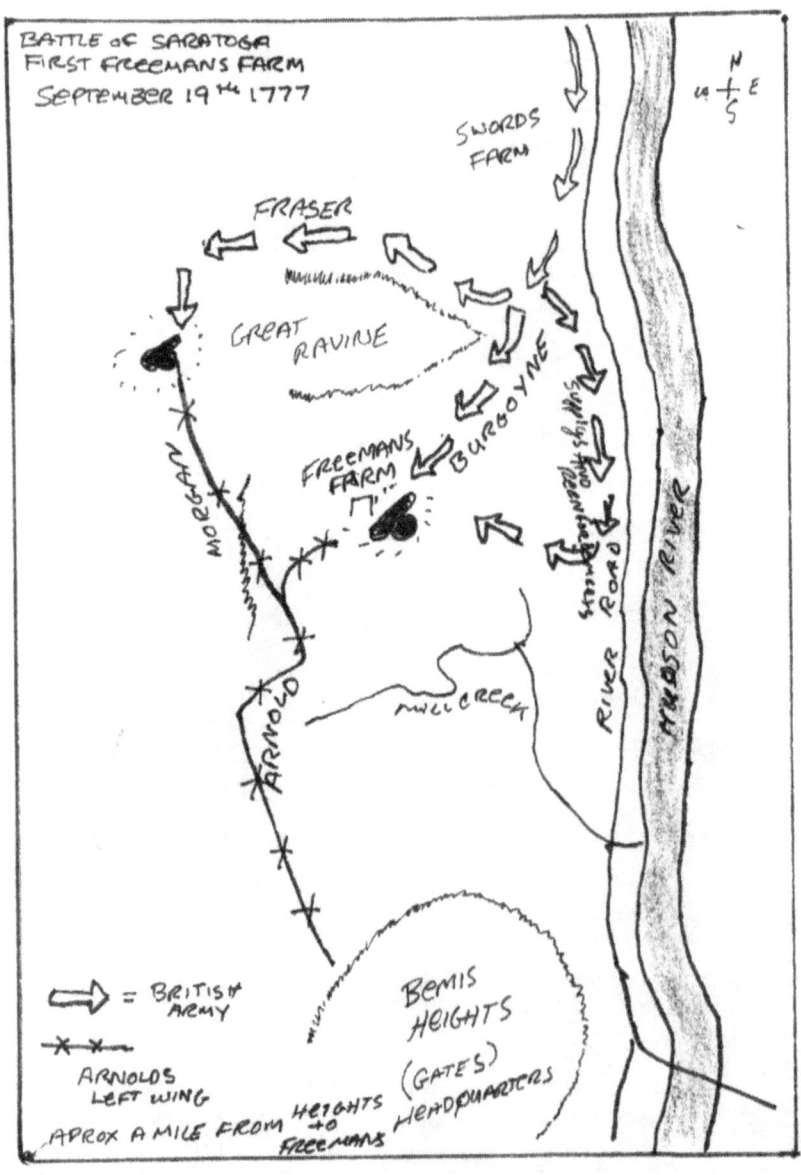

Map 9

CHAPTER TWENTY

A LONG & PAINFUL WINTER FOR ARNOLD & AMERICA

While Benedict was fighting Burgoyne, George Washington had his hands full. General Howe made a move against the American army at Brandywine Creek. Both sides suffered heavy losses and Washington was driven back.

By late September, British forces under Howe occupied the Capital at Philadelphia. Congress relocated the capital first to Lancaster, Pennsylvania and then to York, Pennsylvania. The only good news of the campaign season was the defeat of Burgoyne's army. As Washington retreated across the Pennsylvania hills, he ordered Gates to send reinforcements. But Gates was slow to react, perhaps wanting Washington to stumble.

For his victory at Saratoga, Gates had a medal in his honor struck by Congress. He then designed a vicious political campaign to elevate himself, to the point of trying to replace Washington. Benedict's long recovery gave him no chance to defend his actions or relay the truth about General Gates.

Over the next five months, Benedict was flat on his back, trying to recover while enduring horrible pain. The surgeons wanted desperately to amputate his leg, but Benedict wouldn't allow it. They put his leg into a device called a traction box, wired down so the leg couldn't move. Benedict felt like a wounded, caged animal trapped in his own body. His leg had to be re-opened to remove bone splinters. That leg atrophied terribly and became a full two inches shorter than the other leg.

Benedict survived the ordeal but would be crippled and in pain for the rest of his life. However, he wasn't the kind of man to be kept down. He had a special shoe with a two-inch lift made for him and he was determined to ride and walk again, someday.

As he had been in a prone position for so long, he continuously asked for information on how the war effort was going. Many of his officers and troops visited him regularly, which lifted his heart. It also gave him much time to think.

Benedict believed strongly about the cause of liberty. He dreamed of a new country where men were created equal. Those were high words, but he sometimes became bitter when he saw how rank, privilege, bloodlines and wealth trumped the actions and efforts of so many. He also thought about how the members of Congress had written of sacrificing their lives, property and sacred honor. But it seemed to him, he was one of the few willing to put deeds and actions above words.

As he looked death in the face, Benedict's business was nearly broken, and many stepped harshly on his honor. If he recovered, he was determined to set some things straight. 1

One of Benedict's more distinguished visitors during his recovery was the Marquis de Lafayette. Lafayette had arrived from France, seeking adventure and glory in the fight for American freedom. He attached himself to George Washington. He had heard of this fighting General Arnold and wanted to meet him. Lafayette heard from Benedict and other officers truthful accounts of how the Battle of Saratoga really went down. 2

But the Marquis was an aristocrat's aristocrat. On returning to Congress, he still gave credit for Burgoyne's defeat to Horatio Gates, since he was the ranking general in the field and higher in status than Benedict. Lafayette's betrayal, actions and manner just fueled the fire within Benedict. He did not trust the French and really hoped they wouldn't be any part of the new America.

He had watched men bleed and die for the cause of liberty and the end of British tyranny. Why would they want to align themselves with another monarchy? Especially one where the elite and privileged used men like pawns for the cause of furthering themselves. When Benedict heard of Lafayette's alliance with Gates, he knew he was right not to trust the French. He had lost faith in many of the elites in Congress. Even his 'excellency' George Washington was acting at times more the part of a king and not a general.

Benedict had gone into action quite naïve, but now he knew merit and actions weren't always enough. There were those who, without honor, would elevate themselves. It was a very long and painful winter for Benedict, but by spring he was very slowly regaining his health.

Washington was in a desperate situation at Valley Forge. He surely needed the assistance of men like Benedict, who could get things done. He wrote to Benedict of "an earnest wish to have his services in the ensuing campaign" and promised "a command which I trust will be agreeable to yourself and of great advantage to the public." 3

That February, Washington did get some good assistance as Benedict was recovering. Baron Von Steuben, a German volunteer who claimed to have military experience in the German army, attached himself to the Washington entourage through Congress. Washington made him acting inspector general in charge of training troops.

Steuben wrote that the men were literally naked; the officers that had coats had them of every color and make. The arms were in horrible condition. They were covered with rust and half without bayonets. Many could not fire a single shot. With regard to discipline, no such thing existed. Steuben is owed a great debt from our country. He took his position very seriously and slowly formed the rag-tag army into a fighting force.

But food, supplies and morale were still horribly low. Contrary to popular belief, Washington and his upper staff did not bother to suffer as his men were. Inside a very comfortable brick home used as headquarters, the staff had servants and enjoyed a regular supply of food fit for the upper class they were.

Washington rarely walked among the troops and never without guards. Throughout the war, he faced as many as six mutiny attempts.

Benedict could not take the hospital life any longer. He hired a cart to take him home for a while, so he could see his boys and his sister Hannah. On the journey there, he penned a letter back to Washington on March 12th of 1778. His trip to home was delayed by a couple of weeks, as the rough ride in the cart caused his leg to re-open. More bone splinters had to be removed. 4

The attending surgeons said the cleansing process "will be a work of time" and take perhaps two to six months. Benedict informed Washington that it was with utmost regret that he could not form any judgment, regarding when he might "repair to headquarters" and "take the command your Excellency has been so good as to reserve for me."

Benedict finally made it back to his home in New Haven and got some well-earned rest, although he was still in pain from his wounds and subsequent surgeries performed to remove bone splinters from his leg. It did his heart good to spend some time with his family. But Arnold's sense of duty wouldn't let him rest for very long.

The fallen General Arnold knew his country was at a pivotal moment. The British were occupying Philadelphia. Washington was backed up to the hills of Pennsylvania at Valley Forge and preparations for the following campaign were sure to begin soon. Benedict then decided to travel to Valley Forge by carriage since he couldn't ride yet. Not even a shattered leg would prevent him from fulfilling his sense of duty to his country.

On May 6th of 1778, Washington received news that France had entered into alliance with the now-recognized United States. George was ecstatic and proclaimed a day of rejoicing throughout the whole army. He ordered 13 rounds of cannon fire and loud huzzahs for the king of France and the American states. With Lafayette at his side, he then reviewed his troops.

Washington must have wondered how Benedict would receive the news. The next day, in an appeasing way, he wrote to Benedict to say that he had received a gift of epaulets and sword knots that he reserved for Benedict when he arrived. He knew the French alliance was mostly a result of the American army's actions at Saratoga, during the defeat of Burgoyne. He also knew that Benedict was no fan of the French and hoped his fighting general would be placated by the generous gift. 5

Washington did not expect to hear from Benedict for months. As he sat in his cozy headquarters at Valley Forge, with his servants and Lafayette, suddenly the whole camp erupted into loud huzzahs. The men were cheering wildly. On investigation, Washington discovered that Benedict had arrived by surprise, in a carriage, on May 21st of 1778. 6

The men were joyful. Their fighting general was back! Washington must have been more than a little jealous that he could not raise that kind of support from his men. Lafayette seemed quite bewildered. He wrote that he had never seen so much "adoration" for a common officer.

As Benedict settled into camp, Washington presented him with the gift of epaulets and sword knots. They began going over plans for the upcoming campaign season.

In May, British General Howe – because of his poor showing the previous year – was replaced by British General Henry Clinton. Clinton, fearing a blockade of French ships, withdrew his troops from Philadelphia and brought them back to New York City.

Americans began re-occupying the capital in Philadelphia by mid-June. Washington decided Benedict should take command of defenses in Philadelphia while he recovered from his wounds and reached condition to take the field. 7

Washington also had an ulterior motive. This assignment would separate Benedict from his adoring troops. He knew well that the cesspool of backbiting politics in the capital would probably ensure Benedict was no threat to his command. Lafayette also thought the politics of Congress would eat alive a lower-class general like Benedict.

Lafayette and Washington were getting a bit paranoid. George had just barely survived an attempt by Horatio Gates to replace him as commander-in-chief. Word was spreading, especially among the troops, who had really won the Battle of Saratoga.

George was beginning to see Benedict as a possible threat to his power. But he had trust in Benedict since he knew Benedict didn't really have any political aspirations, as men like Gates had. Nonetheless, he would keep an eye on Benedict, since no one could muster troop support like he had.

Arnold's visit to Valley Forge turned out to be a turning point in his military career. Washington's and Lafayette's jealousy of Benedict's adoring troops would cause Washington to decide never to give him a field command again.

CHAPTER TWENTY-ONE

CAPITAL COMMANDER & INTRODUCTION TO POLITICS 1778

By June of 1778, Benedict assumed command of the Patriots' capital city. Washington attempted an attack on the returning British army, which resulted in the Battle of Monmouth, in New Jersey. The two-day fight was pretty much a standoff, as Charles Lee, one of Washington's generals, ordered a retreat against his orders. British General Henry Clinton's forces marched back to New York City.

On June 19th of 1778, General Arnold declared martial law in Philadelphia. Congress returned to the capital city in July of 1778. Washington set up temporary headquarters at West Point, New York. From West Point, Washington continued monitoring British General Clinton's actions through an extensive spy ring he created and maintained to watch Clinton's movements and other interests he had throughout the colonies. 1

The spy ring was extremely secretive and would later be known as the Culper spy ring. It was not even discovered until 100 years after the war was over. It could be said that it was the forerunner of today's C.I.A.

Also, that June, France and Spain declared war against Great Britain and France sent a fleet of ships to attempt a combined siege of British forces in Rhode Island. The whole effort failed because of slow American troop movements and bad weather for the French fleet. The French were forced to move their ships to Boston for repairs.

Benedict also learned that Parliament put together a serious peace offering. Britain, after Arnold's defeat of Burgoyne and rumors of France entering the war, was heavily in debt and many were sick of conflicts.

Members of the British Parliament put together a Parliamentary Peace Commission and presented their offers to Congress while it was meeting in York, Pennsylvania during the occupation of Philadelphia. 2

The British offered nearly everything America requested, including self-rule. However, Britain did expect former treaties were to be respected, and thought the new country should end its borders at the Appalachin mountains. Many congressmen, including Jefferson, Patrick Henry, George Mason, Franklin and Washington, already had interests and investments in the Ohio Valley and in other Indian-held territories west of the Appalachins.

All of Great Britain's peace offerings were promptly rejected. When Benedict received this information, he was quite disgusted. Hadn't what the men were fighting for been simply independence, not increasing the land holdings of wealthy colonists?

Benedict also discovered that the peace offer information was being purposely withheld from the public. As Benedict took command of the situation in Philadelphia, he soon learned about all the worst elements of capital politics.

✕

A well-organized group of very zealous radicals called the Constitutional Party confronted Arnold with demands of how he should handle citizens suspected of collaboration with the British during the long occupation of Philadelphia. They insisted on severe punishments that included hanging. 3

One of Arnold's fiercest antagonists was a young lawyer by the name of Joseph Reed. He was a Pennsylvania delegate to the Continental Congress. But he stepped down to assist the state's attorney general in prosecuting 23 suspected Loyalists for treason. He opposed the martial law enforced by Benedict and was especially angry that Arnold would not allow hangings.

Reed made Arnold his main adversary and tried his best to discredit Arnold's reputation. He wanted to get Arnold out of town by any means possible.

Benedict refused to comply with their demands. He recognized the citizens were only trying to survive the occupation and he wanted reconciliation. His actions infuriated the blood-thirsty, zealous patriots and they accused Benedict of high-handedness and of having the emblems of a military dictator. Since Benedict insisted on maintaining order, they began a smear campaign against him.

It didn't take long for Arnold to be entirely sick of the whole political scene in Philadelphia. By July 19th of 1778, he wrote a letter to Washington. Since he could not yet ride well because of his wounded leg, he thought he could command a ship and lead a naval thrust into British supply lines. 4

Washington wrote back to say he had no opinion of the naval service requested by Benedict. By denying his request, Washington had Benedict where he wanted him. 5

Benedict went on the offensive with Congress and he became the first advocate for veterans' rights. He badgered Congress with his memories of men bleeding and dying during service to their country, while Congress had made no provisions for their widows and children.

Arnold attended many parties where he formed a fund-raising campaign for at least some of the veterans. He took a special interest in the family of his friend, General Joseph Warren, who died in battle at Boston. When he found out that Warren's family was left destitute, Benedict gave 500 silver dollars of his own money to help them. He sent it to Boston with John Hancock, who was returning to Boston. 6

Benedict asked Warren's family to call on him, first, for any expenses and he promised to pay those with thanks. His compassion shamed Congress into taking an interest. They made some effort to provide assistance for fallen veterans and their families, at least in the case of officers. Subsequentially, Benedict would give over 3,000 pounds just to the Warren family.

By September of 1778, Benedict finally found something positive in Philadelphia. He met an attractive young girl he would eventually become engaged to. Her name was Margaret 'Peggy' Shippen. She was the daughter of a wealthy Neutralist.

Benedict fell madly in love with Peggy. She was described as intelligent, vivacious and very beautiful. She, as well, was very attracted to the handsome and energetic General Arnold. Their formal courtship throughout the coming winter season would keep him in much better spirits.

In October of 1778, Benedict had to deal with a British attack on Little Egg Harbor in New Jersey, south of Philadelphia. The British linked with some privateers and attacked the harbor. Since Arnold did not have enough troops, he immediately sent 100 militia to reinforce a regiment that was on its way for defense.

Only 50 of the militia showed and that was not a sufficient force to stop the carnage. The Brits landed nearly 500 men and they burned all the houses, as well as eight or ten vessels in the harbor. The militia did manage to move most of the valuable goods and part of the vessels farther north some 30 miles to keep them from enemy hands. 7

On October 23rd of 1778, George Washington replied to Arnold's report on the fighting at Egg Harbor.

Washington wrote: "I am sorry at the destruction of property in Egg Harbor, but in attending to the general objects of war, we must at times submit to such losses or depend on the exertions of the militia for their prevention." No troops were offered to assist General Arnold. 8

The Egg Harbor attack seemed to provoke much anger in Arnold. The last time he saw a town burned out, he mounted his horse and went into battle. Not one, but two horses were shot out from under him.

What about the common people and their property? Where was Washington's support of the troops? Washington had said that at times such losses must be submitted to.

After the Egg Harbor incident in November of 1778, Arnold addressed Congress again about putting together a Navy that he would be glad to lead, as he did on Lake Champlain. He felt a huge need to harass the British ships freely navigating the coast. But Congress couldn't muster the support. Arnold wondered if Congress really cared for the common people of the country. 9

The political wrangling was getting to be more than Benedict could bear. His main adversary, Joseph Reed, was appointed president of the Supreme Executive Council of Pennsylvania and he began flexing his newly acquired political muscle.

Reed finally caused Arnold to snap. Arnold challenged two of the war board members to a duel. They backed down but continued their political attacks.

In late January of 1779, Arnold made a business trip to look into a real estate deal. He still had a business to run. He penned a letter to Peggy on February 8th of 1779. "I daily discover so much baseness and ingratitude among mankind that I almost blush to be of the same species." 10

On the same day Arnold wrote to Peggy, Reed had eight charges of abuse of powers against Benedict published in the newspapers. As he did in the field, Arnold took the offensive. His honor and reputation meant everything to him, and he wasn't about to let anyone slander his good name.

Arnold demanded that Congress conduct a court of inquiry to examine his actions. He expected to be cleared of any charges. The Constitutional Party asked for a delay to get time to collect evidence. All of the charges were trumped-up and there was no proof to move forward.

By mid-March of 1779, Benedict reached out to John Jay of Congress to ask that charges against him be cleared speedily. He then resigned his command in Philadelphia and the same day wrote a letter to General Washington. It stated his true feelings. 11

He wrote:

"As soon as my wounds will permit, I shall be happy to take a command in the line of the Army and at all times of rendering my country every service in my power. The final determination of the charges must make both the President and the Council appear to the world in their true colors as a set of unprincipled, malicious scoundrels who have prostituted their honor and truth for the purpose of gratifying their private resentment against an innocent person." 12

Also, in March of 1779, in preparation for his upcoming wedding to Peggy, Benedict had the opportunity to purchase one of the finest properties in Philadelphia – Mount Pleasant. John Adams described it as the most elegant seat in Pennsylvania.

Since Congress had always treated Arnold as second class, it must have gratified him to own a property that was finer than the elites owned. He did have to get a mortgage on the property, but he still had assets in New Haven that he could sell to pay for it, if need be.

Also, Congress was still reviewing expenses Arnold had submitted in the Canadian Campaign. He expected payment to also help cover the cost of buying the new property. He had given up his flagship, the *Peggy* – along with its cargo – in Quebec's harbor during the enemy attack there.

On April 8th of 1779, Peggy and Benedict were married. By April 14th of that year, Benedict found out he was acquitted of most of the charges against him. But Congress requested a court martial by the Army to answer the remaining charges. Benedict was incensed and wrote to Washington to get on with it.

The bickering and timing of getting on with his court martial seemed to drag on forever.

By May 5th of 1779, Arnold wrote to Washington: "If your excellency thinks me a criminal, for Heaven's sake, let me be immediately tried and if found guilty, executed. I want no favor. I only ask justice." 13

On May 7th of 1779, Washington set a trial date of June 1st of 1779 – at least the second or third postponement.

In early May of 1779, Benedict received a long, heart-felt letter from British Colonel Beverly Robinson. He was one of the heads of Loyalist King's American Regiment on the British side. The letter appealed to Benedict his sense of duty to his country. 14

Arnold had great respect for Colonel Robinson. Benedict had given up his business, family ties while risking his life and his honor to give to his country. But he recognized that so did Colonel Robinson.

Before the war, Robinson was actually an acquaintance of patriots like Washington and he had huge properties and land holdings on the east side of the Hudson River. He gave it all up to follow his principles of supporting his king and country, on the side of Great Britain.

Robinson's letter seemed to have quite an effect on Benedict. The letter lavished praise on Arnold for his activity and bravery. Robinson tried to convince Benedict that he was on the wrong side and if he came to the British side it might steer the country away from France and independence under Britain.

Benedict was actually given more honor and respect from the British than he was receiving from his own countrymen.

In the letter to Arnold, Robinson made it clear that if Arnold switched allegiances he would be honored and welcomed by Great Britain. This letter certainly affected Arnold and made him possibly think in a different direction.

It wasn't long after Robinson's letter that most historians point to evidence of Arnold's first contact with the British. 15

CHAPTER TWENTY-TWO

CAMPAIGN SEASON IS ON & OUR FIGHTING GENERAL IS STUCK IN LIMBO

Arnold was becoming more and more frustrated. He had given up his command in Philadelphia and was getting no support from Congress or Washington for anything. He opened a door to possibly offer his service to Great Britain. His contact would be British Major John Andre.

Andre was described as handsome, artistic and very highly educated. He was a true romantic. He loved painting, poetry and played the flute. He was fluent in English, French, German and Italian. It was said that he enlisted in the British Army to mend a broken heart after a long courtship had ended.

He was sent to Germany for two years of special training. By 1774, he had obtained the rank of lieutenant and was shipped off to Canada. He was involved in the American siege of St. John's and was taken prisoner by General Richard Montgomery. 1

As a prisoner of high rank, he was sent south through Lake Champlain to Lake George and on to the Hudson, along with 700 other prisoners. Along the way, officers of rank like Andre were much better treated than the regular British soldiers.

At stops along the way south, they were housed and fed at some prominent locations. One of his stops was an elegant mansion called the White House. It was owned by Joshua Hett Smith. We will hear much more about Smith later on in the story.

Andre would later be transferred to Lancaster, Pennsylvania. As a ranking officer, he was allowed to stay with a local farm family instead of a prison compound like the soldiers faced. He was moved into the home and family of Caleb Cope, a German Pennsylvania farmer, where his ability to speak German served him well.

He gave art lessons to the family's oldest son and became a close friend of the family. At the end of 1776, he was put on a prisoner exchange list and sent to British General Howe in New York City.

While in New York, Andre presented to General Howe a memoir he wrote about observations in the colonies. Howe was quite impressed, and made him an aide to British Major General Charles Grey.

Grey was an adversary associated with Washington in the Battle of Brandywine Creek, Germantown, and the Battle of Monmouth. But he was also part of the invasion force that led to the occupation of Philadelphia. During the long British occupation, Andre attended events where he wrote poetry and played flute for the 'Ladies of Philadelphia.' One of those ladies was Margaret 'Peggy' Shippen, Benedict's future wife.

Peggy, being from a neutralist family, was quite smitten by the dashing young officer and he with her. Andre may have even considered courtship, but times as they were, would not allow it. Nevertheless, they remained very good friends. Peggy would have told Benedict that Andre was a man of honor he could trust.

As British General Clinton had succeeded General Howe in New York City, Andre was promoted to a major in 1778 and was appointed to Clinton's staff.

Clinton, seeing Andre's talent and resourcefulness, made him head of British intelligence. That appointment gained the resources of intelligence he needed to penetrate Philadelphia.

But we must also keep in mind that Washington's spy ring – later known as the Culper Spy Ring – may also have known of Andre's position as head of intelligence, and they would be keeping an eye on him. The spy ring may have reported Andre's friendship with Peggy to Washington and he may have kept this information as future ammunition in case Arnold got too popular.

It's possible that Benedict, fearing the downfall of independence and worries for his new wife, children and sister in Connecticut, may have entertained some kind of an outlet, in case the situation for the colonies went badly.

That Benedict or Peggy could have even contacted Andre in 1779 seems highly improbable. But it is possible that Andre may have contacted them, as British Colonel Beverly Robinson had. Andre may have wanted to keep in contact with Peggy, with Benedict's famous fighting style. He might have thought she would someday be an available widow and he did care for her deeply. 2

As spring rolled into summer, Washington was still busy trying to analyze British General Clinton's plans for the force entrenched in New York City. Clinton had Washington pinned down or in retreat.

Arnold finally got a court martial date of June 1 – but received another postponement. The British attacked up the Hudson River and captured Stony Point. That action kept the army too busy for trials. 3

In July, Benedict sent another plea to get on with his trial. Also, in July, General 'mad' Anthony Wayne retook Stony Point on the Hudson. He earned the reputation of 'mad' by charging the British with the orders to use bayonets only. The fort was retaken by the American side and he captured nearly 500 British soldiers.

Also, that summer, the American army defeated Loyalists and Indian bands in Elmira, New York and launched a retaliatory campaign against the tribes responsible for the massacres of settlers. Some 40 Indian towns were burned down throughout the Finger Lakes region. 4

Washington and Congress had also promised veterans that for their service they would be paid with land grants if they remained with the cause. Washington had his eye on the land of central New York for that purpose.

Arnold was frustrated and sitting on the fence. He reached out to Britain through Major Andre and they pushed back, knowing he had no command position. They requested information they could use. Benedict did supply information, but nothing of any great importance.

He hadn't really decided on making a jump to the British side. It would be a great deal of risk for him, but he was going to keep the option open because of the way he was being treated by our side. He wasn't about to make the move without rank and some financial guarantees.

Since Benedict gave up his position of authority in Philadelphia, lawlessness began to brew in the streets. Mobs of Constitutionalists and overzealous patriots were demonstrating and looking for loyalists to hang or burn out. 5

By October, he had to request an armed guard to move about the city. He also put down one demonstration by pulling his pistols. Another reason he wanted protection was that Peggy had become very pregnant.

Almost a year had passed since Arnold had demanded his inquiry and had to deal with Congress, which was represented by Reed. Finally, in December enough officers were available to hold Arnold's court martial hearing. 6

CHAPTER TWENTY-THREE

1780 – ARNOLD TEETERING ON THE EDGE & SO IS AMERICA

Why He Went to the Other Side Explained

By the winter of 1779, Washington set up his winter encampment in Morristown, New Jersey. The weather became very frigid and snowy in December and January. Blizzards hit the Northeast and the Hudson River froze nearly to the harbor.

Supply shortages and morale hit rock bottom. When January 1st rolled into view, many enlistments expired, and men were leaving in droves. Desertions occurred daily, far outnumbering the remaining enlisted force.

Mutiny also became a serious problem. Washington would write: "In every line of the Army the most serious features of mutiny and sedition are sensed." To control the problem, he would eventually even have some of the offenders shot and hanged – a move that wouldn't endear men to Washington's side. 1

Arnold would also write that year to General Nathanael Green to say that 1,500 troops of all ranks should be used to surround Congress and make them listen to reason. The Army should not starve in a land of plenty.

By January 21st Arnold finally got his court martial on the eight charges holding him in limbo. He defended himself, answering each charge, one by one. His accusers could find nothing less than honorable about Benedict's conduct in Philadelphia.

But the court did find Arnold guilty of two minor charges. The claim was that he allowed a merchant ship, in which he had investments, to leave port when others could not, and that he used government wagons to move cargo to the ship. Congress approved the findings of the court martial and suggested Arnold be turned over to Washington for reprimand.

The whole affair was a little more than a hand slap and the charges were probably a way to placate the Constitutional Party. But letting any charges stand was more than Benedict could bear. He felt that his very honor had been assaulted.

He wrote a letter to his good friend, Silas Deane:

March 22, 1780
"Sir,

I believe you will be equally surprised with me when you find the court martial having fully acquitted me of the charge of employing public wagons, or defrauding the public, or of injuring or impeding the public service. Yet in their next sentence say, 'as requests from him might operate as commands,' I ought to receive a reprimand. For what? Not for doing wrong, but because I might have done wrong; or rather, because evil might follow the good that I did!

I have proposed to the Board of Admiralty an expedition, which will require three or four hundred land forces to act in conjunction with the ships. The matter rests with General Washington. If men can be spared and my plan takes place, you will hear from me soon. If it should not, I propose going to Boston with the intention to take the command of a private ship. 2

I am, &c.,
B. Arnold"

Arnold was disgusted with Congress. He thought justifiably that our forefathers were disappointments to many, especially to those in the military.

Although Benedict had a channel open to Britain through Andre, he may have given up on Congress and was losing any faith in Washington. He still had not given up on his country. He still had the troops and people he loved to fight for.

In December and January, British Commander Clinton was forcing a mass deployment of troops to attack the southern states. Up to 8,000 troops, ships and supplies were heading toward Charleston, South Carolina.

Previously, on March 6th, Arnold had been approached by the Naval Board about a plan to intercept the British forces moving south. He knew the army was pressed for men and he worked day and night to formulate a battle plan that would not strain the Army.

Arnold knew of many ships he could refit for war. They already had experienced crews. He knew well the high seas between New York and the Carolinas. He could sail out of the Chesapeake Bay and hit the British broadside, as he did in Valcour. His plan rested on Washington's response and he begged Washington for a chance. He limited his need for troops to only 400 men.

On March 19, 1780, he had some joyous news to give also. Peggy gave birth to a son. 3

Everyone seemed to know the British were moving offensively southward, except General Washington. He still was obsessed with using the French in combination with American troops to drive the British out of New York.

On March 28, 1780, Benedict received the devastating news that Washington denied his troop request and his naval plan was abandoned. 4

Then, on April 6, Washington finally gave Arnold his official public reprimand. It seemed all too much to Arnold. To make matters even worse, Congress's Board of Treasury finished their review of Arnold's Canadian campaign expenses. They said Benedict owed them $1,000 – the money he needed for the mortgage on his new house. 5

On top of all the politics he endured, the last straw came down. On May 12th of 1780 – after a long siege – Charleston, South Carolina fell into the hands of the British. America surrendered over 5,000 troops, equipment, powder and other supplies.

During the siege, all were concerned. Arnold hoped that since the commander of the southern Army was in such need and his old friend Daniel Morgan was already in the south, he would be the obvious choice to take the southern command.

But of all the people in the world, Congress went over Washington's head and appointed Horatio Gates on May 17th of 1780. At that point, Arnold felt very, very angry and crushed.

Since 1774, he went into battle as a militia captain, funded by his own pocket. He took Ticonderoga and captured the cannons America needed to chase the British from Boston, then took over the entire Champlain Valley and changed the course of the war.

He then took on a mission as colonel, battling to the walls of Quebec through impossible odds. While suffering a horrible leg wound, Benedict then saved more than 500 men at Fort Anne. As our first Commodore, he later fought off the Royal Navy and saved Washington's fleeing army from certain defeat.

At Ridgefield, Arnold had two horses shot from under him and he still didn't quit. He volunteered on a mission to relieve Fort Stanwix and then came back in time to defeat Burgoyne at Saratoga, again crippling his leg.

Instead of gratitude, Benedict was betrayed by Lafayette, who gave Gates the honor of his victory. He was brought up on charges by Reed and the Pennsylvania Council. Congress told Arnold they were owed money by him! Washington would not support his efforts and even reprimanded him.

Now, the final blow. While he was in Philadelphia without a command, Congress gave the southern command to Gates. Arnold also found out that his victory at Saratoga could have brought peace with Britain in 1778 if congressmen didn't have investments west of the Appalachians.

Arnold also had a deep resentment of the French alliance. He considered the French an enemy of his Protestant faith. He also felt their monarchy enslaved their own people.

Arnold, a man of action, reached his limit.

I believe mid-May of 1780 was Arnold's tipping point. This is the very curious thing many will find hard to understand.

Arnold now felt he had two roads in front of him if he simply wanted to make the statement that he felt his country was wrong and had wronged him.

The best and safest course of action would be to march into Congress, resign his commission, sell one of his two properties and go back to the apothecary and sea trade business. He certainly left a legacy as America's only real winning general and would be remembered as our greatest war hero.

The whole country was now a war zone and the economy was in tatters. The Continental currency suffered so much inflation it was hardly worth the paper it was printed on. It would be difficult, but this plan was the safest route to take.

There are some historians who say financial pressures turned Arnold. I feel that is more than ridiculous. If I had to list who was the most generous patriot with personal funds invested in the American Revolution it would be Benedict Arnold, hands down.

Arnold funded many of his missions from his own pocket. In Quebec, he even gave up one of his ships for the cause. When the old artillery officer Colonel John Lamb got orders to put an artillery division together without funds, he went to Arnold and got what he needed.

Many more times, Benedict found himself in financial hot water by loaning and giving money to people he knew could never pay him back.

What many will find hard to understand is that in May of 1780 Benedict was not thinking of himself. He considered himself a true patriot and a man of principles and honor.

He decided that as risky as it would be, he needed to lead a charge back to the British side. He seriously felt the country he loved would be far better off under its former footing, rather than what he saw being formed and going forward.

CHAPTER TWENTY-FOUR

THE FRENCH ALLIANCE RAMPING UP – ARNOLD'S ALLEGIANCE WINDING DOWN

In June and July of 1780, Benedict opened more urgent communications with the British. The lines of communications were risky and negotiations seemed futile. Benedict had given them some information, but they were not that interested. Arnold had just gone through court martial and had no post in the line of the Army.

By July 11, Benedict had penned a letter to Andre, complaining of unanswered letters. He even suggested that he "cooperate for the advantage of all parties or end the correspondence for the mutual safety of all concerned." 1

If Arnold's letters had been intercepted, you need to ask by whom? Washington had a very intensive spy ring that no one at the time was aware of. It would later be labeled the 'Culper Spy Ring.' All correspondence between and among armies was always in jeopardy. Being a courier in 1780 was a very dangerous job.

By the 12th of July, Arnold wrote again to Andre, piquing British interest. He said he was hoping to get the command at West Point. 2

He said, "the present struggles were like the pangs of a dying man, violent but of short duration." He also stated that "the mass of the people were heartily tired of the war and wished to be on their former footing."

The very same day, the French arrived en mass in Newport, Rhode Island. General John Baptiste Rochambeau and Admiral Charles Louis d'Arsac landed seven ships of the French line with 6,000 troops and 1,000 sailors.

Adding to Benedict's frustration and dismay over the war situation, bad news came from Charleston, South Carolina. It fell and America suffered its worst war defeat. The British captured over 5,000 prisoners and seized over 300 pieces of artillery. The British had moved all their main thrusts to the south. Benedict realized that if only Washington had approved of his naval plan, the British would have at least been slowed down. But Washington seemed to be still fixated on New York.

On July 17th Benedict requested four months pay for the purchase of horses and equipment so he could report to Washington to gain a field command. 3

By late July, Benedict got significant British interest from Andre and British General Clinton. On the 24th of July, Andre expressed an interest in doing the negotiations himself if they could be set up near West Point. 4

By the end of July, Benedict was totally sick of politics and being stuck in limbo. He reported to Washington's temporary headquarters, just above Stony Point on the west side of the Hudson. Then, he crossed the river to Washington's main headquarters, which were now in Peekskill.

CHAPTER TWENTY-FIVE

AUGUST 1780 – ARNOLD TAKES HIS WEST POINT POST SERIOUSLY

On August 1st, Washington – in his general orders for the day – gave Arnold a post of very high honor. He was appointed to the command of the left wing of Washington's main army. 1

We have always been told that Arnold protested in favor of the West Point command. We have only Washington's word for that. But Arnold did already inform the British he would be at the Point and that he had lobbied with Schuyler for that West Point position.

Also, to command the left wing would probably force him to cooperate with the French.

But the next day the left wing went to Lord William Stirling. On August 3rd, Arnold received a letter from Washington. It told him to report to the command of West Point. 2

The post at West Point was certainly not a type of post that Benedict would have picked on his own. Historians now tell us the importance of the Point. They refer to it as the 'Gibraltar of America' or the 'Key to the Continent.' Now, we hold it in esteem because that's where American military officers are trained.

But in 1780, without an enemy army in the north – thanks to Arnold – West Point wasn't much more than an over-fortified supply depot. Historians also tell us that West Point was an object of importance to the British. The previous year, the British tried and failed to hold Stony Point, a post ten miles south of West Point on the Hudson. General Anthony Wayne routed the Red Coats out with a surprise bayonet charge and captured 500 British regulars.

The British could not possibly hold West Point without control of all the posts between West Point and New York City. They did not have the manpower to even consider trying. Besides, they had already shifted their attention to the southern colonies.

On August 5th, Benedict set up his headquarters at Robinson House. The Robinson House was the estate previously owned by British Colonel Beverly Robinson before the war broke out. To serve his king and country as a Loyalist, he had to abandon his properties. 3

Robinson House was across from the Point and a little south. From there – with the use of his barge – Arnold could easily reach the fortifications at the Point and the main river crossing in Peekskill. For its time, Robinson House was a very plush estate and Benedict was looking forward to showing his wife, Peggy. He hoped she and the baby could join him there.

We have also been told repeatedly in history books that Arnold spent his time weakening the defenses at West Point. I have found no evidence to support this. In fact, I found many instances where he strengthened all the fortifications there with what he was given. If anyone weakened West Point, it was George Washington.

On August 5th, Washington instructed Arnold to remove any unnecessary personnel. He believed militia could do the job. 4

Also, in early August, the famous Polish engineer Colonel Thaddeus Kosciuszko, who helped Arnold scout Bemis Heights, saw no future in continuing to fortify the works at West Point. He requested a field command in the south. It was granted, but Washington insisted he needed him as an engineer, not a field officer. He was replaced at West Point by French engineer Major Jean Villefranche. 5

On August 8th, Arnold sent a letter to Washington, stating the need for more experienced troops, teams of horses and supplies. On August 11th, Washington told him to "proceed in working with materials which he found on hand." 6

August 12th, Arnold wrote again to Washington. He gave a report of the militia on hand and listed many problems at the garrison. But he assured 'His Excellency' that with "such men and materials as I have, I will do all that could be done." 7

That didn't sound like someone weakening defenses.

In mid-August, the army changed quartermaster generals and Colonel Pickering was appointed to the department. Benedict wasted no time in requesting that supplies needed be provided immediately. 8

He especially needed fresh teams of horses to help raise the sinking chain on the Hudson River. A chain with huge links had been stretched across the river at West Point to impede any large ships that tried to sail past without being slowed or stopped. The chain was beginning to sink and needed fresh timbers to raise and re-float it.

In August, Benedict didn't completely forget his contacts with the British. He kept looking for ways to possibly use flags to set up a meeting. By the end of August, the French alliance was ramping up and so were Arnold's contacts with Andre'. Benedict, to risk his move to the British side and finalize plans, wanted assurance and a face-to-face meeting with the British. He wrote to Andre' on August 30th to say he wanted a meeting in ten days. He complained again of letters with no answers and/or late answers. 9

He was also looking for contacts with Loyalist ties. He thought he found one in Joshua Hett Smith.

CHAPTER TWENTY-SIX

JOSHUA HETT SMITH

Joshua Hett Smith was a member of the group I referred to earlier in the book as an underground survivalist. He was a very bright young lawyer who came from a long-established and wealthy family in New York. The Smith family had many properties in New York City and vast stretches of land going up the west side of the Hudson River.

He had always shown Patriot leanings, but Joshua clearly thought he was smart enough to play both sides. No one really seemed to trust him on the American side – mainly because of his brother William Smith. Joshua's brother was a very staunch Loyalist and he was the chief justice in New York City. He considered himself an Englishman above all else. 1

Joshua Smith resided in a large estate on the west side of Haverstraw Bay. His home was commonly referred to as the 'White House.' The White House was a stopping point for every elite group traveling on the west side of the Hudson. Joshua lived there with a large staff of slaves and servants. His estate was surrounded by tenant farmers he leased land to and traded with.

One of the regular visitors to the White House was George Washington. Also, men like Adams, Jefferson or anyone of importance in the area would make Smith's property a stopping point. Even after Arnold defeated Burgoyne, the General was given lodging there as he traveled toward Boston as a prisoner of war. But one curious guest traveling through in 1776 was none other than a young lieutenant, John Andre'.

Andre' was on his way toward Pennsylvania as a prisoner of war after he was captured by Montgomery at Fort St. John's. Joshua Smith knew almost everyone in the area. He reached out to Arnold soon after he took his post at West Point. On August 16th he offered his service for intelligence, as he had a good view of the ship traffic on Haverstraw Bay. He also offered his home as a resting point for Mrs. Peggy Arnold when she arrived from Philadelphia and waited for Arnold to retrieve her with his barge.

Smith asked Arnold for help with permission and flags, to help save starving women with children who needed to re-unite with family in New York City. 2

I'm sure Benedict thought Joshua Hett Smith, with all of his contacts on both sides, could be a good asset in his plans to contact the British. Joshua had another project he was working on that kept him traveling by ferry across the Hudson River. One of his nephews was basically trapped on the British side of the lines. He was hoping to get permission from Washington or the governor of New York to assure that the boys could re-unite with their father and see his brother William in New York City. But no one seemed to want to give permission to help a Tory family re-unite. 3

So, on every trip across the Hudson he would stop at Peekskill and visit his cousin Colonel James Livingston, who was in charge of the post there.

CHAPTER TWENTY-SEVEN

COLONEL JAMES LIVINGSTON

Livingston was in command of the crossing point and post in Peekskill. He was originally recruited by a man who was one of Benedict's strongest enemies, Colonel John Brown. He was involved in the intelligence network under Phillip Schuyler back in 1776.

Brown rubbed Benedict the wrong way during the Canadian campaign. To make a long story short, there was a squabble over the rank Brown said was promised to him by Montgomery, just before he was killed. Brown was in charge of some captured British officers' possessions. Benedict thought Brown dishonorably helped himself to those.

Arnold called him out on the matter and Brown took offense. For the rest of his career, Brown sought to go after Arnold and his reputation. 1

Brown recruited Livingston to form the first Canadian regiment to fight for America. Livingston completed the task and his regiment fought with honor through Saratoga and beyond. Many were still with him in Peekskill.

Livingston and his cousin, Joshua Hett Smith, would soon play a pivotal role in the Andre' and Arnold story.

As you will see, I believe the evidence will show that Livingston, during his many days at the ferry crossing, was also an agent for Washington's and Tallmadge's spy ring.

CHAPTER TWENTY-EIGHT

ARNOLD GETTING BOLD & SLOPPY WITH HIS SECRET COMMUNICATIONS

On August 30th of 1780, Arnold sent a letter to Andre. He complained of slow response to letters and hoped he could set up a meeting in the course of ten days. 1

The next day, Andre was recommended for a promotion to become an adjutant general for the British army, which he received.

Arnold began the process of setting up a meeting he thought could be done honorably through the use of flags. He would try to arrange the meeting through Colonel Elisha Sheldon of the 2nd Dragoons. They were an elite mounted group of soldiers in a fast-moving cavalry unit that was in charge of the forces watching the enemy lines. Unknown to Arnold, this was the same outfit that Washington's head of intelligence rode in. He was Major Ben Talmadge.

Benedict wrote to Sheldon on the 1st of August and again on the 7th to say he was trying to set up a channel of intelligence. On the 7th, Andre contacted Sheldon by a letter signed by 'John Anderson', Andre's code name. Andre' said he would be at Dobbs Ferry the 11th at 12:00 noon. 2

While all this intrigue was going on, so was the war. By September, more detailed reports were coming up from the southern campaign.

General Horatio Gates finally showed his true colors. He gathered his forces in Hillsborough, North Carolina and marched south toward Camden, South Carolina. He thought he would easily rout the British forces there. Unfortunately, he ran into a sizable column of British regulars under the command of British General Lord Charles Cornwallis. Against the wishes of his officers, Gates decided to engage the British in battle.

The decision proved disastrous for the southern army. A bloody battle ensued, causing 750 casualties and close to 1,000 men captured by the British. As the battle raged, Gates and his aides rode hard north, supposedly seeking assistance.

By nightfall, Gates was a good 60 miles north of the battlefield. Gates was accused of cowardice in the face of the enemy and would never fully regain his honor. A very embarrassed Congress had to ask Washington to appoint a new southern commander.

When Benedict received the news of Gates' performance, he must have felt quite vindicated. He probably expected to be called by Washington to take the southern command.

Benedict would have been the obvious choice. His good friend, Daniel Morgan, was in the south already and Arnold had the proven battle experience to get the job done. But Arnold was never even asked. Washington knew if he sent Arnold south and he found a way to defeat Cornwallis, Benedict would be the hero of the entire nation.

By mid-September, Washington had other ideas for Arnold.

In early September, Arnold was sent an express letter from Washington, stating he had intelligence that the British were looking to attack the Hudson Highlands.

Arnold ordered 60 flat-bottom boats to proceed to Colonel Livingston's post in Peekskill, in case they needed to evacuate the ferry crossing and move north toward West Point. 3,4

Washington agreed with Arnold's defensive strategy. On September 6th of 1780, Washington held a council of war. The war was definitely shifting south, and he wanted officers' opinions on what strategy would be best and he wanted detailed situation reports from all of his officers by the 10th of September. 5

Arnold wasn't summoned to the meeting, so he was sent a copy.

On September 9th and 10th of 1780, Arnold received letters from Colonel John Jameson of lower Salem and White Castle, as well as from Colonel Sheldon of the 2nd Dragoons. 6

They told Benedict they were aware of 'John Anderson' (Andre's code name) and also aware that Arnold was setting up a meeting to gain intelligence. Arnold wrote back to Sheldon to let him know of his hope to contact 'Anderson' and that he would be near Dobbs Ferry.

Arnold said if Anderson showed in his quarter, he wanted him escorted to his position near Dobbs Ferry. 7

As Benedict worked to set up a September 11th meeting with Andre, all the flags going back and forth in the area were raising many suspicions of what was going on.

CHAPTER TWENTY-NINE

ARNOLD'S FIRST MEETING WITH THE BRITS LITERALLY ALMOST SUNK

Just before Arnold's proposed British contact, he was clearly not sure of what direction he was going to take.

On September 10th, he sent a letter to Andre to say he suspected the correspondence he sent on the 7th may have been intercepted. He also vented his frustration that Andre wasn't being careful enough and told him he must get to American lines by "stealth." 1

Andre planned to attend the meeting set with Colonel Beverly Robinson, going with the use of flags near Dobbs Ferry. The very day of the meeting, as Arnold arrived at the area near Dobbs Ferry, he sent a letter to Washington. He said he had found some cannons at West Point.

Benedict explained that the cannons were unserviceable for combat, but he intended to use them as signal guns to set up a warning beacon south of the Point. They would be an alarm if the British made a move up the river. 2

If Arnold intended to turn West Point over to the British, why would he be setting up warning beacons?

The morning of his meeting, Arnold left Robinson House in his barge, rowed by his eight bargemen, and made his way south toward Dobbs Ferry. He took a break at Joshua Smith's landing on Haverstraw Bay.

Smith inquired about the series of flags, recently passed along the south end of the bay. Benedict told him the meaning of the flags would be explained in a short time.

Arnold, with his bargemen and a flag of truce, then proceeded south toward Dobbs Ferry and the British warship, the *Vulture*. The ship was now in the area, carrying Robinson and Andre'.

As Arnold approached the enemy lines, a gunboat that was unaware of the meeting opened fire on Arnold's barge. The cannonball just missed its mark, nearly sinking the barge. Benedict made a quick retreat back to the western shore, as the British continued their barrage of cannon fire for the next five hours.

Arnold waited in the area above Dobbs Ferry till nearly 3 o'clock in the afternoon, hoping Robinson or Andre' would find a way to approach him by use of flags, but no one showed.

Robinson would later write to Arnold on the 16th to say that he was greatly disappointed in not seeing Mr. Smith at the time appointed. Benedict, in his known correspondence, never mentioned using Joshua H. Smith for the meeting so there must be more to this story than we have been told. 3

This has never been answered.

Benedict then took his barge back north to Joshua Smith's White House where he was pleasantly surprised. His wife Peggy and their baby had just arrived at Smith's on their way from Philadelphia.

I'm sure they had a fine meal at Smith's and a happy reunion. Arnold then took Peggy and the baby the next morning, by barge, across the river back to his Robinson House headquarters.

CHAPTER THIRTY

THE PLOT THICKENS
Arnold Explores a Route to the British Side
Washington Finds a Way to Get Rid of Arnold

On September 12th of 1780, Benedict crossed over the Hudson River and settled Peggy and the baby into their new headquarters at the Robinson House. After he showed Peggy around, they began to settle in.

That day, Benedict penned a letter to Washington. The letter seemed quite routine. It concerned him retaining his personal bargemen and a problem Colonel Hay had with getting flour for the troops. Also, there was the matter of bateaus that he had sent to Colonel Livingston in case of evacuation.

The very first sentence of the letter caught my attention!

Arnold wrote that he was "enclosing a copy of a council of war, held on the 6th of September 1780." 1

Later on in this story, Andre is captured with, supposedly, a dangerous parcel of papers found in his boot. One of those papers was a copy of a council of war, dated September 6th. How do real historians explain how this copy got from Washington's desk into Andre's boot?

I will now attempt to explain how I think it happened. Arnold's next letter – he wrote the same day – really gets to his feelings at the time.

Benedict penned a letter to Major General Nathanel Greene, who previously, before he advanced in rank, was the quartermaster general. Arnold was actually looking for where he could get a supply of paper. Colonel Pickering, now quartermaster, informed him he didn't have the stores or money to purchase paper.

But the letter to Greene was interesting, as I think it gave Arnold a chance to vent his feelings at the time. He wrote about General Horatio Gates' performance at Camden, South Carolina: "I cannot avoid remarking that his conduct on this occasion has in no way disappointed my expectations or predictions on frequent occasions."

He also wrote about Congress: "It is a matter much to be lamented that our army is permitted to starve in a land of plenty. There is a fault somewhere; it ought to be traced up to its authors and if it was preferred, they ought to be capitally punished. This is in my opinion the only measure left to procure a regular supply to the army in the future." 2

Over the next few days, Arnold began to put together another plan to meet with the British. This time, he would have them come to him. He let Andre' know on the 15th. He suggested that if he came by stealth up the east side of the Hudson, the officers in the area – Sheldon, Jameson or Tallmadge – would all be under instructions to escort him under guard to his headquarters.

Benedict also offered that if that was not agreeable, he would send someone they could trust, by water on the night of the 20th to Dobbs Ferry or to the warship *Vulture*. He also suggested Andre' be disguised to keep the matter a secret. 3

Two days prior to that, he wrote to Andre' to propose meeting by land or water. Arnold began the preliminaries to set up the meeting. He wrote to Colonel Sheldon, letting him know he was still looking for Anderson – Andre's code name. 4

Arnold also wrote to Major Tallmadge on the 13th of September. He wrote: "If Mr. John Anderson, a person I expect from New York, should come to your quarters, I have to request you will give him an escort of two horsemen to bring him on his way to this place and send an express to me, that I may meet him. If your business will permit, I wish you to come with him." 5

Benedict didn't know Tallmadge was the head of Washington's secret service. Tallmadge most likely was the source of Arnold's intercepted letters, and he also had a Lady Agent 355 working on Andre'.

Tallmadge's lady agent was assigned to gain information relating to Andre'. We don't know anything about her except her agent number – 355 – and she only reported to Tallmadge and Tallmadge only reported to Washington.

To Tallmadge, the game was on!

CHAPTER THIRTY-ONE

BENJAMIN TALLMADGE : A MAN WITH A MISSION & AN AX TO GRIND

By the time Tallmadge received Arnold's letter stating he wanted John Anderson brought to headquarters, I'm sure he should have had all the pieces put together. Tallmadge was not only Washington's head of intelligence – which no one knew – he also had Lady Agent 355 working on Andre'. Even Andre' and Arnold, through their failed meeting attempts, were worried they were raising suspicions.

Benedict had complained of possible intercepted communications. If Tallmadge didn't know what was going on, he certainly should have. I believe he even knew who Anderson – Andre's code name – was. Tallmadge only answered to one person – George Washington. 1

Tallmadge was very, very, highly motivated to capture Andre'.

Benjamin Tallmadge was a graduate of Yale University. His very best friend and roommate when he attended the university was Nathan Hale. Captured by the British, Hale was accused of being a spy. The British hung Hale. He was famously known to say, "I regret I have but one life to give to my country." 2

The capture of Andre' would be seen by Tallmadge as the ultimate revenge. Tallmadge rode with the 2nd Dragoons – an elite, fast moving cavalry – that patrolled enemy lines near White Castle and Greenfield and all around the southeastern shores of the Hudson River, below West Point.

That very week, I believe Tallmadge acquired his main target – Andre'. He was soon to report to Washington that very week, as he would be crossing the Hudson to meet with the French in Connecticut. It is my theory based on who was where, when and their action, that Tallmadge reported his findings of Arnold communicating with the British to Washington. 3

It is my personal assessment that Washington would seize the opportunity. If Andre' could be captured with evidence on him, he could arrest Arnold for treason or just get him to leave his post. Benedict had become a thorn in Washington's side. He was too popular with the troops to be given a large command, and he constantly spoke out against the French alliance. I also believe the French, and possibly Lafayette himself, may have been pressuring Washington to get rid of Arnold. But Arnold negotiating with the British through the use of flags would not be enough evidence for an arrest. Washington and Tallmadge needed papers.

I will now attempt to explain how I think the downfall of Arnold happened.

CHAPTER THIRTY-TWO

A WEEK OF VERY HIGH INTRIGUE

On September 13th, Benedict received a note from Colonel Livingston, stating that Colonel Beverly Robinson of the British had come to "Tarrytown in a barge, under the pretense of a flag, but I think it more probable to reconnoiter the country."

Livingston wanted to give them a check – open fire. Benedict sent a note back to Livingston to be "exceedingly cautious of how we venture small parties as low as Tarrytown." 1

Benedict should have wondered why Livingston was not near his post near Peekskill. Why was he so far south? He happened to be in the same area as Benjamin Tallmadge. I believe this is when Livingston and Tallmadge started planning Andre's capture by using Livingston as an agent.

Arnold also wrote that day to Colonel Lamb, who was in charge of all artillery units.

Benedict wanted two nine-pound, or preferably, 12-pound cannons to be set up as signal guns near Dobbs Ferry "to keep off enemy boats who come up almost every day and insult the post." 2

This was not exactly reducing defenses, as we have been told.

The next day, September 14th, Benedict wrote to Washington, stating his formal opinion on the council of war. He didn't give much hope of routing the British from New York without more reinforcements from the French and he thought the Pennsylvania Lines might be better used to aid the southern colonies since there was no navy to harass the British. 3

The very morning he wrote to Washington, he crossed the Hudson to Joshua Smith's house. He told Smith that he was setting up a secret meeting with the British, and that it would be of great advantage to the country. He wanted Smith's help to escort possibly Colonel Robinson, and especially John Anderson – Andre's code name – for a high-level meeting in secret. He wanted Joshua to go at night on the 20th and bring them to the White House.

I'm sure Joshua wasn't comfortable with the situation, but he had much property at risk. He didn't want to disappoint the area commander, Benedict. Joshua must have already been involved in British contacts, since Colonel Beverly Robinson wrote two days later to say he was disappointed in not seeing "Mr. Smith" at the failed meeting on the 11th. Joshua seemed quite comfortable with playing every side. In his letters, Benedict never named who he was sending as an escort. 4

Joshua probably also informed Benedict that he was taking his family on a trip to Fishkill. He had planned to meet with Governor George Clinton of New York about re-uniting his nephew with their father, Thomas, in New York City. Clinton was in Poughkeepsie, 12 miles north of Fishkill. Benedict offered that they should stop at Robinson House for dinner on their way through. It would give Peggy a chance to entertain.

Benedict made his way back across the Hudson to headquarters, where he had received a message from Washington.

Washington approved of Benedict's new cannon placements and added a note telling him he would be in Peekskill on Sunday evening of the 17th on his way to meet French Admiral Charles Louis Ternay and French General Compte D' Rochambeau in Hartford, Connecticut. He asked Benedict to direct the quartermaster to have a night's forage for 40 horses ready and a captain and guard of 50 men to accompany him. He also told Benedict to keep his trip "to yourself, as I want to make my journey a secret." 5

Arnold sent a note to Andre to tell him Washington would be in King's Ferry on Sunday, the 17th. Apparently, the British didn't get the message, as Robinson said in a letter afterward, he was unaware Washington was there. 6

Benedict then wrote to his friend, Colonel Lamb, that Washington approved of the new cannon placement and he wanted it fully armed with 50 rounds of shot and some grape shot instead of just signal guns. But again, we have always been told that Arnold weakened West Point. 7

The next day, Arnold sent a note to Washington to tell him he had horse forage and guard arranged for his crossing. Arnold also stated that the detailed situation reports Washington asked for in the council of war would be delivered in person by him as he crossed the river. 8

It is my belief that excerpts from Arnold's situation reports will surface later in this story.

CHAPTER THIRTY-THREE

ANOTHER PLAN BEGINS TO HATCH

On the morning of Sunday, September 17th, Joshua Hett Smith had his servants gathered, his wife and two nephews in preparation to make a trip across the river to Fishkill. The small Smith entourage crossed King's Ferry to Verplank Point.

Every time Smith crossed the river, he would stop and visit his cousin, Colonel James Livingston. I'm sure he bragged to his cousin that he was also on a mission to set up British negotiations for General Arnold. As the details were related, he may have said it involved 'Mr. John Anderson' – code for Andre'.

I believe Livingston, acting as an agent for Tallmadge, informed his cousin that 'Anderson' was a person they very much wanted to capture. He wanted Smith's help to accomplish that. Joshua Hett Smith thought this was a very dangerous game with nothing in it for him. He told Livingston that if he got involved, he wanted something, in writing, absolving him of any wrongdoing. He surely didn't want to be on anyone's wrong side, definitely not Washington's or Arnold's. But he was already in the game, so he wanted a 'get out of jail free' card.

Livingston told him that could be arranged, with more details, before he made his way back from Fishkill.

Joshua and company then made their way up to Robinson House, where they were entertained for a mid-day Sunday meal by Peggy, the baby and a number of Benedict's closest officers. The group included army surgeon and Harvard graduate Dr. William Eustis, Colonel Return Jonathan Meigs – who fought with Benedict in Quebec – artillerist Colonel Lamb, Major David S. Franks – who volunteered to be on Arnold's staff back in Albany – and Colonel Richard Varick, who served loyally with Arnold as far back as '76. 1

While they were eating, Benedict told Major Franks they would soon be going across the river to meet for dinner with General Washington, who would be entertained with his entourage at the White House, as they prepared to move 40 horses across the Hudson to Peekskill. Apparently, Joshua Smith had a very large staff since Washington and company would have dinner there even if Smith wasn't home.

Varick and Lamb both approached Arnold before lunch to tell him they really didn't like him associating with Joshua H. Smith. They didn't trust him and thought he was a damn Tory and a snake in the grass. Benedict dismissed their feeling but should have taken their advice.

As the midday meal progressed, Arnold received a letter from Colonel Beverly Robinson, who was on board the warship *Vulture*. He hoped to have a meeting concerning his property that Arnold was using as headquarters. He showed the letter to Lamb, who thought it was improper for a British officer to request a meeting with Arnold. He counseled him to show the letter to Washington. Benedict agreed to do so. 2

After lunch, Smith and family left for Fishkill. Arnold and Franks made their way across the Hudson to meet Washington for dinner. Washington had a very large and impressive entourage. He had his staff of servants also, men like Hamilton, Knox, Lafayette and their aides and their personal staffs. This is how 'his excellency' was expected to travel.

In late afternoon, the large entourage made their way across the Hudson with a guard of nearly 20. Arnold discussed with Washington the letter Robinson had sent him, as he promised Lamb he would do. Washington thought it a civil matter that Robinson should take up with New York's governor, not army officers. He was also said to have noticed with his spyglass the British warship *Vulture*. It was anchored off Teller's Point at the south end of the bay.

Benedict also handed over his detailed situation reports that Washington required from his war council.

They all landed near Verplank Point, then rode into Peekskill, where they spent the night. The next morning, Washington mounted up to ride to his high-level meeting with the French in Hartford, Connecticut. He told Benedict he would be back in five days to spend the night at his quarters at Robinson House and to inspect fortifications at the point. 3

CHAPTER THIRTY-FOUR

ARNOLD WANTS TO MEET WITH THE BRITISH, WASHINGTON MEETS THE FRENCH & TALLMADGE PLOTS REVENGE

As Washington left Peekskill to meet the French command in Connecticut, Benedict went back to Robinson House and fired off a letter to Colonel Beverly Robinson. The letter was quite polite, telling Robinson that he told Washington about his concerns and there was little he could do. 1

Benedict stated he would send an agent Wednesday, the night of the 20th with a boat and a flag of truce. The matter would be of secrecy and honor. He also enclosed a note to Anderson, code for Andre'. He asked that the *Vulture* remain anchored where she was, as he would send someone there or to the landing at Dobbs Ferry, if necessary. His agent would conduct him to a place of safety for a meeting 2

Arnold thought now that he finally had a chance for a meeting with Andre', getting to the warship *Vulture* would be much easier and safer than the landing at Dobbs Ferry, farther down river. Arnold's new agent, Joshua H. Smith, had dropped off Smith's family to stay with relatives in Fishkill, New York. Joshua Smith then traveled to Poughkeepsie, New York to meet with New York Governor George Clinton.

He was hoping to get permission from Governor Clinton to get his nephew – Thomas' son – who was stuck behind the enemy lines in New York City with his other brother, William, so Thomas' family could re-unite.

Smith was promptly turned away by the governor, who politely told him – though he knew the Smith family well – he wasn't about to aid a Tory family. No re-union for the Smiths this year! 3

On his way back, Joshua stopped in Fishkill to tell the boys and his family the sad news, then went back south to Robinson House to aid in Arnold's meeting. On September 19th, Arnold received a letter from Colonel Beverly Robinson from on board the *Vulture*, off Teller's Point. He thanked Arnold for his polite letter and civil expressions to him. But he also included an interesting paragraph, showing how the war had separated people.

He wrote: "Had I known General Washington was with you, I should certainly have made my application to him. As I flatter myself, I should be allowed every reasonable indulgence from him. I beg my best respects may be presented to him. I can have nothing further to say to you at present but must wait a more favorable opportunity of doing something for my family." 4

Colonel Beverly Robinson was a good friend of Washington before the war.

In another interesting letter, before the secret meeting, Arnold wrote an angry note to Colonel James Livingston. Arnold had sent nearly 60 manned boats to Livingston, in case of a needed evacuation of his post. He found out from the man who had just delivered letters under a flag of truce to the *Vulture*, that the British had collected nearly 40 of the boats, but due to neglect, they had washed down river.

Arnold wanted the remaining boats immediately collected and secured from the enemy and those responsible for such neglect to be punished. He also mentioned the cannons he was sending south for his new warning redoubt were on a sloop, instead of bateaus, and he was worried they couldn't pass the enemy vessels on the river. He wanted them better secured and sent down at the very first favorable opportunity. 5

I think he was quite angry with Livingston for not doing a good job at his post. Livingston seemed to be neglecting his post, but I think at the time he was a bit pre-occupied with a secret mission of his own.

When Washington's entourage left Peekskill on the way to Connecticut, three men were all in the same area – Washington, Tallmadge and Livingston. Now this can't be proven and is my speculation. But it's based on who was where, when, who was talking to whom and their actions in the aftermath of what went down.

I believe Tallmadge presented his findings on 'Anderson' to Washington and they used Livingston's association with his cousin, Joshua Smith, to lay a trap to capture Andre'. I will now attempt to show how I think things played out.

CHAPTER THIRTY-FIVE

SEPTEMBER 20TH – THE SECRET MEETING DATE – OOPS!

On the morning of September 20th, Joshua Hett Smith left his family with relatives in Fishkill. He told them he would be back in a few days, as he had important business to do for General Arnold. He made his way south to meet Arnold at Robinson House. They went over the details of the meeting. Benedict gave to Joshua a note for the quartermaster, Major Edward Kierse of Verplank's Point, asking him to provide a boat for the night.

Benedict wanted Joshua to go under a flag of truce to the warship *Vulture*, off Teller's Point. He asked him to escort possibly Colonel Beverly Robinson, and for sure, a merchant named 'John Anderson', Andre's code name, to his home in Haverstraw – the White House – for a secret high-level meeting of great importance to the country. He wanted it done between 11 and 12 at night, as he didn't – at this time – want anything known by the people of the country.

Joshua complained of such a dangerous, unprecedented use of flags at night. But Benedict assured him the mission was known on the *Vulture*- and would not be a problem. Benedict issued to Joshua a pass which I still don't understand.

The pass stated: "Permission is given to Joshua Smith, Esquire; a gentleman named Mr. John Anderson who is with him and his two servants to pass the guards near King's Ferry at all times." 1

We have always been told by historians that the secret meeting designed for the 20th was to take place at the White House in Haverstraw. That's why Smith had the house empty. If you went from the White House to the *Vulture* and back to shore, you wouldn't need to cross at King's Ferry?

He may have intended the pass to be used for the water guards near King's Ferry.

I'm wondering if Arnold intended that Anderson would be disguised as a civilian and instructed Joshua to bring him across at King's Ferry for a meeting at his headquarters at Robinson House. That actually seems possible, based on the wording of the pass. But Andre' and the British Command would never have agreed to that. Regardless, Joshua, not wanting to disappoint the area commander and maybe a little flattered he was asked, agreed to carry out the top-secret mission.

After Joshua met with Arnold, he made his way south to the ferry crossing at Verplank's Point. There, he met with his cousin Colonel James Livingston. I believe Livingston had a far different mission for Joshua. He informed Joshua that Anderson needed to be captured. He told Joshua his mission would be made very simple.

Once Joshua got Anderson on shore, Livingston informed Joshua he was preparing to open fire on the *Vulture* and either sink it or drive it off. And all he wanted Joshua to do was escort Anderson down to Pine's Bridge and leave him there. Someone else would be in charge of the capture.

Joshua probably thought this sounded even more dangerous than the mess he had already got himself into and told Livingston he had to have something in writing to absolve him of wrongdoing, 'a get out of jail free card' which I believe he received.

But Livingston told him there was a problem! He sneaked around the chain of command, bypassing Arnold, to get the ammunition he needed to fire on the ship from Colonel Lamb at West Point. And, he wasn't quite ready to get in position and needed one more day. The evidence of this is a letter from Lamb, dated September 20th.

He wrote:
"Sir, I have sent you the ammunition you requested, but at the same time, I wish there may be not a wanton waste of it, as we have little to spare. Firing at a ship with a four-pounder is, in my opinion, a waste of powder as the damage she will sustain is not equal to the expense. Whenever applications are made for ammunition, they must be made through the commanding officer of artillery at the post where it is wanted." 2

Smith said, if you need another day to get ready, what am I going to tell Arnold?

Livingston said that would be easy. He said Arnold just sent a letter to him, complaining of all the unsecured boats scattered on shore and he wanted someone punished for neglecting them. So, quartermaster Kierse knows, if especially Arnold, requests a boat they are not to be readily available. They were supposed to be drawn up and secured!

Just tell him no boats are available!

Historians have always told us that Smith then had to cross the river to find Kierse, and Kierse told him no boats were available, which makes sense. But I have found it very hard to swallow that IF you weren't purposely buying time, you couldn't find a rowboat on the Hudson River in 1780. I'm sure if a government boat wasn't available, Smith's tenant farmers or he may have even had a boat of his own on his estate. 3

Regardless, very late in the afternoon he ran into one of his tenant farmers, Samuel Cahoon, who was tending his cows. He asked Samuel to take one of his horses and deliver a note to General Arnold across the river, telling him the meeting couldn't take place.

He managed to put the meeting off a day as Livingston requested.

Then, he went home to rest at the White House.

Poor Samuel probably figured he had enough to do but didn't want to deny the higher-class Joshua Smith and reluctantly agreed to his request. It took Samuel most of the night to cross the river and make it to Robinson House, where he left Smith's note with one of Benedict's aides. Then, he had to cross the river to get back to his farm, a hard journey in 1780.

While all of this was going on, Andre' rode from New York City by horseback to get to Dobb's Ferry on the morning of the 20th. When he arrived, he was informed that the *Vulture* had moved upriver toward Teller's Point, almost ten miles past the British lines. He got a gunboat to give him a ride upriver and arrived at about 7 pm. Before he left New York City on his mission, he was given three very specific orders from General Clinton, the head of the British army. 4

The orders were: Do not change out of your uniform, do not go within any American posts and do not carry any papers. This was a dangerous mission and he didn't want to lose his adjutant general.

Andre' met up with Colonel Robinson, who was on board the ship, and they waited all night for a boat and flag to arrive. But none showed. Another failed meeting!

CHAPTER THIRTY-SIX

ANOTHER MISSED MEETING – WHAT'S GOING ON?

When Benedict woke up on September 21st, Smith's tenant farmer Samuel Cahoon, was just leaving Robinson House. His message delivery took all night. Just to give you an idea, the Arnold story wasn't the only thing going on. The ferry crossings and forts were very busy places.

The main part of the American army was south and west toward Tappan, New York, just north of the New Jersey line. Large supply trains had to cross at King's Ferry. Sometimes as many as 50 wagons were backed up there. Small herds of cattle and supplies had to be organized and escorted south. The forts, with hundreds of men, were busy with all kinds of minor details such as providing forage for animals. As many as 200 men did nothing but cut wood to maintain fires and build up supplies for the upcoming winter, using only axes and handsaws.

That morning, Benedict opened Joshua Smith's note telling him his pickup hadn't been made! He covered himself with an accompanying note from Quartermaster Kieres. It said no boats were available. Arnold should have realized by now that he picked the wrong man – Smith – to handle such an important and delicate meeting.

The British on board the *Vulture* needed to know what was going on and what to do next. Andre' penned a letter back to his commander, Sir Henry Clinton. He explained that he had arrived on board the *Vulture* at 7 pm. No one appeared so he said that it was the second excursion he had made with Colonel Robinson and that "a third would infallibly fix suspicions." He thought it best to remain on the ship. 1

Andre' also acted as secretary for the ship's captain, Andrew Sutherland. The captain was upset about a violation of the laws of arms. The previous day, Sutherland noticed a flag of truce on shore and assumed it might be a message from Arnold. He sent a crew to investigate and his men were ambushed by men firing from the bushes. He said, luckily no one was hurt, but he wanted Arnold to know about unlawful and 'treacherous intentions.' 2

It's assumed that Benedict recognized Andre's handwriting and knew he – Andre' – was still on board the *Vulture*. That morning, under a flag of truce, Colonel Beverly Robinson also sent a message to Arnold. It included Sutherland's letter to Arnold.

"Sir, I have been greatly disappointed in not seeing Mr. Smith at the time appointed, being very anxious to conclude our business, which is very necessary and should be done without delay. I can now make a final settlement with him, as my partner – meaning Andre' – upon receipt of the letter I forwarded to him yesterday, immediately set off from New York and arrived here last night. If Mr. Smith will come here, we will attend him to any convenient and safe place." 3

How Robinson knew Smith was Arnold's emissary is not known. But it looked like Benedict's last chance to see what the British could offer if he switched sides. Arnold set off by midday to see if he could fix the situation and arrange the secret meeting himself.

Benedict went to his barge and had his men row him to Verplank's Point, where he saw Colonel Livingston and Quartermaster Kieres, who told Arnold that no boats were available. So, Arnold sent his bargemen into Peekskill Bay to retrieve one and he told Kieres that when a boat arrived, it should be delivered to Minisceongo Creek at Colonel Hay's landing – near Smith's house – and to send an express to him or Smith when it arrived.

He told Livingston and Kieres he was sending Joshua Smith on a mission to gather intelligence and they should make sure the guard boats near King's Ferry knew Smith had permission to pass, any time, day or night. Colonel Livingston was very careful and never mentioned to Arnold that he was preparing to open fire on the *Vulture* at dawn of the next morning.

Arnold then crossed on the ferry, acquired a horse, and made his way to Smith's 'White House.' On his way, he probably passed the tenant farmer Samuel Cahoon, who was just getting back home after delivering Smith's messages. Arnold explained to Joshua Smith that the meeting on the *Vulture* had to be made that night, he had a boat on the way, and he needed to secure some oarsmen. 4

Smith agreed to go, but never mentioned to Arnold that his cousin, Colonel Livingston, was preparing to assault the ship. Smith also was putting away the 'get of jail free card' he received from Livingston. It was filed neatly in his desk in case he needed it. 5

Now, for some odd reason, J. H. Smith decided in the afternoon to ask his tenant farmer Samuel Cahoon to be an oarsman for a midnight trip. He had his own personal servants and staff to pick from, and he had already asked too much from Cahoon.

Cahoon strongly objected to going since he was up all night delivering messages and he had his own chores to attend to. Arnold pushed him to make the journey, and Cahoon said he would need to get his brother Joseph to help row the boat since he was so tired. Joseph also objected and they both thought it was improper to be going in the middle of the night.

At later trials, the Cahoon brothers' testimony shed the most light on how the upcoming, famous secret meeting really went down. 6

Arnold finally promised the Cahoon brothers a fifty-weight of flour – a large amount in 1780 – if they would do the task, along with threats of being reported as disaffected citizens if they didn't go. In 1780, that was a threat that could cause them to lose all of their property. The choice was made for them. Benedict reassured them that everything was aboveboard and only had to be kept from the inhabitants and the common man. This calmed their nerves and they agreed to go.

CHAPTER THIRTY-SEVEN

ARNOLD GETS HIS FACE-TO-FACE MEETING

The midnight meeting was finally set up the night of September 21. The plan was to have Joshua Smith and the Cahoon brothers go by rowboat to the *Vulture* from Hay's Landing – just north of Smith's house – and pick up Colonel Beverly Robinson and Mr. Anderson, then bring them to Long Cove, a landing point about four miles south of Smith's 'White House' on the west side of the Hudson, closer to the ship.

Arnold would be waiting, with Smith's servant and some spare horses, to take them to the White House for the secret meeting. Benedict expected Robinson but especially needed to see Mr. Anderson. How things transpired next came from many sources, but I think the most believable ones came from Colonel Robinson and the Cahoon brothers.

Before Smith and the Cahoons set off, Arnold wrote out three papers for them to take with them.

The first was a pass in case a guard boat intercepted them.

It said: "Permission is granted to Joshua Smith, Esq. to go to Dobb's Ferry with three men and a boy in a boat with a flag to carry some letters of a private nature for gentlemen in New York and to return immediately. He has permission to go at such hours and times as the tides and his business suits."

General B. Arnold 1

The second was a letter for Smith to deliver to Colonel Robinson.

It said: "This will be delivered to you by Mr. Smith, who will conduct you to a place of safety. Neither Mr. Smith nor any other persons shall be made acquainted with your proposals. If they are of such a nature that I can take notice of them, I shall do it with pleasure. If not, you shall be permitted to return immediately. I take it for granted, Colonel Robinson will not propose anything that is not for the interest of the United States, as well as himself." 2

The third was just a piece of four words.

It said: "Gustavus to John Anderson." Gustavus was Arnold's code name, so Andre' would know the information came from Benedict.

The Cahoons and Smith set off on a very dark journey at night toward the warship *Vulture*. They arrived at the ship between midnight and 1:00 am. The ship's crew hollered out to ask who was approaching His Majesty's ship in the middle of the night. Smith also received threats to blow them out of the water or hang them from a yardarm.

Smith explained that he was under the protection of a flag of truce with messages for Colonel Robinson and the ship's captain. Smith went up a rope ladder while the Cahoon brothers nervously waited in the rowboat. Smith was then escorted below deck to Captain Sutherland's quarters, where Colonel Beverly Robinson was also present. I believe Smith wasn't simply on a mission for Arnold, but he intended to do his best to get just Anderson (Andre') off the ship, not Robinson.

The men present poured over Arnold's passes and the letter to Robinson. But Smith also produced the pass from the previous night's mission. It read: "Permission is given to Joshua Smith, a gentleman John Anderson who is with him and his two servants to pass the guards near King's Ferry at all times." 3

As a lawyer, Smith insisted that if anyone went ashore other than Mr. Anderson, it would be a violation of the flag.

While Captain Sutherland and Colonel Robinson discussed the situation, they sent for Mr. Anderson (Andre') who was sleeping in another berth. Joshua used his legal skills to convince Sutherland, Robinson and Mr. Anderson that only Mr. Anderson should go ashore for the meeting. The men finally agreed with Smith's assessment.

Andre' wore a long, blue dress coat over his bright, red military uniform. Though he would never admit it, I'm quite sure Joshua recognized Andre', since he had met Andre' four years earlier when he was a captured British lieutenant staying at the White House, on his way to confinement in Pennsylvania.

Smith, at trial later, would say he thought this man, Anderson, was a merchant, not a British officer. Really?

As Smith and Anderson climbed down the rope ladder and back into the waiting rowboat, Robinson observed that they only had two rowers and a small boat to get back to shore. He offered to escort them and tow them in with an armed barge. But Smith strongly insisted that would be a violation of the flag. This would have also interrupted his secret plan.

The most disturbing action at this point in the story is that Joshua Smith never told Arnold, Robinson or anyone else on board the ship that they were soon to be fired on by cannons, though he was well aware it was about to happen.

The Cahoons then rowed Smith and Andre' into the dark night on the Hudson toward Long Cove, arriving sometime past one in morning.

Arnold was waiting with Smith's servant and some horses, to escort whoever showed for the high-level meeting, to ride to the White House so the talk could take place there. But Andre' told Arnold that what he wanted to say shouldn't take that long and he wanted to get back aboard the *Vulture* as soon as possible. So, Benedict and Andre' went up to a grove of pine trees near the shore to have their discussion.

Benedict told Smith to wait with the Cahoon brothers, near the boat. Being of a higher class than Arnold, Smith wasn't used to being treated as a commoner, and I'm sure he felt dejected by not being allowed to be part of the discussions. 4

As Arnold and Andre' strolled off toward the pine grove, Joshua Smith asked the Cahoon brothers if they were up to rowing back to the warship. Samuel Cahoon complained that he was exhausted from the previous night's ride and Joseph really didn't want any part of rowing back to that ship.

Joshua told the brothers to do what they thought best, which was pretty much telling them they would soon be dismissed. A few hours rolled by and the time needed to get back to the *Vulture*, under cover of darkness, was quickly fading.

Arnold and Andre's meeting in the pine grove went on for a good three hours. No one knows what was discussed there for so long, but every author gets to speculate at this point in the story. I guess it's my turn!

We have often been told they discussed a plan of giving over control of the fort at West Point. To me, this makes no sense. Most British operations had already moved south. For the British to control West Point and all the forts between the point and New York City would have extended their forces too thinly. There was a French army at the east and an American army to their northwest. The British would be risking control of New York City to even try. What they would gain wouldn't be worth the risk.

Benedict needed to have face-to-face assurances from Andre' that if he switched sides, he would receive an equivalent rank and enough money to make up for all – or part – of what he would be giving up.

Arnold knew that going to the British side would cost him the loss of two homes, his ships, his business and risk the lives of his family and his. He gave up nearly everything for America. Now, he would have to start over and give up nearly everything – again – to serve Great Britain.

Andre' had proposals from Sir Henry Clinton in New York. We also don't know if Lady Agent 355 fed any information to Andre'. He probably also expressed concerns for Mrs. Arnold, as they had formed a friendship a few years earlier.

I think Arnold was in the wait-and-see mode and still on the fence. He may have wanted to see if Washington was going to offer the southern command to him and if he would be ignored and passed over yet again. He may have even offered to gather a large group of soldiers and explain to them that he was no longer willing to serve a corrupt congress or a French monarchy. He may have also considered leading a large group of like-minded soldiers and supplies from West Point, down the west side of the Hudson River to New York City.

It sounds strange, but I think Benedict wanted to do what he thought was best for his country. That's why he needed a face-to-face meeting.

Benedict had some major decisions to make.

CHAPTER THIRTY-EIGHT

ALL HELL BREAKS LOOSE—ANDRE TRAPPED BEHIND ENEMY LINES

As the eastern sky was just beginning to brighten, Smith went up to the grove of pines and Arnold asked Smith to take 'Mr. Anderson' (Andre') back to the *Vulture*. Smith protested strongly, saying the tides were against them and the hands – the Cahoons – were too tired to make the journey.

I don't believe Smith had any intention of going back to that ship, since he knew it was soon to be attacked. So, Benedict directed Smith to return the boat to Hay's Landing and if the Cahoons were too tired, they were to leave it wherever they pleased. He then escorted Andre' to the horses he had waiting near Long Cove. Benedict, Andre', and Smith's servant rode up to the 'White House.'

As Smith went back to dismiss the Cahoons and secure the boat, his cousin, Colonel Livingston, came through with his plan. A ship-to-shore battle roared across the Hudson! Smith and the Cahoons ditched the boat near the plains by the White House and walked up the hill toward Smith's home.

Arnold and Andre' arrived and dismounted the horses at the White House, as servants put the horses away in the stable. Benedict and Andre' went upstairs at the White House, where Andre' removed his blue dress coat, revealing his bright red British uniform. When Smith came in from his walk, Benedict told Smith that Andre' borrowed the uniform from a man in New York – out of foolish vanity. Joshua Smith certainly would have known that was an odd excuse! Smith had to know that Andre' was a British officer, though he would never admit it. 1

Smith, Andre and Arnold all watched the ship-to-shore battle from the upstairs windows. Colonel Beverly Robinson described the battle in a letter back to Sir Henry Clinton.

"On Thursday night, they brought down to Teller's Point: one 6 pounder and a howitzer – probably a 4 pounder. They entrenched themselves on the very point and at daylight on Friday morning began a very hot fire on us from both, which continued for two hours and would have been longer, but luckily their magazine blew up.

It was near high water and the tide very slack and no wind filled the sails, so that it was impossible – though every exertion was made with auxiliary boats – to get the ship turned out of their reach sooner. Six shots hulled us, one between wind and water. Many others struck the sails and rigging and the boats on deck. Two shells hit us, one fell full on the quarter deck, another near the main shrouds." 2

The auxiliary boats finally towed the ship out far enough into the channels of the Hudson so they could move down the river, out of range. Only Captain Sutherland was hurt by a splinter on his nose, but Livingston accomplished his mission by driving the *Vulture* down river.

I'm not sure how many Americans were hurt by British fire or when the magazine blew up. But Andre' – watching from Smith's window – must have felt sick while he watched the *Vulture* slowly move out of sight. Now, many decisions needed to be made.

CHAPTER THIRTY-NINE

HOW TO GET MR. ANDERSON (ANDRE) BACK?

Arnold suggested – probably encouraged by Smith – that they could go by land down through Westchester to Kingsbridge, on the east side of the Hudson. But Andre' objected strongly to this idea. When Arnold left around ten in the morning, Andre' later stated, "It was settled in the way I came I was also to return." 1

Benedict had to get back to headquarters at Robinson House, as shortly, Washington and his entourage were due back from their French meeting and were to stay the night at Robinson House and inspect the Point. On September 22, 1780, Arnold left three passes issued for Joshua and Anderson, one by water, two by land:

First by water, the one Andre' expected to be used:

"Joshua Smith, Esq. has permission to pass with a boat and three hands and a flag to Dobbs Ferry on public business and return immediately."

The next two passes were to go by land to satisfy Smith:

"Joshua Smith, Esq. has permission to pass the guards at White Plains and return, being on public business by my direction."

"Permit Mr. John Anderson to pass the guards at White Plains or below if he chooses, he being on public business by my direction." 2

So, when Benedict left the White House, Andre' was still in his bright red uniform and they were settled that Smith was to return him to the *Vulture* or Dobbs Ferry by boat that evening with a pass and a flag. But he left a contingency plan with Smith and the passes by land, if necessary. Andre's fate and return journey were now in the hands of Joshua Smith.

Joshua never even made an attempt to secure any oarsmen. Andre' paced back and forth upstairs in the White House, all day. He insisted to Smith that he must return by boat. He had his orders from Clinton not to leave his uniform, not to go within any enemy posts and not to carry any papers. The battle of wills between Smith and Anderson went on all afternoon. Smith told Anderson there was no way he was going to make the journey south by water after seeing the ship-to-shore battle with the *Vulture*. Besides, he had another mission of his own.

As the sun began to set, Joshua won the argument. Andre' felt he had no choice but to go with Smith over land. Smith, after a nap, offered some of his clothes to Anderson – Andre' – since he surely couldn't cross on the ferry with a British uniform on. As sunset moved in quickly, Joshua instructed his servant to ready three horses, as they would soon be off to the ferry.

Mr. Anderson, Joshua Smith and Smith's servant headed north toward the ferry crossing. Along the way, they met a soldier who Joshua knew. At the west side was a group of soldiers who later remarked about how 'chatty' Smith was. Smith was because there were some of Livingston's officers posted at the ferry. The soldiers offered a convivial bottle of grog they were sharing to Joshua. 3

Joshua dismounted his horse and chatted with the men as Andre' nervously waited by the ferry crossing with Joshua's servant. They boarded the ferry with their horses and were poled by the ferry men into the deep water. The men manned the sweeps – large, wide oars to propel the craft – across the Hudson. Smith joked with the ferry men that they would be rewarded for a swift journey. When they reached the landing at Verplank's Point on the other side, Joshua gave eight dollars to one of the men, for their good work and swift efforts.

As they led the horses off the ferry, Joshua made a stop at his cousin Colonel Livingston's quarters. Since it was now dark, Livingston offered the men something to eat and drink. A rather mortified Andre' rode on slowly, leaving Joshua to visit with his cousin. Joshua would have to catch up because Andre' had no interest in stopping at an American post.

This is the point where I deviate from history, without evidence, except for what would happen later in the story. I'm quite sure Livingston toasted Smith to a drink on a well-accomplished mission and told him all he had to do was drop him off at Pines Bridge with directions to White Castle.

This is also where Joshua's $1,000 loan to quartermaster Kierse to forward to dispatchers probably paid off. I believe Livingston then sent an express to Tallmadge to let him know his prize was on the way!

Joshua then mounted his horse and caught up with Andre' and his servant. They rode slowly through the night through Peekskill, then turned east onto Compound Road – at least what was called a road in 1780. By eight or nine that night it must have been tough going when they encountered a group of Westchester militia commanded by Captain Ebenezer Boyd.

What is very unusual and interesting now in the story, if you look closely at the map provided, Compound Road was certainly not the best or quickest way to get Andre' back to the British lines. The Albany Post Road along the Hudson River would have been the logical route. But that is not where Benjamin Tallmadge and his 2nd Dragoons were posted.

Joshua Smith seemed to know almost everyone in the area. Captain Boyd took their passes near the firelight so he could read them and was satisfied when he realized they had permission from General Arnold to be on the road. But Boyd warned them, traveling much farther – especially at night – was extremely dangerous. And it was.

In 1780, the lines between the armies were patrolled by very vicious gangs of men. There were gangs loosely affiliated with what the British people called cowboys, and gangs loosely affiliated with the American cause – the skinners. 4

These bands robbed travelers, looking for communications they could sell to the highest bidders. They kidnapped people for ransom, they took firewood and food from local merchants and farmers. The only cause they truly served was their own survival and they didn't really care who they hurt to accomplish it.

Boyd told Smith it would be smarter to go back toward Peekskill to Andrew Miller's farm and try to get lodging there and go again in the morning. He mentioned that they had just heard shots south of his post. Seeing the wisdom in Boyd's warning, Smith led Anderson (Andre') and his servant back up Compound Road to the Miller Farm.

The Millers had little to offer but a single bed where Joshua and Anderson spent the night. Their servant probably slept better outside with the horses. Andre' barely slept. He knew if he was discovered behind enemy lines – with a feigned name – and out of his uniform, he would be labeled a spy and the penalty would be death.

Andre' stirred awake before dawn and asked Smith's servant to ready the horses. Just before daylight, they offered payment to Miller for the lodging. He refused to take the money and explained that he had no food to offer them since the cowboys had robbed them and he had just enough to feed his wife and family.

Smith, Andre' and Smith's servant rode south near where they were stopped the previous night. On duty now was the local depot commissioner by the name of Ebenezer Foote. He examined their passes and Smith inquired as to who was on duty on the lower roads. Foote told Smith that the area below Pines Bridge was patrolled by the 2nd Continental Dragoons under the command of John Jameson. I think Joshua Smith was just confirming what he already knew. 5

A little farther south, they stopped at the home of Isaac and Sarah Underhill, where they hoped to get some breakfast and feed for the horses. The horses were tended to, but the Underhills had also been robbed by the cowboys and all they had to offer was some suppon to eat. Suppon was mush made of milk and boiled water and Indian corn. It was the best they could do.

Joshua Smith payed the Underhills and told Mr. Anderson this was as far as he could escort him. They were only about two to three miles from Pines Bridge. Joshua told Anderson that about a half mile beyond the bridge the road forked. Left went toward White Plains and right to Sing

Sing and Tarrytown. He said the safest route to take was to go left when he hit the fork.

Andre' asked Smith for some spare cash if he had any. Joshua gave eight dollars to him, about half of what he had. Andre' offered his gold watch to Joshua in return for his help. Joshua refused. But he asked Andre' if he would deliver a message to his brother William in New York City. Andre' agreed to do that. If this was a written message, it disappeared for all time. If it was a verbal message, did Andre' explain he couldn't carry papers? This message to William Smith from Joshua Smith has never been explained. 6

Andre' and Smith parted company. Smith and his servant headed north.

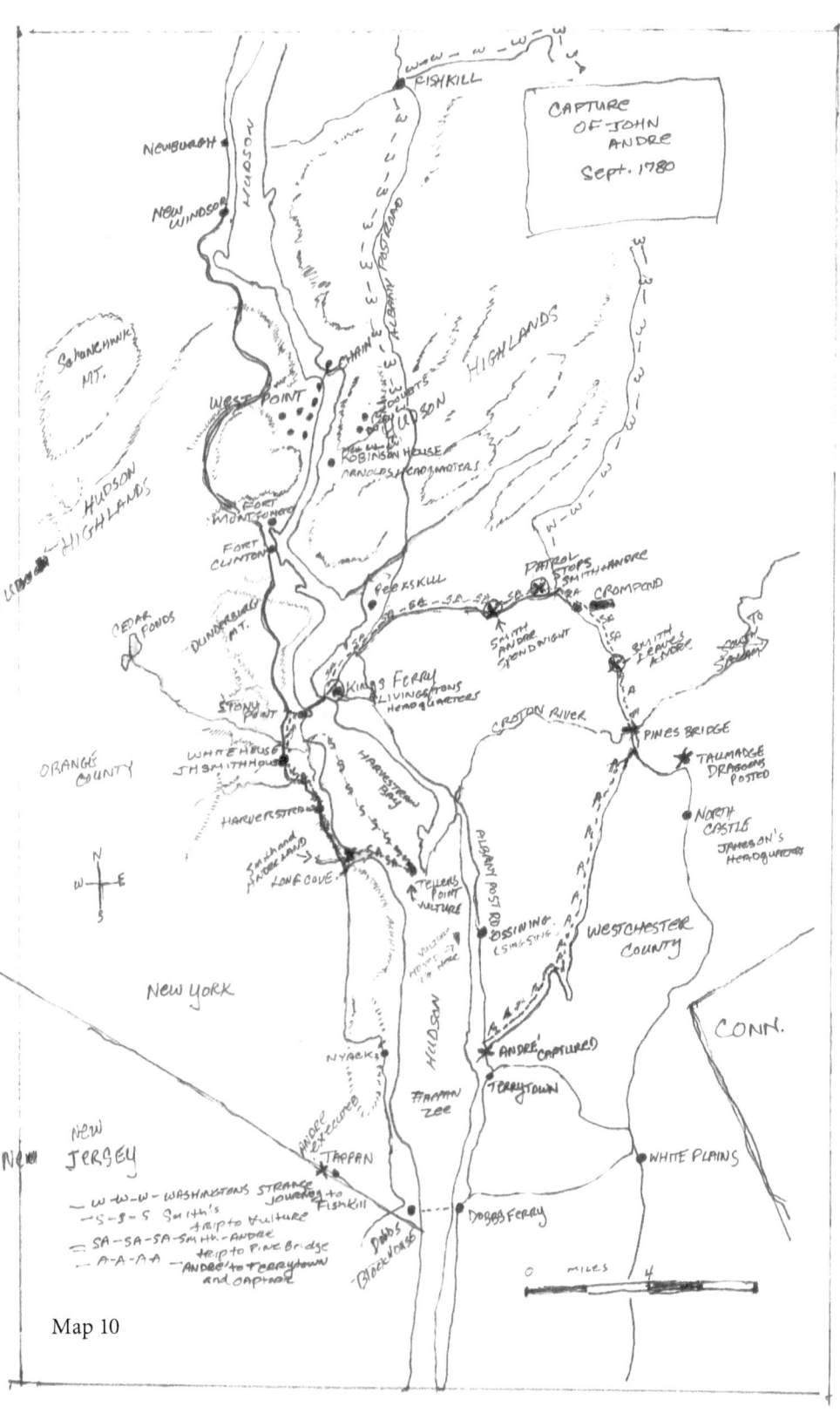

Map 10

CHAPTER FORTY

THE FAMOUS CAPTURE

Andre rode on southward and crossed Pines Bridge. A half mile beyond, he encountered the fork in the road. He really didn't trust Joshua and instead of following his directions to go left, he took the road to the right toward Tarrytown. It is my belief that if he went to the left, he would have ridden directly into the hands of Benjamin Tallmadge and the 2nd Dragoons who were waiting to arrest him.

By going to the right, Tallmadge's plan was almost foiled. Around 10 am, as Andre' rode on toward Tarrytown, three men stepped out into the road and leveled their muskets at him. They ordered him to dismount. The men have been described as militia, volunteers and patriots, but most likely they were skinners.

The truth was revealed many years later by Benjamin Tallmadge himself. When one of the men applied for funds from Congress, Tallmadge insisted they had been paid enough already and that they were only trying to rob Andre'. Their names were John Paulding, Isaac Van Wart and Abraham Williams. 1

Only Paulding could read. Andre' thought at first they were British loyalists but found out they were Americans. He produced his pass from General Arnold, but that didn't impress them. They had Andre' strip down and searched his clothes. We have always been told they found papers in Andre's boot, stocking or heel of his boot, revealing to the men they had captured a spy!

This made a very good story, but I really don't believe any papers were on Andre' other than his pass and possibly the letter from Joshua Smith to his brother William. Andre' tried to bribe the men to let him go, promising payment but they knew if they let this man – Andre' aka Anderson – go they would never hear from him again.

They knew the word was out in no-man's land that troops were on the lookout for Anderson. But their best bet was to take him to the nearest post where they might get a reward. So, the three men took Anderson on a nearly 12-mile march to North Castle, and they arrived around 5:30 pm. They presented their prisoner to Colonel John Jameson, who was now commander of that post.

Jameson rewarded the three men – who had already taken Anderson's money – but also gave Andre's gold watch and his horse to them as a reward. They went happily on their way.

By now, Benjamin Tallmadge was getting upset because he planned to capture Anderson, but he never showed on the road to North Castle. He began backtracking toward Pines Bridge with his horse regiment. On his way back through, he may have even encountered the three men leading their new horse and he may have asked them where they got the horse. They may have said it was a reward for a captured prisoner. This is my speculation.

At this point, Colonel John Jameson wondered what he should do with this man Anderson and he did exactly as he was ordered to by Arnold, previously. He assembled an armed guard and sent Anderson to Robinson House headquarters. Not long after Anderson left with his armed guard, Benjamin Tallmadge – the unknown head of Washington's secret service – showed up at Jameson's post.

All hell broke loose. Tallmadge took control of the situation and had Anderson recaptured. I believe this is when the dangerous parcel of papers appeared! That afternoon, Jameson penned three letters he wrote, two of which he sent to Lieutenant Solomon Allen, who was in charge of escorting Anderson to Robinson House. He wanted to have Anderson retaken as a prisoner and put under secured guard in lower Salem. (Letter 1) 2

Jameson enclosed a strange letter to Arnold – that he was nervous about sending – informing General Arnold about Anderson's capture and he gave a detailed description of dangerous papers that he was sending on to Washington. It was strange, if Arnold was suspected of treason. Why inform him of Andre's capture with details about papers, unless you wanted him to flee? (Letters 2,3)

The third letter from Jameson, sent by special courier, went directly to Washington.

"Enclosed you will receive a parcel of papers taken from a certain John Anderson, who has a pass signed by General Arnold. I have sent the prisoner to General Arnold. He is very desirous of the papers and everything being sent with him, but I think they are of a dangerous tendency. I thought it more proper your Excellency should see them." (Letter 3) (4)

Jameson wrote to Washington four days later to apologize for sending the letter that warned Arnold, but he wanted Washington to know he consulted Tallmadge before sending it. He was afraid he would be in trouble. At this point, most authors infer that Jameson was confused but it looks likely he was coerced. 5

Now would be a good time to take a hard look at this 'dangerous parcel of papers.'

CHAPTER FORTY-ONE

THE DANGEROUS PARCEL OF PAPERS

(Papers transcribed in the papers section of this book.)

Exactly what was in this large parcel of papers that would implicate Arnold of treason? Remember that Andre' had very specific orders to not carry papers.

#1 – An estimate of the number of men necessary to man works at West Point and in the vicinity and dated September of 1780 was signed by French engineer Villefranche. Why? If Arnold was sending information to the British, why use the papers authored by another officer?

#2 – What about artillery orders? The following 'disposition of the corps is to take place in case of alarm.' Signed by Major Sebastian Bauman, commander of artillery.

#3 – Return of ordnance in the forts and batteries at West Point and its dependencies. Signed by Major S. Bauman, Major Commander of Artillery. Dated September 5, 1780.

#4 – Estimate of forces at West Point and its dependencies. Unsigned and dated September 13, 1780.

#5 – A double-sided sheet describing the construction of various redoubts, dated September 1780 but not signed.

Documents 1, 2 and 3 came from other officers. I thought that seemed strange. Why weren't these officers investigated or implicated?

Documents 4 and 5 were not signed by General Arnold but were said to be in his handwriting.

Also note all the dates are more than a week prior to Arnold's meeting with the British, and days before Washington's trip across the Hudson to meet with the French.

I had a highly accredited handwriting expert examine documents 4 and

5, and he verified that most likely they were in Arnold's handwriting. So, the next question I had was why weren't they signed and why did they seem so random? 1

Remember when Arnold crossed the Hudson and he presented Washington with his detailed situation reports? These could have easily been extracted from the documents Benedict turned in to Washington. That would explain why they were unsigned if they were parts of a larger report.

I never once saw any un-signed correspondence of General Arnold.

Document 6 was the kicker. It was a copy of the report of the Council of War held in Bergen County, dated September 6, 1780. As previously mentioned, on September 12th Arnold enclosed this copy of the Council of War report in a letter to Washington! So, how did this document get from Washington's desk and into Andre's possession?

To me, all the documents presented as evidence of Arnold's treason not only seem questionable, but could have easily been cherry-picked from Washington's desk, between the time he left Peekskill for his French meeting, and Andre's capture. To me, it's very obvious these documents were planted on Andre' to implicate Arnold. 2,3.

CHAPTER FORTY-TWO

TALLMADGE GETS THE CAPTURE UNDER CONTROL—NOW THE PARCEL OF PAPERS

Once Tallmadge got the situation at North Castle completely under control, he finally got to meet his prize, John Anderson (Andre'). I'm sure he knew who Anderson was from his Lady Agent 355, who had been working on Andre'.

Andre' knew his fate. Tallmadge, who wouldn't leave Andre's presence, informed him that his best friend was Nathan Hale and that Andre' would soon suffer the same sentence as Hale did. Tallmadge and 20 dragoons escorted Andre' to South Salem, where on the next morning – September 24th of 1780 – Andre' asked for a quill and paper. He wrote a very elegant confession of his circumstances directly to General George Washington to tell him his prisoner was not John Anderson, but John Andre', adjutant general of the British army! 1

In the letter, Andre' explained how he became a prisoner under a feigned name and out of uniform, but he never mentioned any papers. But someone was waiting for those papers. Washington needed them in case Arnold didn't leave his post. The plan was to get Benedict simply to flee his post, but if he remained, they needed the paperwork to arrest him for treason. The messenger delivering the so-called dangerous parcel couldn't find Washington and returned to his post, where the letter from Andre' was added.

Tallmadge and Jameson received word that Washington changed his plans and was now in Fishkill, not on the way to Robinson House. Washington had completed his very high-level meeting with the French in Hartford. His entourage received a 13-cannon salute from the French.

General Washington hoped to talk the French into combining forces, then attacking and driving the British from New York City. But the French wanted more reinforcements. They also probably wanted to know who Washington was going to assign the post of commander of the southern army. The obvious choice would be General Arnold, but the French knew Arnold wanted nothing to do with their alliance. To them, Arnold was a problem. I believe Washington told them that problem was soon to be taken care of.

As Washington wrapped up his discussions with the French, he was hoping to receive word from Tallmadge that his capture of Anderson had been made and now he could approach Arnold with the parcel of papers. But where were they? No cell phones back then for a quick answer.

Washington needed to buy some time. Because Livingston needed an extra day to drive off the *Vulture*, in addition to Andre' taking the wrong road, his whole plan was a day and a half behind. So, instead of going directly back to Robinson House, he took his entourage through the high, mountainous land near the Hudson to Fishkill.

As Washington dined that night in Fishkill, one of his many guests was Joshua Hett Smith, Esq. I doubt Smith knew how high his involvement went in the plan to capture Anderson. But just his presence told Washington that at least part of the plan had succeeded. However, the papers still hadn't arrived! Washington wanted confirmation of Andre's arrest and the paperwork before confronting Arnold.

Washington was due at Robinson House the next morning to see Arnold and inspect the works at West Point. He was quite well-known to be very punctual and never late.

Just to give you an example, I read in the Washington papers that one morning he wanted the army mustered out at three am. But he wanted to go easy on the troops, so he stated in his orders that anyone late was not to receive more than 40 lashes.

On September 25th, Washington seemed to be taking his time. As his 40-horse entourage made its trip from Fishkill to Robinson House, Washington veered off the road to inspect the southern redoubt across from West Point. His men complained they were heading for breakfast! Supposedly, Washington told them, 'I know all of you young men are in love with Mrs. Arnold. You may go for breakfast and tell her not to wait for me.' (paraphrased)

I believe Washington went to the redoubt to buy a little more time and he may have hoped that through his spyglass he could catch a glimpse of

Arnold's barge going south if he took the bait Tallmadge would be sending to him. 2

Two days prior – after he dropped off Anderson – Joshua Smith rode directly to Robinson House and he was there by dinner time. He privately informed Arnold that he didn't take Anderson back to the *Vulture* but took him overland and left him near enemy lines at Pines Bridge.

At dinner, an altercation took place. Arnold's closest aide, Colonel Richard Varick, really didn't want his general associating with the likes of Joshua Smith. He thought he was a rascal and a Tory, maybe even a spy. At first, Benedict took offense and he saw that the whole matter was upsetting Peggy. After Benedict calmed down, he told Varick he would no longer associate with Mr. Smith. 3

But, on the morning of September 25th of 1780, Arnold was still awaiting the arrival of General Washington for breakfast. Noon was quickly approaching and not normal behavior for General Washington. Benedict was probably considering – in his mind – if he was going to take the offers proposed by Great Britain. Maybe, he would wait and see if Washington might offer the southern command to him.

Benedict sat at the table, surrounded by his men, which was normal in Arnold's headquarters. His men were always welcome to be with him. He considered his closest officers his family.

But now, something else happened!

CHAPTER FORTY-THREE

DECISION MADE!

As Benedict was waiting, some of Washington's entourage began filtering into headquarters. Peggy greeted them, then went upstairs to feed her baby.

Then, Arnold was approached by Lieutenant Solomon Allen of the 2nd Dragoons. He had a dispatch for him. When Benedict opened it, his heart sank. The letter explained that Anderson (Andre') was now a prisoner and he had a dangerous parcel of papers that had been sent on to Washington! 1

Benedict went upstairs to see Peggy and told her the decision to go over to Great Britain had been made for him. He was sure Washington was coming to arrest him for treason and he must flee! 2

The news was far too much for Peggy to bear and she fainted. Arnold laid her on the bed and went downstairs. He told Major Franks to summon the post doctor because Peggy was ill. Benedict then went outside and mounted a horse. He told the men he was heading for the Point and he would soon be back.

He made a quick ride down the ravine by Robinson's Landing and ordered his bargemen there to prepare to set out immediately. The men probably thought they would turn upriver to the Point, but Arnold directed them south toward Haverstraw Bay.

I'm sure Arnold's bargemen wondered what the hell was going on! They rowed the entire length of the bay, just past Teller's Point, where Arnold spotted the warship *Vulture* anchored off Sing Sing.

He set up a flag and ordered his men to move alongside the ship. The men must have been a little crazy with fear.

Arnold explained to his men that he was going over to the standard of

Great Britain and he offered to give them good positions if they would go with him. Two of the crew took Arnold's offer, but the others became prisoners. When the *Vulture* arrived downriver, British General Sir Henry Clinton pardoned and released the crew members who didn't join under Britain's flag. 3

Colonel Beverly Robinson was on board the ship at the time and so was her captain, Andrew Sutherland. Arnold announced that Andre' had been captured and he told them what he knew. Benedict and Robinson both wrote letters to Washington and left them under flag at the local blockhouse at Dobbs Ferry. The ship sailed to New York City, arriving there about 3 pm. 4

Arnold's world was now changed forever.

CHAPTER FORTY-FOUR

WASHINGTON HAS A BIG MESS TO CLEAN UP & IT MUST GO HIS WAY

Washington finally arrived at Robinson House headquarters around 11 am for breakfast with his full entourage. He inquired about where General Arnold was. He was told Arnold just left within the hour to go to the Point. Washington still hadn't received the parcel of dangerous papers and he knew that when it arrived – if it arrived – he would either have to confront Arnold or hopefully, Arnold had left town.

General Washington grabbed a quick bite to eat and took Generals Knox and Lafayette with him to cross the river to West Point. When he arrived, he was greeted by Colonel Lamb and he asked where Arnold was. Lamb said he didn't know. Washington hoped he was gone, but since he was across the river, he inspected the work at West Point. By the time he recrossed the river in Lamb's barge and got back to headquarters, it was now nearly 4 pm.

Finally, the parcel of dangerous papers had been delivered. The plan by Washington and Tallmadge had worked perfectly. The Arnold problem had been solved. But there were many questions and loose ends to tie up. Washington looked over the now-revealed papers, along with Andre's letter. Peggy went into hysterics and lost control of herself. Many authors like to say her hysterics were an act, but I believe she was truly at the point of a nervous breakdown. 1

Here she was. The man she loved fled to avoid treason charges and she was left deep behind American lines. Peggy didn't know if she would ever see Benedict again. She had seen what happened to people accused of treason and being loyalists. She had witnessed people hung from trees and buildings, people tarred and whipped, with their houses burned or confiscated. I think she was petrified to the point of insanity.

One of the men wrote that this was the only time in the war when Washington lost his composure and broke down. It was said that Washington's dismay was due to the brave General Arnold going to the other side. Now, who could he trust?

I think it weighed heavy on his heart to further himself and to satisfy the French. He had literally just sold America's greatest patriot down the river. Washington was seeing in Peggy not only the destruction of Arnold, but his family, as well.

As Washington regained his composure, he got to work. He and his aides wrote to every officer in the vicinity, right down to the wood cutting parties. He notified everyone of Arnold's great dye of treason and informed them the object was to give up West Point and prepare for attack that wasn't coming. 2

Oddly, to the officer – Colonel Livingston – just south of headquarters and in charge of Verplank Point and the ferry crossing, Washington wrote only one sentence, "I wish to see you here immediately and request that you will come without least delay." 3

I believe Washington wanted to make sure Livingston told his story correctly. Also, an armed guard was sent that night to Fishkill to arrest Joshua Hett Smith and have him brought to headquarters. Smith was taken from his bed that night. Also, that very evening, he received the letters from Arnold and Colonel Beverly Robinson.

In his letter, Arnold insisted that his actions of late were based on the principle of the 'love of my country.' He asked no favor for himself and said, "I have too often experienced the ingratitude of my country to attempt it."

Arnold appealed to Washington's humanity to protect Mrs. Arnold and said she was good and innocent as an angel. He also added:

"In justice to the gentlemen of 'my family,' Colonel Varick, Major Franks and also Joshua Smith, are totally ignorant of any transactions of mine that they had reason to believe were injurious to the public." 4

Colonel Robinson's letter simply informed Washington that by the rules of war, Andre' was under the flag and direction and passes of General Arnold and he should be released. 5

Joshua Smith arrived under guard the next morning and was heavily interrogated, as they wanted to implicate him as part of the treason. Lafayette seemed to take personal interest in seeing Smith hung with Andre', even testifying at his upcoming trial. But Smith's defense – at least for now – was that he was just following the requests of Commander Arnold's directions as a good American and had no idea Mr. Anderson was a British officer.

He was given permission to write to his brother Thomas to turn over Andre's uniform which was in a room upstairs in his house at Haverstraw. At the end of his note, Smith said, "Remember me to your family." I'm sure he thought the gallows might be a real possibility. 6

Washington then wrote to Congress and the governor of New York to inform them of the darkest dye of treason. When our forefathers got news of Arnold – the most popular general – going to the British side, they panicked. If any soldiers decided to follow Arnold's example, the war would be over, and they might hang! 7, 8

A man who was a hero to the entire nation quickly became portrayed as the most evil traitor in American history! Men like Franklin and Adams – who had always supported Arnold – now turned 180 degrees on him. And the politicians controlled the presses.

General Nathanael Greene summed it up best in a letter he wrote about Arnold. "Never since the fall of Lucifer, has a fall equaled his." 9

CHAPTER FORTY-FIVE

THE CLEAN-UP CONTINUES & ANDRE'S TRIAL BEGINS

The next huge problem Washington had was the three men – skinners, militia, volunteers – who picked up Andre'. They not only had to get their story straight, but they had to be the ones who found the dangerous parcel of papers that would implicate Arnold. When Andre' took the wrong road past Pines Bridge, the men became a major part of the story.

The three men were immediately summoned to headquarters at Robinson House. Colonel John Jameson wrote a very telling note to Washington:

"Sir,
This will be delivered to you by John Paulding, one of the young men who took Major Andre' and who nobly refused any sum of money that he should demand. The other two young men who were in company with him are not yet found: As soon as they arrive, they will be sent on."

He also went on to say he was sorry he wrote his note to General Arnold, warning him to make his escape. But he was afraid he would be in trouble and made it clear the note was approved by Major Tallmadge! 1

So, let's recap what we've learned so far about the cleanup operation: The three men – Paulding, Van Wart and David Williams – who captured Andre' while trying to rob him turned him in for a reward. They were given Andre's money, his gold watch and his horse, but they really hit the jackpot. They also became the most highly decorated soldiers in the Revolutionary War. Washington bestowed on them the first medals ever awarded to any soldier in the United States – the Medal of Valor. They were also given lifetime pensions, and each received a farm in New York state. Not bad payment for robbing somebody!

Colonel Livingston's part in the capture also was addressed. He retired from the service three months after Benedict's defection. Livingston was given 3,500 acres in upstate New York near Tyre in the Finger Lakes region and later received another 1,000 acres in the Ohio Valley. Quartermaster Major Kierse received $1,000 from Joshua Smith to forward dispatches which he never had to pay back.

After Arnold's defection, Lady Agent 355 knew too much and was never heard from again. We can only speculate on her fate. The only thing left to keep total control of the story was Andre' himself, but he couldn't get a chance to talk. That would soon be taken care of.

Washington also insisted that Arnold would never get a platform from which to talk. He later gave Lafayette orders that if Arnold were ever captured, he must be killed.

The following day, Peggy still seemed in shock, but calmer. In Benedict's request to Washington after he boarded the warship, *Vulture*, he had asked to have Peggy taken to her family in Philadelphia or to him in New York, 'as she may choose.' 2

We have been told she was a huge part of his decision to jump sides, but just that phrase in his letter tells me principle was driving him more than any influence by Peggy. She decided to go to friends and family in Philadelphia and Major Franks began escorting her home on the 27th. Even with her baby, Peggy still seemed in shock.

The next thing to wrap up was planning a trial for Andre' and Smith. Washington wasted no time in putting together a legal team. He had already requested that Judge Advocate John Laurance, Esq. report to headquarters "without delay" on September 26th of 1780. 3

Orders were given for a heavily armed guard of over 50 dragoons to escort Andre' and Smith to main headquarters in Tappan, New York. In the orders, it was stipulated that Smith and Andre' would not be allowed to talk to each other and were to be kept in separate boats on the journey south and kept in separate houses when they arrived. Tallmadge would be Andre's shadow and was to stay with him every second, from his capture until the end. 4

Tallmadge also supervised every inch of the journey south. No one knew at the time that he was head of Washington's 'secret service.'

As the large force made their way toward Haverstraw Bay, Joshua Smith requested a stop at his home – the White House – so he could retrieve papers for his defense. Tallmadge allowed it.

You might ask, what possible papers did he have for defense?

I think he had a 'get out of jail free' card from Livingston. When Joshua entered his home office, it had been ransacked and there were no papers! He asked to talk to his brother to see what had happened, but Tallmadge would not allow it. 5

Just a little side note: A lot of the truth on what and how things happened could have been made much clearer if people asked and valued the testimony of the African American slaves. I'm sure they were privy to conversations they overheard, but slaves were almost made to be invisible in 1780. The sin of slavery cast a long shadow. I'm sure the slaves knew who ransacked Joshua H. Smith's house.

Tallmadge and 50 dragoons with their prisoners re-mounted their horses and continued to Tappan.

CHAPTER FORTY-SIX

THE TRIALS AT TAPPAN

Major Tallmadge had already informed Andre' what the result of his trial would be. He was caught under a feigned name, out of uniform and passing within American posts – the definition of a spy. Papers or no papers, he would hang. And Andre' knew it! I'm sure Tallmadge could have warned Andre' that if he protested the papers, his friend Peggy would pay the price.

Tallmadge and six dragoons marched Andre' into the room for his trial. Presiding were General Nathanael Greene and a number of Washington's select officers. 1

Andre' felt he should be treated as a soldier who fell into enemy hands. The British argument was that he left the *Vulture* under a flag of truce – in uniform – and was directed by Arnold, given passes and was just trapped unwillingly behind the lines and he should not be considered as a spy. The whole proceeding didn't take long. After questioning Andre', they excused him to his room. They deliberated and passed sentence that afternoon. Death!

That evening, Andre' received permission to write to British Commander Clinton in New York City. His letter never mentioned papers, only changing out of uniform and passing through the enemy posts and not following Clinton's orders. He seemed to blame only himself and didn't want Clinton to feel any remorse. The letter read like a last will and testament, even asking that his mother and three sisters be taken care of. 2

The British sent Andre's dress uniform and the next morning, Washington sent approval of the board's opinion and set his execution for five pm on the following day. Washington was then deluged with letters, from as high up as British General Clinton, who wanted discussions on the matter. Clinton offered large prisoner exchanges. Some of Washington's own officers admired Andre's courage and manners. Those officers thought maybe they could even exchange Andre' for Arnold. 3

Washington delayed the execution for another day, while Smith's trial was just starting. Benedict offered to exchange himself for Andre'. But British General Clinton told him his offer brought honor, but even if Arnold was his own brother, he could not allow it.

On October 1st, Arnold appealed again to Washington's humanity, explaining how Andre' fell to enemy hands under his direction and that Clinton then offered 40 men who could be exchanged.

He wrote: "I call Heaven and Earth to witness that your Excellency will be justly answerable to the torrent of blood that may be spilled in consequence." 4

Andre' wrote to Washington to request that he, at least, die an officer's death by a firing squad. It seemed that almost everyone was moved by Andre's plight and mannerisms. But I feel Washington could not risk any talk by Andre'. He ordered that Andre' be hung at noon, October 2nd of 1780. Andre's hanging was a huge affair. 5

He was led out by 500 infantrymen, four abreast with fife and drums. He was taken to a wagon – pulled by two horses – with a rope hanging over it. Andre' was instructed to climb on the wagon. His sentence was read, and he brushed the executioner aside, not wanting his dress uniform to be soiled. He attached the rope around his neck by himself. He was given the opportunity to say his last words.

"I have nothing more to say, gentlemen, but that you all bear witness as I meet my fate as a brave man."

He handed his clean white handkerchief to the men. It was tied over his eyes and his hands were secured behind his back. With that, the officer in charge dropped his drawn sword and the team of horses lunged forward. Andre' had won the hearts of both sides, but now his part in the story was over. 6

Now, Joshua Smith's trial was in progress. Smith was a very highly educated lawyer. He thought his best way out was to just tell the American side what they wanted to hear. He played completely innocent, just being a good American trying to grant the wishes of General Arnold and that he had no idea Andre' was anything but a merchant.

Smith thought what he was involved with was for the good of the country. Nobody really believed him, nor did they like him. But in this defense, they had no real evidence. Joshua Smith was acquitted of treason. But he was never told the verdict. The military court just sent him to another prison, hoping the civil authorities could come up with some evidence that would justify his hanging.

A year later, Smith still didn't know he was acquitted, and he realized that eventually someone would hang him. His wife – with the help of a number of 'underground survivalists' – sneaked him out of prison. He was wearing woman's clothes, and by stealth, they helped to get him to the British in New York City.

When Smith got to the British side, he just told them what they wanted to hear. They didn't believe him. Many on the British side thought he had a great deal to do with Andre's capture. Years later, in an effort to clear his name, he wrote a book called *An Authentic Narrative of the Causes Which Led to the Death of Major Andre', Adjutant General of His Majesty's Forces in North America.*

Smith's whole involvement in his double-sided life cost him everything. Not only his reputation, but his property in America, as well. 7

Van Schaick Mansion, Cohoes, NY. Built circa 1735. The mansion is located where the Mohawk and Hudson Rivers intersect. The Van Schaik Family loaned ten thousand in gold to help form a northern army, but Congress never paid them back. The Mansion was used as headquarters in the planning of the Saratoga Campaign. *Courtesy of the General Peter Gansevoort chapter of DAR.*

British General "Gentleman John" Burgoyne portrait by Sir Joshua Reynolds. Lead the Northern attack on America. He was later defeated at Saratoga, turning the tide of the war. He credited only General Benedict Arnold for his defeat. *Courtesy Library of Congress.*

Washington Headquarters at Valley Forge. Contrary to popular belief, not much suffering here. Washington staff and servants were separate from what the soldiers endured. *Courtesy Library of Congress.*

General Marquis de Lafayette, French aristocrat, sought glory in the cause of American Revolution. A friend of Washington, he betrayed Arnold by giving credit of the victory at Saratoga to Gates. Public domain, *courtesy of the US Postal Service, 1977*

John Andre, head of British intelligence, Arnold's contact with the British, and friend of Mrs. Arnold, sentenced to hang by Washington. Public domain, *courtesy of New York Public Library*

The White House, Mansion of Joshua Hett Smith on west side of the Hudson. Photo by George William Nash, 1905, *The New York Historical Society*

Colonel Beverly Robinson House seized as property of a loyalist, and used as headquarters for General Arnold, on the East side of the Hudson, 1780. Photo of Gustavus W. Pach, *New York Historical Society.*

Major Benjamin Tallmadge by John Trumbull. Head of Intelligence for George Washington, (no one knew this at the time) wanted revenge (his best friend was Nathan Hale.) *Courtesy Library of Congress.*

Model of British warship HMS Vulture at West Point Museum, U.S. Military Academy, constructed to scale by Bernhard Schulze.

Depiction of André's ambush, from Harper's Weekly, October 2, 1880. According to Tallmadge, the three men were just attempting robbery.

Self-portrait of Major John Andre on the eve of his execution. Public domain, *courtesy of Yale University Art Gallery.*

Copy of a sketch done by John André himself on the morning of his execution. This shows his last day as a free man, being rowed to shore in Haverstraw Bay. Public domain, *courtesy of the New York Public Library.*

CHAPTER FORTY-SEVEN

THE AFTERMATH – THE WAR WAS FAR FROM OVER

Right after Andre' was hung, Arnold angrily penned a chilling short note to Washington.

He considered Andre's hanging "A wanton execution of a gallant British officer in cold blood." He warned Washington that if anything happened to Peggy and his baby, "I will revenge their wrong in a deluge of American blood." 1

Peggy was in Philadelphia only for a short time. Within a couple of weeks, the politically based press demonized General Arnold. The situation in Philadelphia became too dangerous to harbor her there. By the end of the month, on October 27th, the Supreme Executive Council of Pennsylvania – Reed's cronies – gave Peggy an order of eviction. She had to leave Pennsylvania within two weeks. 2

Some friends helped her and the baby get to New York City to be with Benedict. On October 7th, Arnold wrote a long, heartfelt letter to the 'inhabitants of America.' He wanted to explain the reasons why he left the service of the United States and took up the standard of Great Britain.

If you want to know the 'whys' of our greatest war hero, who became disillusioned with our forefathers, you can view it in the letter section of this book. Benedict felt we were duped by a self-serving congress that was deceiving the public, prolonging the war and causing so much suffering. 3

Benedict went on to chide Congress for not accepting the Parliamentary Peace Commission of 1778. In favor of an unnatural and what he felt was an unholy alliance with the monarchy of France, he was compelled to act upon his principles. His letter was published in Loyalist newspapers, but that was just preaching to the choir. American papers were controlled by politicians and they were far too busy demonizing Arnold to care what he had to say.

Arnold then received permission to try and recruit some of his old comrades to form an American division to fight for Britain. He put forth a proclamation:

"To the officers and soldiers of the Continental Army who have the real interest of their country at heart and who pre-determined to be no longer the tools and dupes of the congress or France." He had some success, but not in large numbers, as he had hoped. 4

The war in the south was now raging and British General Clinton sent Benedict on a mission to disrupt American supply lines in Virginia. Benedict led a force of 1,600 men up the James River and captured Richmond.

It was said that Arnold got word to Thomas Jefferson, offering to spare the city unharmed if they would give up the supplies and tobacco. Jefferson refused and the British burned most of the city. One place we can visit today is the Berkeley Mansion on the James River in Virginia. Arnold had orders to burn the mansion. He allowed the soldiers to ransack the property and burn the furniture. However, he spared the building that stands today.

Washington sent Lafayette on a mission to try and stop Arnold's mission in Virginia. He gave Lafayette a very chilling order. He told Lafayette that if Arnold were ever captured, he must be killed. He didn't want Arnold to have a platform to talk from. Arnold's mission on the James River was a complete success for the British. 5

But Benedict didn't seem to fight as aggressively for Great Britain as he did for America. Maybe it was just because of his war wounds. He seemed to only be following and completing his orders.

To him, his conflict wasn't with the people of his country or the soldiers. It was with the elitists in Congress and the French. A couple of weeks later, after Arnold took Richmond, America had a southern victory that helped turn the tide of the war in America's favor.

On January 17th of 1781, the Battle of Cowpens happened. The American forces were led by Benedict's old friend Daniel Morgan. He fought in the same fearless style Benedict used in Saratoga.

The British suffered a humiliating defeat at Cowpens. It would eventually enable British General Lord Cornwallis to get back up to Yorktown. But, before Yorktown, Benedict was recalled back north and was sent on a raid in his home state of Connecticut, near New London. Just before Arnold left on the raid in August of 1781, Peggy gave birth to their second child in New York City.

When Benedict went on the raid in September, he gave orders to spare civilian property. But the British soldiers got out of hand and most of New London burned, earning Benedict a new title in the American press – 'America's Nero.' The idea of the raid was to put pressure on Washington to keep his forces in the north.

Washington was getting word that British General Lord Cornwallis had backed up to Yorktown. At Yorktown Cornwallis was trying to set up a military base of operations to control America's supply traffic on the Chesapeake Bay. After surviving yet another mutiny attempt with the help of French General Rochambeau, Washington made a very quick march south. There, he supervised the Siege of Yorktown so he could take complete credit and accept the surrender of General Cornwallis. 6

That situation gave Washington the decisive victory he had long been searching for. It would be what he needed to propel 'His Excellency' to the presidency or kingship he desired.

CHAPTER FORTY-EIGHT

ON TO LONDON & CANADA

General Arnold earned the respect of the British during his two missions in Virginia and Connecticut. He proved he could lead in a scarlet uniform as well as in a blue one.

By December of 1781 – after Yorktown – Benedict took Peggy and their two children on a voyage to London. He hoped to convince Parliament to stay the course. But they were already sick of the war and were entering peace negotiations.

Arnold also asked and received an audience with King George. He explained that this new country – America – would be trading with someone and he hoped it would be Britain and not France. He asked King George, since America really didn't have a navy, if he could do what he could to protect American merchant shipping.

Benedict and Peggy stayed in London for a while. After the war started drawing down, thousands of Loyalists became refugees, and most had their property seized. Many were loaded onto ships and were sailed up to Canada. They were dropped off to make a new start.

Benedict, Peggy and his growing family eventually purchased a large merchant ship and made it to New Brunswick, Canada. Benedict and his older sons, Richard and Henry, revived his mercantile trade, running goods from the West Indies to Canada.

For a while, Benedict fell into his old habits. He over-extended himself financially by loaning money to people who could not pay him back. When he tried to call in some of the debts to keep his creditors away, it almost caused riots in the streets.

Arnold managed to finally become quite successful in his trading ventures. On one trip to the West Indies, Arnold was captured by the French on the Island of Guadalupe, in the eastern Caribbean region. He was accused of being a British spy and was sentenced to be hanged. He bribed one of his guards and managed to escape. He again went into action. His hatred for the French spurred him on to organize forces and a militia. He forced the French out of control of the island. 1

King George was so grateful for Arnold's efforts that he awarded him 13,400 acres in Canada for "his very gallant and meritorious service in Guadalupe."

It took several years of very hard work to build his business in New Brunswick. Benedict's war wounds began to get the best of him. He moved Peggy and his family back to London. Peggy and Benedict enjoyed a very close and happy marriage. Peggy always referred to Benedict as 'her general.'

They had seven children. Four boys and a girl made it to adulthood. Benedict died after a week of severe illness and great suffering, as described by Peggy. The date was June 14th, 1801. He was 60 years old. 2

Peggy took over the management of Benedict's rather extensive estate. It was quite unusual for a female to do that in 1801. She was very proud that she managed to pay with honor all of Benedict's debts and had enough left to provide for her family. She was always a devoted wife and mother. Peggy had nothing but praise for her general. She died just three years later by cancer at the age of 44.

Benedict had three sons by his first marriage and four sons and a daughter with Peggy. Between marriages, while he was serving in Canada, Benedict also fathered an illegitimate son. He kept track of that son and provided for him in his will.

Benedict's loving sister Hannah would remain very close to the boys she raised, especially Richard and Henry. In his will, Benedict left most of his Canadian assets to them, with an annuity for Hannah. 3

All of his sons would go on to serve with honor in the British military.

CHAPTER FORTY-NINE

VERY IMPORTANT CONCLUSIONS & QUESTIONS

Most historians have taken the easiest path to continue to demonize General Arnold, as set forth since September of 1780. But, to me, they have never come up with a plausible reason to answer why our greatest war hero would abandon the cause and go over to Great Britain. The usual answers given are money, the influence of Peggy or something inherently selfish.

After nearly 40 years of looking into the subject to answer the questions – for myself – I have come up with four major conclusions.

I believe I can say with confidence that General Arnold was the greatest war hero in the history of the United States. Someday, I hope, his efforts and actions will be honorably recognized. I also believe that without his contributions, America would have never won the war for independence.

I also have found that General Arnold was a man of extreme honor. He would have defended his honor by duel if necessary. He also was a man of integrity and principle, but above all he was a man of actions. He truly believed that principles and words meant nothing if not followed by actions. He also believed those actions were what he should be judged by. When Arnold went to the British side during the war, he was – in his mind – doing what he thought was best for his country. And love of his country was his driving principle. I also feel it's obvious that the evidence shows there is a high probability that the papers indicating Arnold's treason charge were actually planted on Andre' to get Arnold to flee or stand trial.

I feel Arnold was treated badly and dishonorably by Congress. If Congress or Washington had approved of Arnold's naval plan or offered him the Southern Command, he probably never would have entertained going over to Great Britain.

I know that my body of work will be immediately torn down by prominent historians. Therefore, I have made a list of questions, and I hope that before this work is discredited, readers will please make an honest evaluation, and try to answer them as I feel I have.

Arnold's early contacts

• If Arnold made any decision to go to the British side in 1779, how do you explain his desperate attempts to gain a post in the army or form a navy, up to May of 1780?

• Do you really think Washington and Lafayette weren't jealous and nervous about Arnold when all the men at Valley Forge erupted in cheers when he arrived? And why, after that day, would General Arnold never get to command regular battlefield troops again?

Peggy

• As strong-willed a person as Arnold was, do you really think that Peggy – from a Neutralist family – who was 19 years his junior and a female in 1780, could be an influence on Benedict's decisions?

• I know Peggy and Benedict were in love, but doesn't the concept of Peggy's influence seem a little far-fetched?

• If Peggy was a major influence on Benedict's decisions, why when he made his 'escape' to New York City, did he write to Washington and ask him to send her to Philadelphia – or to him in New York – or whatever she chose?

Veterans

• When little Egg Harbor was attacked, or when Arnold presented his naval plans, where was Washington's support?

• Why have very few historians ever remarked on Arnold's efforts in Philadelphia to raise funds for the families of fallen soldiers?

Arnold's political problems

• How is it that no one looks into Washington's friendship with Joseph Reed, the man who brought charges against Arnold in Philadelphia? Was Washington trying to remove Arnold politically? Before West Point?

West Point

• Why is it never explained that without a British northern army

– thanks to Arnold – West Point in 1780 wasn't much more than an over-fortified supply depot, too far north for the British to gain anything by its control? Especially with all their efforts going south.

• We've always been told that Arnold weakened the defenses at West Point. Can any evidence be found to show that he weakened defenses *prior* to September of 1780?

• How can anyone explain all the effort Benedict put forth in setting up warning beacons and redoubts just days prior to his 'escape' – or defection – to the British?

• If Arnold was set on giving up West Point and settled on going to the side of Great Britain, why did he still need a face-to-face meeting with the British Andre' for assurances?

Tallmadge

• No one knew Major Benjamin Tallmadge was Washington's head of his secret service. Arnold referred to slow response and unanswered letters. Tallmadge had a lady Agent 355, working on Andre'. We are led to believe no one knew Arnold was talking to the British?

• Isn't it odd that Tallmadge just happened to be in the same area where Andre' was captured and remained with him until he was hung?

Smith and Livingston

• Isn't it significant that Livingston and Joshua Smith were not only cousins, but they met every time Smith crossed the Hudson? No one remarks that on the morning of Arnold's defection and 'escape' he was confidently waiting to give Washington an inspection of West Point. Did he feel ready for an inspection?

• When Livingston wrote a note to Arnold to tell him that Robinson was passing flags near Tarrytown, no one questioned why Livingston was so far south of his post in King's Ferry? Nor why he happened to be in the same area as Tallmadge?

• When Livingston wasn't ready to fire on the *Vulture* and he needed more time, is it believable that a rowboat couldn't be found on the Hudson in 1780?

• How do you explain so many unsecured boats, just a few days prior, that the British were collecting nearly 40 of them?

• Why did Livingston go around the chain of command to fire on the warship? Why didn't Smith tell Arnold or anyone else on the ship that the boat was about to be attacked?

• Why when Arnold recrossed the Hudson to fix his failed meeting and meet with Livingston, didn't Livingston inform Arnold of his preparations to attack the '*Vulture*'?

The Evidence

• Wasn't it odd that Smith produced the prior day's pass and pushed to get only Anderson (Andre') off the boat, and not Robinson? Isn't it strange that Smith also refused an armed barge to take Andre' to shore?

• With all the staff available to Joshua Smith, he couldn't come up with oarsmen to row Andre' to Dobb's Ferry? He had a pass to do it.

• Why was Quartermaster Kierse given a loan of $1,000 to forward dispatches for Smith?

• Why did Smith, on his way across the Hudson, have another private meeting with Livingston?

• Why didn't Smith take Andre' on the easier route along the Hudson instead of the road to Pines Bridge?

• When Andre' was dropped off at Pines Bridge, Smith twice mentioned giving Andre' a message for his brother Thomas in New York City. What happened to the message that Andre' agreed to deliver?

• Isn't it odd that the three men who captured Andre' were so highly rewarded?

• Colonel Jameson didn't seem to recognize any treason plot until Tallmadge came on the scene. And if it was obvious, why would Jameson send the warning letter to Arnold? And why was Jameson so intent on telling Washington that the letter to Arnold was sent with Tallmadge's consultation?

• How about the 'dangerous parcel' of papers? Nothing signed by Arnold and most of the papers were signed by other officers? No one questioned that?

• Did anyone notice that all the dates on the 'dangerous parcel of papers' were well in advance of the British meeting and prior to Arnold's handing in his detailed situation reports to Washington?

• Now, the big question. How did the copy of the Council of War report from September 6th – that Arnold sent back to Washington – make its way into Andre's boot?

Washington's actions

• Isn't it odd that Washington took a harder and different route back from the French meeting and ended up in Fishkill, where he met with Joshua Smith?

• What was Washington's slow journey from Fish Kill to Robinson House and around West Point, if he wasn't buying time?

• No one noticed that in Andre's letter to Washington –identifying himself and his situation – he never mentioned papers?

• When the treason was discovered, why was every officer in the area notified to prepare for the attack except for Livingston? Why did Livingston have to report to headquarters immediately?

• Why did the three men who captured Andre' have to be immediately rounded up to report to Washington?

• When Andre' and Smith were taken to Tappan for trial and Smith asked for permission to retrieve papers at his home for his defense, what possible papers could he have had? And, who ransacked his house?

• When Andre' got permission to write to British General Clinton, did you notice he never mentioned papers?

• Unless you wanted Andre' permanently silenced, why couldn't he have been exchanged for many prisoners?

• What happened to Lady Agent 355 and why was she never heard from again after September 1780?

• Why did Livingston retire three months after September 1780 and receive two very large tracts of land?

• Why was Lafayette ordered by Washington that if Arnold was ever captured he must be killed? Unless you didn't want him to talk.

....

I feel there are almost as many questions as answers, but the evidence to me points to the planting of papers on Andre' in order to get Arnold to leave or go on trial.

Because Arnold was considered by Congress to be second class, and his outspoken views against the French alliance, Washington and Congress were not about to let General Arnold's popularity and military skills elevate him to the top.

I can't imagine if Arnold's naval plan was approved, or if he was offered the southern command and he was the man who defeated Cornwallis, how different America's history would have been.

Hopefully, this book answers the who, what, when, where and why. I also hope readers find that an honest and truthful look into history can be just as fun and interesting as ongoing legends.

The End

BIBLIOGRAPHY & SOURCES

BOOKS

Benedict Arnold, Revolutionary Hero by James Kirby Martin

A Hero and A Spy, the Revolutionary War Correspondence of Benedict Arnold by Russell M. Lea

Valiant Ambition: George Washington, Benedict Arnold & The Fate of the American Revolution by Nathaniel Philbrick

The Wilderness War: A Narrative
The Wilderness Empire: A Narrative by Allan W. Eckert

Benedict Arnold's Army: The 1775 American Invasion of Canada During the Revolutionary War by Arthur S. Lefkowitz

An Authentic Narrative of the Causes Which Led to the Death of Major Andre', Adjutant General of His Majesty's Forces in North America by Joshua Hett Smith, print date 1809 – available at www.forgottenbooks.com

Accomplice in Treason: Joshua Hett Smith and the Arnold Conspiracy by Richard J. Koke

George Washington and Benedict Arnold: A Tale of Two Patriots by Dave R. Palmer

Bloody Mohawk: The French and Indian War and American Revolution on New York's Frontier by Richard Berleth

Benedict Arnold: In the Company of Heroes by Arthur S. Lefkowitz

Founding Myths: Stories That Hide Our Patriotic Past by Ray Raphael

Arundel by Kenneth Roberts

Turncoat by Stephen Brumwell

The Tragedy of Benedict Arnold by Joyce Lee Malcolm

DIGITAL SOURCES ONLINE

The Library of Congress
The George Washington Papers
Clements Library Archives
Canadian National Archives
New York Archives

SITES PERSONALLY VISITED BY THE AUTHOR FOR INFORMATION OVER 40 YEARS – NOT ALL LISTED BUT WOULD RECOMMEND:

Crown Point Museum
Champlain Maritime Museum
Fort Ticonderoga and Museum
National Battlefield of Saratoga and Museum
Philip Schuyler Mansion at Albany, New York
State of New York Museum
VanSchaick Mansion at Cohoes, New York
Oriskany Battlefield Memorial
General Herkimer Home at Herkimer, New York
National Museum at Fort Stanwicks, Rome, New York
West Point Military Museum, West Point, New York
USS Constitution, Boston Harbor
Battlefields at Lexington and Concord
Colonial Williamsburg, Williamsburg, Virginia
Yorktown Museum and Battlefield, Yorktown, Virginia
Old Statehouse Museum and Freedom Trail, Boston MA
Steuben Memorial State Historic Site, Remsen, New York
Valley Forge National Historic Park, Valley Forge, Pennsylvania
George Washington's Mount Vernon Estate, Mount Vernon, Virginia
Berkeley Plantation, Charles City County, Virginia

ACTUAL LETTERS

Letters 1 - 8 are transcribed documents supposedly found in Andre's boot. Letter 9: A chilling note from Arnold to Washington. Letters 10 - 12: Arnold's letter of of explanation back to the "Inhabitants of America" These letters have been provided so readers can see the actual documents for themselves.

1   *Estimate of the number of men necessary to man the works at West Point & in the vicinity, Sept. 1780.*

Fort Arnold	620
Fort Putnam	450
Fort Webb	140
Fort Wyllys	140
Reboubt No. 1	150
Redoubt No. 2	150
Redoubt No. 3	120
Redoubt No. 4.	100
Redoubt No. 5	130
Redoubt No. 6	110
Redoubt No. 7	78
North Redoubt	120
South Redoubt	130
Total	2,438

Villefranche, Engineer
(The artillery men are not included in the above estimate.)

2

Artillery Orders:
The following disposition of the corps is to take place is case of an alarm.

Capt. Daniels with his Company repair to Fort Putnam, detach an officer with 12 men to Wyllys Redoubt, a non-commissioned officer with 3 men to Webb Redoubt, and the like number to Redoubt No. 4.

Captain Thomas and Company to repair to Fort Arnold.

Captain Simmons and Company to remain at the North and South Redoubts at the east side of the river until further orders.

Lieut. Barber with 20 men of Captain Jackson's Company will repair to Constitution Island; the remainder of the company with Lieut. Masons will repair to Arnold.

Capt. Lieut. George and Lieut. Blake with 20 men of Capt. Treadwell's Company will repair to Redoubt No. 1 & 2, the remainder of the company will be sent to Fort Arnold.

Late Jones' Company with Lieut. Fisk to repair to the South Battery.

The Chain Battery, Sherburne's Redoubt, and the brass field pieces will be manned from Fort Arnold. As occasion may require.

The commissary and conductor of military stores will in turn wait upon the commanding officer of artillery for orders.

The artillery officers in the garrison, (agreeable to former orders) will repair to Fort Arnold and there receive further orders from the commanding officer of artillery, S. Bauman, Major Commt. Artillery.

3

Return of Ordnance in the Forts & Batteries at West Point and its dependencies, Sept. 5th, 1780.

S. Bauman, Major Comdt. Of Artillery

<u>Forts</u>

Arnold	Garrison Carriage	– 1 Iron 24 lb., 6 / 18 lb.
	Stocked Carriage	– 1 Iron 12 lb.
	Travelling Carriage	– 1 Brass 4 lb., 3 Iron 3 lb.
	Mortars	– 5 Brass 10", 5 / 5", 1 / 4"
Putnam	Garrison Carriage	– 5 Iron 18 lb., 2 / 12 lb.
	Travelling Carriage	– 2 Brass 5 lb., 1 / 4 lb.
	Mortars	– 4 Brass 5"
V. Pt / S. Pt	Travelling Carriage	– 1 Iron 18 lb.
	Stocked Carriage	– 2 Iron 12 lb.
	Mortars	– 2 Brass 5", 1 / 4"
	Howitzers	– 1 Iron 8"
Con. Isl.	Garrison Carriage	– 4 Iron 12 lb., 1 / 9 lb., 5 / 6 lb.

<u>Batteries</u>

South	Garrison Carriage	– 4 Iron 18 lb., 1 / 12 lb.
Chain	Garrison Carriage	– 1 Iron 12 lb.
	Stocked Carriage	– 2 Iron 12 lb.
Lanthorn	Garrison Carriage	– 2 Iron 9 lb.

<u>Redoubts</u>

No. 1	Garrison Carriage	– 1 Iron 12 lb., 4 / 9 lb.
No. 2	Garrison Carriage	– 2 Iron 9 lb.
No. 4	Garrison Carriage	– 2 Iron 6 lb.
Meigs	Garrison Carriage	– 1 Iron 6 lb.
	Travelling Carriage	– 1 Iron 4 lb.
North	Garrison Carriage	– 3 Iron 18 lb., 3 / 12 lb.
Sherman	Garrison Carriage	– 2 Iron 6 lb.
	Stocked Carriage	– 3 Iron 6 lb.
South	Garrison Carriage	– 1 Iron 12 lb., 4 / 6 lb.
Webb	Garrison Carriage	– 1 Iron 12 lb., 1 / 4 lb.
	Stocked Carriage	– 2 Iron 6 lb.
Wyllys	Travelling Carriage	– 2 Iron 18 lb., 3 / 3 lb.

4

Estimate of the forces at West Point and its dependencies, Sept. 13th 1780

A brigade of Massachusetts Militia & two regiments of rank & file New Hampshire Inclusive of 166 Bateaus Men at Verplank's and Stony Points.	*992*
On command & extra service at Fishkill, New Windsor, etc, etc who may be called in occasionally.	*852*
3 regiments of Connecticut Militia under the Command of Colonel Wells on the lines near N. Castle.	*488*
A detachment of New York levies on the lines.	*115*
Militia	*2,447*
Colonel Lamb's Regiment	*167*
Colonel Livingston at Verplank & Stony Pts.	*80*
Continental	*247*
Colonel Sheldon's Dragoons on the lines, ½ Mounted	*142*
Bateau Men and Artificers	*250*
Total	*3,086*

5

Remarks on works at West Point, Sept. 1780

Fort Arnold - built of dry fascines, wood in a ruinous condition, incomplete, and subject to take fire from explosive shells.

Fort Putnam – The stone is wanting great repairs, the wall on the east side broke down and rebuilding from the foundation at the west and south sides have been a spiked barricade on the west side broke in many places. The east side is open, two bomb proofs, a provision magazine, and a slight wooden barrack. A commanding piece of ground lies 500 yards west between the fort and Redoubt No. 4, Rocky Hill.

Fort Webb – Built of facings and wood, a slight work, very dry and liable to be set on fire as the approaches are very easy, without defenses save a slight spiked barricade.

Fort Wyllys – Built of stone 5 feet high and 15 feet thick, the work above plank is filled with earth 9 feet thick.
No bomb proofs among the batteries within the fort.

Redoubt No. 1 – On the south side, wood is 9 feet thick, the west, north, and east sides are 4 feet thick.
No cannon in the works, a slight and single abattis,
no ditch or picket. Cannon on two batteries, no bomb proofs.

Redoubt No. 2 – The same as No. 1, no bomb proofs.

Redoubt No. 3 – A slight wood work 3 feet thick, very dry,
no bomb proofs, a single abattis, easily set on fire, no cannon.

Redoubt No. 4 – A wooden work about 10 feet high and 4 or 5 feet thick, the west side faced with a stone wall 8 feet high
and 4 feet thick. No bomb proof, two six pounders, a slight abattis, a commanding piece of ground 500 yards west

North Redoubt – On the east side of the river built of stone 4 feet high, above the stone, wood filled in with earth, very dry, no ditch, a bomb proof, three batteries without the fort, a poor abattis, a rifling piece of ground 500 yards south of the approaches under cover to within 20 yards. The work easily fired with faggots dipped in pitch etc.

South Redoubt – Much the same as the north, a commanding piece of ground 500 yards due east, 3 batteries without the fort.

6

At a Council of War, held in Camp Bergen County, Sept. 6th, 1780   Present – The Commander-in-Chief

The Commander-in-Chief states to the council, that since he had the honor of laying before the General officers, at Morristown, the 6th of June last, a general view of our circumstances, several important events have occurred, which have materially changed the prospects of the campaign.

That the success expected from France, instead of coming out in one body and producing a naval superiority in these seas, has been divided into two divisions. The first of which only consisting of seven ships of the line, one forty-four and three smaller frigates, with five thousand land forces, had arrived at Rhode Island.

That a reinforcement of six ships of the line from England having reinforced the enemy, has made their naval force in these seas amount to nine sails of the line. Two fifties, two forty-fours, and a number of smaller frigates, a force completely superior to that of our allies and which has in conference held them blocked up in the harbor of Rhode Island till then 29th. Ultimately at which period the British fleet disappeared and in no advice of them has since been received.

That accounts received by the alliance frigate, which left France in July, announces the second division to be confined in Breft with several other ships by a British fleet of thirty-two sails of the line and a fleet of the allies of thirty-six or thirty-eight ships of the line ready to put to sea from Cadiz to relieve the Port of Breft.

The most of the states in their answers to the requisitions made of them, give the strongest assurances of doing every thing in their power to furnish the men and supplies required for the expected cooperation. The effect of which, however, has been far short of our expectations, for not much above one third of the levies demanded for the Continental Battalions, nor above the same proportion of militia have been assembled, and the supplies have been so inadequate that there was a necessity for dismissing all the militia, whose immediate services could be dispensed with to lessen our consumption, notwithstanding which the troops now in the field are severely suffering for want of provision.

That the Army at this post and in the vicinity in operating force consists of 10,400 Continental troops and about 400 militia, besides which is a regiment of Continental Troops of about 500 at Rhode island left there for the assistance of our allies, against any attempt of the enemy that way and two Connecticut State Regiments amounting to 800 at North Castle.

7

That the times of service for which the levies are engaged will expire on the first of January, which if not replaced, allowing for the usual casualties, will reduce the Continental Army to less than 6,000 men.

That since the state to the council above referred to, the enemy have brought a detachment of about 3,000 men from Charleston to New York, which makes the present operating force in this quarter between ten and eleven thousand men.

That the enemies force now in the southern states has not been lately ascertained by any distinct accounts, but the General supposes that it cannot be less than 7,000 (of which about 2,000 are in Savannah) in this estimate, the decrease by the casualties of the climate is supposed to be equal to the increase of force derived from the disaffected.

That added to the loss of Charleston and its garrison accounts of a recent misfortune are just arrived from Major General Gates, giving advice of a general action, which happened on the 16th of August near Camden, in which the Army under his command met with a total defeat and in all probability the whole of the Continental Troops and a considerable part of the militia would be cut off.

That the State of Virginia has been sometime exerting itself to raise a body of 3,000 troops to serve till the end of December 1781, but how far it has succeeded is not known.

That Maryland had resolved to raise 2,000 men of which a sufficient number to compose one battalion was to have come to this Army. The remainder to recruit the Maryland Line, but in consequence of the latest advice, an order has been sent to march the whole southward.

That the enemy's force in Canada, Halifax, St. Augustine, and at Penobscot, remains much the same as stated in the preceding council.

That there is still reason to believe the Court of France will prosecute its original intention of giving effectual succor to this country as soon as circumstances will permit; and it is hoped the second division will certainly arrive in the course of the fall.

That a fleet greatly superior to that of the enemy in the West Indies and a formidable land force had failed sometime since from Martinique to make a combined attack upon the Island of Jamaica, that there is a possibility of a reinforcement from this quarter also to the fleet of our ally at Rhode Island.

8

The Commander-in-Chief having thus given the council a full view of our present situation and future prospects, requests the opinion of each member in writing, what plan it will be advisable to pursue, to what objects our attention ought to be directed in the course of this fall and winter, taking into consideration the alternative of having or not having a naval superiority, whether any offensive operations can be immediately undertaken and against what point, what ought to be our immediate preparations and dispositions, particularly whether we can afford or ought to fend any reinforcements from this Army to the southern states, and to what amount the General requests to be favored with these opinions by the 10th instant at farthest.

9

Arnold's chilling note to Washinton

To His Excellency General Washington

                                                              New York, October 5, 1780

Sir

    The wanton execution of a gallant British officer in cold blood may be only the prelude to further butcheries on the same ill-fated occasion. Necessity compelled me to leave behind me in your camp a wife and offspring that are endeared to me by every sacred tie. If any violence be offered to them, remember I will revenge their wrongs in a deluge of American blood.

                                                                                         B. Arnold

10

To the Inhabitants of America

New York, Oct. 7th, 1780

I should forfeit even in my own opinion, the place I have so long held in yours, if I could be indifferent to your approval and silent on the motives which have induced me to join the king's arms.

A very few words, however, shall suffice upon a subject so personal, for to the thousands who suffer under the tyranny of the rulers in the revolted provinces, as well as to the great multitude who have long wished for its defeat, this instance of my conduct can want no vindication, as to that class of men who are criminally prolonging the war from sinister views, at the expense of the public interest, I prefer their hostility to their applause. I am only, therefore, concerned in this address to explain myself to such of my countrymen as want abilities or opportunities to detect the trickery by which they are duped.

Having fought by your side when the love of our country activated our arms, I shall expect from your justice and sincerity, what your deceivers, with more art and less honesty, will find it inconsistent with their own views to admit.

When I quitted domestic happiness for the perils of the field, I conceived the rights of my country in danger, and that duty and honor called me to her defense. A remedy of grievances was my only object and aim; however, I agreed in a step which I thought hastened the declaration of Independence; to justify the measure many plausible reasons were urged, which could no longer exist. When Great Britain, with the open arms of a parent, offered to embrace us as children and grant the wished for remedy.

And now that her worst enemies are in her own bosom, I should change my principles, if I conspired with their designs. Yourselves being judges, was the war the less just because fellow subjects were considered as our foes? You have felt the torture in

(Continued next page)

which we raised our arms against a brother, God incline the guilty protractors of these unnatural dissentions to resign their ambition and cease from their delusions in compassion to kindred blood.

I anticipate your question: was not the war a defensive one until the French joined in the combination? I answer, that I thought so. You will add, was it not afterwards necessary till the separation of the British empire was complete? By no means; in contending for the welfare of my country, I am free to declare my opinion, that had this end been attained, all strife should have ceased.

I lamented therefore the political tyranny and injustice, which with a sovereign contempt of the People of America, studiously neglected to take their collective sentiments of the British proposals of peace. And to negotiate under a suspension of arms, for an adjustment of differences, as a dangerous sacrifice of the great interest of this country to the partial views of a proud, ancient, and crafty foe. I had my suspicions of some imperfections in our councils, on proposals prior to the parliamentary commission of 1778; but having then less to do in the cabinet than the field (I will not pronounce dogmatically as some may, and perhaps justly, that Congress have veiled them from the public eye), I continued to be guided in the negligent confidence of a soldier. But the whole world saw, and all America confessed, the overtures of the second commission exceeded our wishes and expectations. If there was any suspicion of the national liberality, it arose from its excess.

Do any believe that we were at that time really entangled by an alliance with France? Unfortunate deception! And thus they have been duped by a virtuous gullibility, in the incautious moments of unrestrained passion, to give up their fidelity to serve a nation counting both the will and the power to protect us, and aiming at the destruction both of the mother country and the provinces. In the simplicity of common sense, for I pretend to no deceptive reasoning, did the pretended treaty with the Court of Versailles amount to more than an overture to America? Certainly not, because no authority had been given by the people to conclude it, nor to this very hour have they authorized its ratification, the Articles of Confederation remain still unsigned.

In the firm persuasion, therefore, that the private judgement of any individual citizen of this country is as free from all conventional restraints since, as before the insidious offers of France. I preferred those from Great Britain, thinking it infinitely wiser and safer to cast my confidence upon her justice and generosity, than to trust a monarchy too feeble to establish your independence. So perilous to

(Continued next page)

her distant dominions, the enemy of the Protestant faith, and fraudulently avowing an affection for the liberties of mankind, while she holds her native sons in subservience and chains.

I affect no disguise, and therefore frankly declare that in these principles, I had determined to retain my arms and command for an opportunity to surrender them to Great Britain, and in contriving the measures for a purpose, in my opinion, as grateful as it would have been beneficial to my country; I was only solicitous to accomplish an event of decisive importance, and to prevent, as much as possible in the execution of it, the effusion of blood.

With the highest satisfaction I bear testimony to my old fellow soldiers and citizens, that I find solid ground to rely upon the clemency of our sovereign and abundant conviction that it is the generous intention of Great Britain, not only to have the rights and privileges of the colonies unimpaired, together with their perpetual exemption from taxation, but to add such further benefits as may consist with the common prosperity of the empire. In short, I fought for much less than the parent country is as willing to grant to her colonies, as they can be to receive or enjoy.

Some may think I continued in the struggle of those unhappy days too long, and others that I quitted it too soon. To the first I reply, that I did not see with their eyes, nor perhaps had so favorable a situation to look from, and that to one common master I am willing to stand or fall. In behalf of the candid among the latter, some of whom I believe serve blindly but honestly in the ranks I have left, I pray to God to give them all the lights requisite to their own safety before it is too late; and with respect to that kind of critics whose hostility to me originates in their hatred to the principles, by which I am now led to devote my life to the reunion of the British Empire, as the best and only means to dry up the streams of misery that have deluged this country, they may be assured that, conscious of the integrity of my intentions, I shall treat their malice and accusations with contempt and neglect.

ENDNOTES

This book is the culmination of nearly 40 years of part-time research. My quest was always to answer questions to satisfy my own curiosity. A book was never my intention until I realized the story I learned, and explanations of General Arnold's actions were not being told.

Therefore, I never collected source materials along the way and in these footnotes I had to rely on secondary sources. I tried to find books that were well-researched and backed up by primary historical sources.

I must again acknowledge the great and detailed work of the authors listed in the following footnotes. The books and page numbers I referred to should be easily obtained by readers to answer their questions about history, particularly the story of General Arnold and the Revolutionary times.

CHAPTER ONE
Mainly observations – early American studies
1. Monticello – tournarrative@monticello.com – Charlottesville, VA
2. Mount Vernon – tournarrative@mountvernon.com
3. 1st Continental Congress archive documents – Philadelphia, PA Oct. 1774
4. Descriptions of affected citizenry – good description found in narrative of *Death of Major Andre*, by J.H. Smith, pages 26 & 27
5. Letters from Clinton-Sullivan Campaign – see *The Wilderness War*, by Allan W. Eckert – detailed descriptions with letters, pages 299-421

CHAPTER TWO
1. Extensively researched descriptions from *Benedict Arnold, Revolutionary Hero*, by James Kirby Martin – "A Childhood of Legends" pages 11-32
2. Descriptions of early Arnold clan, *Benedict Arnold's Army*, by Lefkowitz, p. 1-3
3. Letter from Hannah Arnold to Benedict Arnold, Norwich, April 12th of 1754 – Pierpont Morgan Library, New York City
4. Authentic narrative by J.H. Smith, 1809, unknown poet, page 170
5. Arnold store sign and advertisement – New Haven Colony Historical Society, New Haven, Connecticut
6. Well-documented description – *Benedict Arnold, Revolutionary Hero*, by James Kirby Martin – "A Person to be Reckoned with in New Haven" pages 41 & 42
7. Boles incident, also documented and described in *Benedict Arnold, Revolutionary Hero*, by James Kirby Martin – "A Person to be Reckoned with in New Haven," pages 43 & 44
8. Description of Arnold's estate, *Benedict Arnold's Army*, by Lefkowitz, pages 3 & 4

9. June 9th, 1770 letter from Benedict Arnold to B. Douglas, Esq. of New Haven. Describes his outrage at "wanton cruel and inhumane murders committed in Boston by the soldiers. Good God!" Description of letter from *Benedict Arnold, Revolutionary Hero*, by J.K. Martin – "Irrepressible Acts of Martial Resistance" pages 57 & 58

CHAPTER THREE
1. *Benedict Arnold, Revolutionary Hero*, by James Kirby Martin –"Irrepressible Acts of Martial Resistance," pages 62 & 63
2. Ibid., page 63
3. Ibid., page 63
4. Letter from Benedict Arnold to Joseph Warren and the Honorable Committees of Safety, April 3rd, 1775 – description of Fort Ticonderoga's condition and ordnance that could be obtained – *A Hero and a Spy*, by Russell M. Lea, page 15
5. Letter from Massachusetts Committee of Safety to Benedict Arnold, commander of a body of troops on an expedition to subdue and take possession of Fort Ticonderoga from Benjamin Church, chairman of the Committee of Safety, dated May 3rd, 1775, *Benedict Arnold, Revolutionary Hero* by J.K. Martin – pages 65 & 66
6. Well-documented descriptions of Arnold's actions prior to attack on Fort Ticonderoga. *Benedict Arnold, Revolutionary Hero*, by J.K. Martin, pages 68 &69
7. Report relayed at talk on Fort Ticonderoga, but quote is unsubstantiated.
8. Letters about Ticonderoga from Easton, Allen and Arnold. Easton, Allen and Edward Mott tried to downplay or ignore Arnold's role and who should be in command. Arnold wrote to the Committee of Safety at Cambridge on May 11th of 1775. He claimed he was the "first person who entered and took possession of the fort." Letter from Benedict Arnold to Massachusetts Committee, May 11th of 1775 & letter from Ethan Allen to Massachusetts Provincial Congress, May 11th of 1775 – well-documented and described in *Benedict Arnold, Revolutionary Hero* by J.K. Martin, pages 72 &73

CHAPTER FOUR
1. Letter to Massachusetts committee of Safety, May 14th of 1775, from Benedict Arnold. Described ordnance seized for Cambridge, also seized preparations to move on St. John's – documented and described in *Benedict Arnold, Revolutionary Hero*, by J.K. Martin – pages 74 & 75. Letter can also be viewed in *A Hero and A Spy*, by Russell Lea – pages 28 & 29
2. Letter to Committee of Safety at Cambridge from Crown Point by Benedict Arnold, dated May 23rd, 1775. Describes mission to St. John's and meeting with Allen and mentioned detailed need of supplies with P.S. Describes fate of Allen mission. *A Hero and A Spy*, by Russell Lea – pages 35-37
3. Letter from Guy Carlton to Lord Dartmouth at Montreal on June 7th, 1775. Documents of American Revolution, 1770-1783 – letter referenced in *Benedict Arnold, Revolutionary Hero*, by J.K. Martin – page 78
4. Descriptions of events, *Benedict Arnold, Revolutionary Hero*, "The Provincial

Politics of Rebellion" Page 91

5. Letter to Continental Congress from Benedict Arnold at Crown Point, dated May 29th of 1775 – *A Hero and a Spy*, by Russell Lea – pages 43 & 44

6. Letter to Benedict Arnold from the inhabitants of Lake Champlain, July 3rd of 1775 – representatives of nearly 600 families. Can be seen in *A Hero and a Spy*, by Russell M. Lea, page 60

(* All letters recorded in one place, thankfully, in *A Hero and a Spy*, by Russell M. Lea)

CHAPTER FIVE
No footnotes necessary.

CHAPTER SIX

1. Letter to Continental Congress written by Benedict Arnold from Albany dated July 11th of 1775. He explained his situation and events in the northern theater – *A Hero and A Spy*, by Russell Lea – page 66

2. *Benedict Arnold, Revolutionary Hero*, by J.K. Martin, pages 98-101

3. Letter from Hannah Arnold to Benedict Arnold from New Haven, written in June 1775 – Also, a good description from *Benedict Arnold, Revolutionary Hero*, by J.K. Martin, pages 102 & 103

4. *Benedict Arnold, Revolutionary Hero*, "Into the Howling Maine Wilderness" pages 104-106

CHAPTER SEVEN

1. Letter to Continental Congress from Benedict Arnold while in Albany, July 11, 1775 – *A Hero and A Spy*, by Russell Lea – page 66

2. Letter to Benedict Arnold from George Washington, September 14, 1775, acknowledging Benedict Arnold's new rank as colonel and orders for command of Quebec expedition, with objectives. Also detailed orders from George Washington to Benedict Arnold, same date. Letters can be viewed in *A Hero and a Spy*, by Russell Lea – pages 69-73

3. Letter from George Washington to Phillip Schuyler, from Cambridge August 20, 1775 George Washington Papers – a digital archives by date

4. Letter to Capt. Colburn from Benedict Arnold, August 21, 1775. Arnold inquires about Colburn's ability to build 200 light bateaus. *A Hero and a Spy*, by Russell Lea – page 68

5. *Benedict Arnold, Revolutionary Hero*, by J.K. Martin, "Into the Howling Maine Wilderness" page 114

6. Ibid., pages 114 & 115

7. Ibid., pages 116-118

CHAPTER EIGHT

1. *Benedict Arnold, Revolutionary Hero*, by J.K. Martin, "Into the Howling Maine Wilderness" Detailed descriptions of preparations and send off, pages 117-121

2. Ibid., pages 121-123

3. *Benedict Arnold's Army*, by Lefkowitz – Detailed descriptions of mission's start, pages 55-63

4. Letter to George Washington from Benedict Arnold at Fort Western, September 25, 1775. Details of trip up to this date, George Washington Papers, archived by date, also *A Hero and A Spy*, by Russell Lea – pages 75-77

5. Ibid., *Benedict Arnold, Revolutionary Hero*, by J.K. Martin, detailed worries about Chief Natanis, pages 120 & 121

6. Ibid., *Benedict Arnold, Revolutionary Hero*, by J.K. Martin, page 122 – also letter from Benedict Arnold to George Washington from Fort Western, dated September 27, 1775 – George Washington Papers, digital archives by date, also *A Hero and A Spy*, by Russell Lea – pages 75-77

7. Letter to Washington from Benedict Arnold, second portage from Kennebec to Dead River, October 13, 1775, George Washington Papers, digital archives by date, also *A Hero and A Spy*, by Russell Lea – pages 77 & 73

8. Ibid., *Benedict Arnold, Revolutionary Hero*, by J.K. Martin, detailed descriptions, page 124 – also Benedict Arnold's journal entries of October 3rd and October 8 – 10 of 1775

9. Dr. Isaac Senter's Journal – see October 24th & 25th entries. Also *Benedict Arnold, Revolutionary Hero*, by J.K. Martin – "Hannibalian Breakthrough to Quebec," pages 134 & 135

10. Morison Journal, Morison's description, Oct. 27, 1775 See *Benedict Arnold's Army*, by Lefkowitz – pages 156 & 157

11. Dr. Isaac Senter's Journal, November 1, 1775 – see in *A Hero and A Spy*, by Russell Lea – page 83

12. Letter from Benedict Arnold to George Washington from Chaudière Pond, dated October 27, 1775 – *A Hero and A Spy*, by Russell Lea – pages 81 & 82

13. Journal entry by Private Abner Stocking, November 2, 1775 – also, description of trials of Jemima Warner and death of her husband. See in *A Hero and A Spy*, by Russell Lea – pages 83 & 84

14. Entries from Dr. Isaac Senter's journal, November 4, 1775 – also *Benedict Arnold Revolutionary Hero*, by J.K. Martin, pages 140-142

15. From journal of Private John Joseph Henry, dated November 7, 1775 – full letter in Benedict Arnold, *A Hero and a Spy*, by Russell M. Lea, page 84

16. Dr. Isaac Senter's Journal, November 5, 1775 – also *Benedict Arnold, Revolutionary Hero*, by J.K. Martin, pages 140 & 141

CHAPTER NINE

1. Letter to George Washington from Benedict Arnold from Point Levi, November 14th of 1775. Describes situation across river from Quebec and preparations for crossing river – see *A Hero and A Spy*, by Russell Lea – pages 87 & 88

2. *Benedict Arnold's Army*, by Lefkowitz – pages 194-199

3. *Benedict Arnold, Revolutionary Hero*, by J.K. Martin – "Hannibalian Breakthrough to Quebec" pages 147-144.

4. Letter to George Washington from Point Aux Trembles by Benedict Arnold,

November 20th of 1775. Explained severe shortages of ammunition and clothing, anxious for General Montgomery to arrive. Benedict thought if only he was 10 days sooner Quebec would have fallen – see *A Hero and A Spy*, by R. Lea – pages 89 & 90

5. Letters from Arnold to Montgomery, November 14th of 1775. Better descriptions of events and more detailed. *Benedict Arnold, Revolutionary Hero*, by J.K. Martin – pages 129-150

CHAPTER TEN

1. Letter to General Schuyler from Richard Montgomery from Holland House, near the Heights of Abraham, December 5th of 1775 – *A Hero and A Spy*, by Russell Lea – page 94.

2. *Benedict Arnold, Revolutionary Hero*, by J.K. Martin – "Liberty or Death at the Walls of Quebec" page 163 – Describes various attempts to make city submit, also mentions the death of Jemima Warner.

3. Ibid., page 161 – more detailed descriptions

4. Long narrative from Dr. Senter's Journal, dated Sunday December 31st of 1775. Describes in detail the day's events as he learned from the wounded at his field hospital: "Oh, liberty! Oh, virtue! Oh, my country!" seemed the language of all – see Dr. Isaac Senter's journal, by dates of entries

5. Ibid. Senter's journal

6. Ibid. Senter's journal

7. Express letter from Benedict Arnold to General Wooster, Montreal from a field hospital set up for care of those wounded during the attack on Quebec on December 31st of 1775 – explained the sad news of assault, asked Wooster to forward express of news to Congress and Washington. *A Hero and A Spy*, by Russell Lea, pages 98 & 99

CHAPTER ELEVEN

1. Letter from Benedict Arnold to Honorable Continental Congress from camp before Quebec, January 11th of 1776 – *A Hero and A Spy*, by Russell Lea – pages 106-108

2. Papers of Thomas Jefferson, better description in *Benedict Arnold, Revolutionary Hero*, by J.K. Martin – page 184

3. George Washington Papers, digital archives by date – January 19th of 1776. Also see *Benedict Arnold, Revolutionary Hero*, by J.K. Martin – page 187

4. Benedict Arnold letter from Holland House, March 26th of 1776 see *Benedict Arnold, Revolutionary Hero*, by J.K. Martin – page 190

5. Journals of Continental Congress – 34 volumes, entry dated January 10th of 1776 – Benedict Arnold received promotion to Brigadier General on January 10th of 1776, but he would get the news much later – see *A Hero and A Spy*, by R. Lea – page 106

6. Letter to General Schuyler from Benedict Arnold at Montreal, April 20th of 1776 – explained his situation of leaving camp in charge of Wooster, also supply problems. Quitting the Canadian Campaign may be only choice left. *A Hero and A Spy*, by Russell Lea – pages 128 & 129

7. *Benedict Arnold, Revolutionary Hero*, by J.K. Martin – "Reduced to a Great Rabble" pages 201-203

8. Letters containing situation reports of Canadian campaign from commissioners to Canada and John Hancock, President of Congress, written from Montreal, on May 10th of 1776 – see *Benedict Arnold, Revolutionary Hero*, by J.K. Martin – pages 203 & 204

9. Ibid. pages 211-215

10. Ibid. page 214

11. Ibid. page 215

12. Ibid. Also letters from Commissioners of Canada to John Hancock, President of Congress written from Montreal, May 27th of 1776 – also Arnold's report to commissioners – see *A Hero and A Spy*, by R. Lea – pages 133-135

13. Letter from Benedict Arnold to Horatio Gates from Chambly, May 31st of 1776 – see *Benedict Arnold, Revolutionary Hero*, page 217

14. Letter from Benedict Arnold to Commissioners of Congress from Montreal, June 2nd of 1776 – see *A Hero and A Spy*, by R. Lea – pages 136 & 137

15. Letter from Benedict Arnold to Philip Schuyler at Chambly – see *Benedict Arnold, Revolutionary Hero*, by J.K. Martin – page 219 – also A Hero and A Spy, by R. Lea – page 140

CHAPTER TWELVE

1. Record of Council of War held at Crown Point on July 7th of 1776. Members:
Major General Philip Schuyler, President
Major General Horatio Gates
Brigadier General J. Sullivan
Brigadier General Benedict Arnold
Brigadier General Frederick Woedtke

2. Many letters explaining the situation of the huge British force about to move south on Lake Champlain and idea of forming a navy following letters to explain the desperate need
Arnold to General Sullivan – June 16th of 1776
Resolution of Congress – June 17th of 1776
Letter to the President of Congress from George Washington – June 17th of 1776
Philip Schuyler to George Washington – June 24th of 1776
Arnold to George Washington from Albany – June 25th of 1776
Philip Schuyler to George Washington from Albany – July 1st of 1776
Above letters can be seen in *A Hero and a Spy* by Russell M. Lea – ages 140-146

CHAPTER THIRTEEN

1. Letter from Benedict Arnold to Major General Gates from Skenesboro on July 24th of 1776 – details on ship construction progress. Cheshire's Mills producing 4,000 feet of boards per day – see *A Hero and A Spy*, by Russell Lea – pages 153 & 154

2. Letter from Benedict Arnold at Skenesboro to General Gates at Ticonderoga – list of ships, guns carried, number of men needed per ship – see *A Hero and A Spy*, by Russell Lea – pages 158 & 159

3. Journal of Lt. Bayze Wells – August 29th of 1776 – description in *Benedict Arnold, Revolutionary Hero*, page 254

4. Letters from Benedict Arnold to General Gates written from Isle LaMott, September 18th of 1776; Bay St. Amand; Isle of Valcour, September 28th of 1776 – see *A Hero and A Spy*, by Russell M. Lea, pages 174-180

5. Letter from Benedict to Gates from Valcour – October 10th of 1776 – *A Hero and A Spy*, by Russell M. Lea – page 182

6. Description of events of Battle of Valcour in letter from Arnold to Major General Schuyler written from Ticonderoga on October 15th of 1776 – see *A Hero and A Spy*, by Russell Lea – pages 194 & 195 – also found by Russell Lea in "Naval Documents of American Revolution" in U.S. Government Printing Office in Washington, DC – British perspective situation report from Guy Carleton to General Burgoyne written on board the *Maria* off the Isle of Valcour in October, after battle – see *A Hero and A Spy*, by Russell Lea – pages 196 & 197

CHAPTER FOURTEEN

1. Description in *Benedict Arnold, Revolutionary Hero*, by J.K. Martin, page 285
2. Better description in *Benedict Arnold, Revolutionary Hero*, by J.K. Martin, page 290
3. Ibid., pages 291 & 292
4. Ibid., page 292
5. Ibid., page 297
6. Ibid., page 300
7. Ibid., page 301
8. Ibid., page 302
9. Ibid., page 303
10. Ibid., pages 306-308
11. Letter from George Washington to Benedict Arnold – March 3rd of 1777, see in *A Hero and A Spy*, by Russell M. Lea – pages 217 & 218
12. Letter to George Washington from Benedict Arnold – March 11th of 1777 – see in *A Hero and A Spy*, by Russell Lea – pages 220 & 221

CHAPTER FIFTEEN

1. Letter from Benedict Arnold to General Alexander McDougall – April 27th of 1777, 10 am – view in *A Hero and A Spy*, by Russell Lea – page 228
2. Better description in *Benedict Arnold, Revolutionary Hero*, by J.K. Martin – pages 316 & 317
3. Ibid., pages 318 & 319
4. Ibid., page 319
5. Benedict's own description in letter to General McDougall on April 28th of 1777 – see in *A Hero and A Spy*, by Russell Lea – pages 229 & 230
6. Better description in *Benedict Arnold, Revolutionary Hero*, by J.K. Martin – page 321
7. Resolution of Congress for Arnold's appointment to Major General – May 2nd of 1777 – See *A Hero and A Spy*, by Russell Lea – pages 234 & 235
8. Better description in B*enedict Arnold, Revolutionary Hero*, by J.K. Martin – page 322

9. Letter from George Washington to the President of Congress – May12th of 1777 – see in *A Hero and A Spy*, by Russell Lea – pages 237 & 238

CHAPTER SIXTEEN
1. Letter from Benedict Arnold to the Hon. Continental Congress – May 20th of 1777 – see in *A Hero and A Spy*, by Russell Lea – page 238
2. Resolution of Congress from journals of the Continental Congress – see in *A Hero and A Spy*, by Russell Lea – page 239
3. Better description in *Benedict Arnold, Revolutionary Hero*, by J.K. Martin – page 327
4. Excerpt of letter from John Adams to Abigail Adams – see in *A Hero and A Spy*, by Russell Lea – page 239
5. More detailed descriptions in *Benedict Arnold, Revolutionary Hero*, by J.K. Martin – pages 332 & 333
6. Letter from George Washington to John Hancock – July 10th of 1777 – see in *A Hero and A Spy*, by Russell Lea – pages 245 & 246
7. Letter to Benedict Arnold from John Hancock – July 12th of 1777 – see in *A Hero and A Spy*, by Russell Lea – pages 246 & 247

CHAPTER SEVENTEEN
1. More detailed descriptions in *Benedict Arnold, Revolutionary Hero*, by J.K. Martin – pages 345-349
2. Ibid., pages 350 & 351
3. Letter from Benedict Arnold to George Washington with vivid descriptions of encounters – July 27th of 1777 – see in *A Hero and A Spy*, by Russell Lea – pages 248 & 249
4. More detailed descriptions in *Benedict Arnold, Revolutionary Hero*, by J.K. Martin – pages 358 & 359
5. Ibid., pages 360 & 361 – more detailed descriptions
6. Ibid., pages 362 & 363
7. Ibid., page 363
8. Note from Philip Schuyler to Benedict Arnold – August 13th of 1777 – see *A Hero and A Spy*, by Russell Lea – page 252

*Also trips to Oriskany Battlefield and family stories of the Battle of Oriskany – three family members in that battle

CHAPTER EIGHTEEN
1. Letter from Benedict Arnold to General Gates – August 21st of 1777 – see *A Hero and A Spy*, by Russell Lea – page 253
2. Letter from Benedict Arnold to General Gates – after war council – August 21st of 1777 – See in *A Hero and A Spy*, by Russell Lea – pages 253 & 254
3. Good description in *Benedict Arnold, Revolutionary Hero*, by J.K. Martin – page 366

4. See letter from Colonel Peter Gansevoort to Benedict Arnold – August 22nd of 1777 – describes retreating St. Leger forces – see *A Hero and A Spy*, by Russell Lea – pages 256 & 257
    *Also accounts in Herkimer County archives

CHAPTER NINETEEN
1. More detailed account in *Benedict Arnold, Revolutionary Hero*, by J.K. Martin – page 361
2. Ibid., page 364
3. Ibid., page 368 – also Van Schaick story, related by Shannon Kehn, member of the Peter Gansevoort Chapter of the Daughters of the American Revolution at Cohoes, NY
4. Ibid., page 368
5. Ibid., page 373
6. Ibid., page 372
7. Ibid., page 373
8. Ibid., page 374
9. Ibid., pages 375-377
10. Ibid., pages 377 & 378
11. Ibid., page 379
12. Later letter describing Arnold's actions by Capt. Ebenezer Wakefield, quotes in *Benedict Arnold, Revolutionary Hero*, by J.K. Martin – pages 379 & 380
13. Notes from James Wilkinson on Battle trying to discredit Arnold late the 19th – see in *A Hero and A Spy*, by Russell Lea – page 264
14. More detailed descriptions of aftermath of September 19th of 1777 – see *Benedict Arnold, Revolutionary Hero*, by J.K. Martin – pages 381-383
15. Letter from Richard Varick on September 22nd of 1777 – see in *A Hero and A Spy*, by Russell Lea – page 269
16. Accolades from other officers and soldiers – see *Benedict Arnold, Revolutionary Hero*, by J.K. Martin – page 384
17. Letter from Benedict Arnold to General Gates on September 22nd of 1777 – explains frustration with Arnold's request to leave camp and join Washington's army – see in *A Hero and A Spy*, by Russell Lea – pages 269-271
18. Two letters from Col. Henry B. Livingston to Gen. Schuyler – See *A Hero and A Spy*, by Russell Lea – pages 272-274
19. Better descriptions – see *Benedict Arnold, Revolutionary Hero*, by J.K. Martin – page 391
20. Ibid., pages 396 & 397
21. Ibid., pages 398 & 399
22. Ibid., page 400
23. Narrative of soldier Henry Dearborn – see *Benedict Arnold, Revolutionary Hero*, by J.K. Martin – pages 402 & 403
    *Also, must credit my trips to Saratoga Battlefield in Saratoga, New York – trips to Schuyler Mansion – New York Public Library digital archives of Schuyler papers – trips and my talks at VanSchaick Mansion in Cohoes, New York

CHAPTER TWENTY

1. Better and more detailed description in *Benedict Arnold, Revolutionary Hero*, by J.K. Martin – "A Violated Right Not Fully Restored" – pages 403-409

2. Lafayette letters-correspondence 1777-1778 – Lafayette trip to Albany – letter to Washington – February 19th of 1778 – see "Washington Papers" – digital archives by date

3. Letter from George Washington to Benedict Arnold – January 20th of 1778 – view in *A Hero and A Spy*, by Russell Lea – pages 293 & 294

4. Letter from Benedict Arnold to George Washington – March 12th of 1778 – George Washington Papers – description also in *Benedict Arnold, Revolutionary Hero*, by J.K. Martin – page 416

5. Letter from George Washington to Benedict Arnold – May 7th of 1778 – view in *A Hero and A Spy*, by Russell Lea – page 296

6. Description based on letters from Henry Dearborn and Lafayette – see in *Benedict Arnold, Revolutionary Hero*, by J.K. Martin – page 423

7. Letter from George Washington to Benedict Arnold – June 18th of 1778 – see in *A Hero and A Spy*, by Russell Lea – pages 299 & 300

CHAPTER TWENTY-ONE

1. Proclamation in Philadelphia by Major General Benedict Arnold on June 19th of 1778 – see *A Hero and A Spy*, by Russell M. Lea – page 300

2. Letter to the "Inhabitants of America" from Benedict Arnold explaining his reasons for switching sides, written on October 7th of 1780 – letter mentioned ignored Peace Commission of 1778 – see *A Hero and A Spy*, by Russell Lea – pages 544-546 – Peace Commission also explained in *Tragedy of Benedict Arnold*, by Joyce Lee Malcolm – pages 229 & 230 – best rendition and explanation of 1778 Peace Commission obtained orally from Randolph G. Flood, Director of Yorktown Museum, Yorktown, Virginia

3. Description *Benedict Arnold, Revolutionary Hero*, by J.K. Martin – see epilogue – pages 428 & 429

4. Letter from Benedict Arnold to George Washington on July 19th of 1778 – see in *A Hero and A Spy*, by Russell Lea – page 303

5. Letter from George Washington to Benedict Arnold on August 13th of 1778 – see in George Washington Papers, digital archives by date

6. Letter to Mercy Scollay from Benedict Arnold on July 15th of 1778 – see in *A Hero and A Spy*, by Russell Lea – pages 302 & 303

7. Letter from Benedict Arnold to George Washington on October 11th of 1778 – see in *A Hero and A Spy*, by Russell Lea – page 311

8. Letter from George Washington to Benedict Arnold on October 23rd of 1778 – see in *A Hero and A Spy*, by Russell Lea – pages 312 & 313

9. Description, including quote to "seize and harass British shipping wherever we found it and create havoc with the British line of supply" – see in *A Hero and A Spy*, by Russell Lea – page 313

10. Letter from Benedict Arnold to Miss Peggy Shippen on February 8th of 1779 – see in *A Hero and A Spy*, by Russell Lea – pages 316 & 317

11. Letter from Benedict Arnold to John Jay, Esq. on March 17th of 1779 – see in *A Hero and A Spy*, by Russell Lea – pages 321 & 322

12. Letter from Benedict Arnold to George Washington on March 19th of 1779 – see in *A Hero and A Spy*, by Russell Lea – page 323

13. Letter from Benedict Arnold to George Washington on May 5th of 1779 – see in *A Hero and A Spy*, by Russell Lea – pages 330 & 331

14. Letter from Colonel Beverly Robinson in May of 1779 – see in *A Hero and A Spy*, by Russell Lea – pages 331-334

15. Transcribed spy letter, not in Arnold's handwriting, referred to as "Monk" letter, signed by General George Monk – see digital archives of Clinton Collection at Clements Library, University of Michigan

CHAPTER TWENTY-TWO

1. Many descriptions of Andre' – see *Turncoat*, by Stephen Brumwell – pages 122-125

2. Letter to Gustavus Monk (Arnold) – July 1779 – see in *A Hero and A Spy*, by Russell Lea – pages 353 & 353

3. Letter from George Washington to Benedict Arnold – June 2nd of 1779 – postponement – see *A Hero and A Spy*, by Russell Lea – pages 345 & 346

4. Clinton Sullivan Campaign – New York Archives – see also *The Wilderness War*, by Allan W. Eckert – pages 327-435

5. Letter from Benedict Arnold to President of Congress Samuel Huntington, Esq. – October 6th of 1779 – see *A Hero and A Spy*, by Russell Lea – pages 361 & 362

6. Court martial details from January 21st of 1780 – see *A Hero and A Spy*, by Russell Lea – pages 365-380

CHAPTER TWENTY-THREE

1. George Washington Papers, digital archives by date – see also George Washington and Benedict Arnold : A Tale of Two Patriots, by Dave R. Palmer "The Black Year"

2. Letter from Benedict Arnold to Silas Deane on March 22nd of 1780 – see in *A Hero and A Spy*, by Russell Lea – page 385

3. Benedict Arnold to George Washington on March 20th of 1780 – see in *A Hero and A Spy*, by Russell Lea – page 384

4. Letter from George Washington to Benedict Arnold on March 28th of 1780 – see in *A Hero and A Spy*, by Russell Lea – pages 385 & 386

5. Letter from George Washington to Benedict Arnold on April 6th of 1780 – see in *A Hero and A Spy*, by Russell Lea – page 386

CHAPTER TWENTY-FOUR

1. Letter from J. Moore, Benedict's code name, to John Anderson, Andre's code name, on July 11th of 1780 – see in *A Hero and A Spy*, by Russell Lea – pages 398 & 399

2. Letter from J. Moore, Benedict's code name, to John Anderson, Andre's code name, on July 12th of 1780 – see in *A Hero and A Spy*, by Russell Lea – pages 399 & 400

3. Letter from Benedict Arnold to Congress on July 17th of 1780 – see in *A Hero and A Spy*, by Russell Lea – page 402

4. Letter from J. Osbourne to J. Carleton included with letter from J. Anderson (Andre's code name) on July 24th of 1780 – see in *A Hero and A Spy*, by Russell Lea – both letters on pages 403-405

CHAPTER TWENTY-FIVE
1. Washington's general orders of the day on August 1st of 1780 – see in George Washington Papers, digital archives by date – also in *A Hero and A Spy*, by Russell Lea – pages 406 & 407
2. Letter from George Washington to Benedict Arnold on August 3rd of 1780 – see George Washington Papers, digital archives by date – also *A Hero and A Spy*, by Russell Lea – pages 408 & 409
3. Letter from Benedict Arnold to Major General Robert Howe on August 5th of 1780 – see in *A Hero and A Spy*, by Russell Lea – page 411
4. Letter from George Washington to Benedict Arnold on August 5th of 1780 – see in *A Hero and A Spy*, by Russell Lea – pages 412 & 413
5. Viewed in letters from Colonel Thaddeus Kosciuszko to George Washington and response – found in George Washington Papers, digital archives by date
6. Letter from Benedict Arnold to George Washington on August 8th of 1780 – see in *A Hero and A Spy*, by Russell Lea – pages 413 & 414 – also letter from George Washington to Benedict Arnold on August 11th of 1780 – see *A Hero and A Spy*, by Russell Lea – page 415
7. Letter from Benedict Arnold to George Washington on August 12th of 1780 – see *A Hero and A Spy*, by Russell Lea – pages 416 & 417
8. Letter from Benedict Arnold to Colonel Timothy Pickering, Quartermaster General, on August 16th of 1780 – see *A Hero and A Spy*, by Russell Lea – page 421
9. Letter to John Anderson (code name Andre') from Benedict Arnold (code name Gustavus) on August 30th of 1780 – see *A Hero and A Spy*, by Russell Lea – pages 425 & 426

CHAPTER TWENTY-SIX
1. Best descriptions of Smith family and Joshua Hett Smith in *Accomplice to Treason*, by Richard J. Koke – Part 1 – pages 3-43
2. Letter from Joshua Hett Smith, Esq. to Benedict Arnold on August 13th of 1780 – see *A Hero and A Spy*, by Russell Lea – pages 418-420
3. Better description in *Accomplice to Treason*, by Richard J. Koke – Chapter 7, page 70

CHAPTER TWENTY-SEVEN
1. See more detailed explanation in *Benedict Arnold, Revolutionary Hero*, by J.K. Martin – pages 194 & 195

CHAPTER TWENTY-EIGHT
1. Letter from Gustavus (Arnold) to John Anderson (Andre') on August 30th of 1780 – see *A Hero and A Spy*, by Russell Lea – pages 425 & 426
2. Letter from Benedict Arnold to Colonel Elisha Sheldon on September 1st of 1780

Letter from Benedict Arnold to Colonel Elisha Sheldon on September 7th of 1780

Letter from John Anderson (Andre') to Colonel Elisha Sheldon on September 7th of 1780

See above letters in *A Hero and A Spy*, by Russell Lea – pages 426-430

3. Letter from George Washington to Major General Arnold on September 2nd of 1780 – see A Hero and A Spy, by Richard Lea – page 427

4. Letter from Benedict Arnold to Colonel James Livingston on September 4th of 1780 – see *A Hero and A Spy*, by Russell Lea – pages 427 & 428

5. Letter from George Washington to Major General Arnold on September 7th of 1780 – see *A Hero and A Spy*, by Russell Lea – page 430

6. Letter from John Jameson to Benedict Arnold on September 9th of 1780 – see *A Hero and A Spy*, by Russell Lea – pages 432 & 433

7. Letter from Benedict Arnold to Colonel Sheldon on September 10th of 1780 – see *A Hero and A Spy*, by Russell Lea – page 433

CHAPTER TWENTY-NINE

1. Letter from Gustavus (Arnold) to John Anderson (Andre') – September 10th of 1780 – see in *A Hero and A Spy*, by Russell Lea – pages 433 & 434

2. Letter from Benedict Arnold to George Washington – September 11th of 1780 – see in *A Hero and A Spy*, by Russell Lea – page 43

3. Letter from Beverly Robinson to Gustavus Monk (Arnold) – September 16th of 1780 – see *A Hero and A Spy*, by Russell Lea – page 443

CHAPTER THIRTY

1. Actual letter from Benedict Arnold to George Washington – September 12th of 1780 – see *A Hero and A Spy*, by Russell Lea – pages 436 & 437

2. Letter from Benedict Arnold to Major General Nathanael Greene – September 12th of 1780 – see *A Hero and A Spy*, by Russell Lea – pages 437 & 438

3. Letter from Gustavus (Arnold) to John Anderson (Andre') – September 15th of 1780 – see *A Hero and A Spy*, by Russell Lea – pages 441-442

4. Letter from Benedict Arnold to Colonel Elisha Sheldon – September 13th of 1780 – see *A Hero and A Spy*, by Russell Lea – page 439

5. Letter from Benedict Arnold to Major Benjamin Tallmadge – September 13th of 1780 – see in *A Hero and A Spy*, by Russell Lea – pages 438 & 439

CHAPTER THIRTY-ONE

1. Letter from Gustavus (Arnold) to John Anderson (Andre') – September 10th of 1780 – see *A Hero and A Spy*, by Russell Lea – pages 433 & 434

2. Description of Tallmadge's relationship with Nathan Hale – well described in *A Hero and A Spy*, by Russell Lea – page 517

3. Based on previous reference to letter from Benedict Arnold to Tallmadge – September 13th of 1780 – *A Hero and A Spy*, by Russell Lea – pages 438 & 439 – also Tallmadge's whereabouts in Lower Salem during Washington's visit to Hartford, Connecticut – also map notes of locations of J.H. Smith, Col. James Livingston and Tallmadge

CHAPTER THIRTY-TWO
1. Notes from Livingston to Arnold – September 13th of 1780 – note from Arnold to Livingston – September 13th of 1780 – see *A Hero and A Spy*, by Russell Lea – page 438
2. Letter from Benedict Arnold to Colonel John Lamb – September 13th of 1780 – see in *A Hero and A Spy*, by Russell Lea – page 439
3. Letter from Benedict Arnold to George Washington – *A Hero and A Spy*, by Russell Lea – pages 440 & 441
4. Letter from Beverly Robinson to Gustavus Monk (Arnold) – September 16th of 1780 – *A Hero and A Spy*, by Russell Lea – page 443
5. Letter from George Washington to Benedict Arnold with ps – September 14th of 1780 – see *A Hero and A Spy*, by Russell Lea – 442
6. Letter from Gustavus (Benedict) to John Anderson (Andre') – September 15th of 1780 – see *A Hero and A Spy*, by Russell Lea – page 443
7. Letter from Benedict Arnold to Colonel Lamb – September 16th of 1780 – see *A Hero and A Spy*, by Russell Lea – pages 443 & 444
8. Letter from Benedict Arnold to George Washington – September 16th of 1780 – see *A Hero and A Spy*, by Russell Lea – page 444

CHAPTER THIRTY-THREE
1. Descriptions of meeting in *A Hero and A Spy*, by Russell Lea – pages 444 & 445
2. Letter from Beverly Robinson to Benedict Arnold from on board Vulture on September 17th of 1780 – see in *A Hero and A Spy*, by Russell Lea – page 445
3. Descriptions of Hudson River crossing – *A Hero and A Spy*, by Russell Lea – pages 445-447

CHAPTER THIRTY-FOUR
1. Letter from Benedict Arnold to Beverly Robinson on September 18th of 1780 – see *A Hero and A Spy*, by Russell Lea – pages 447 & 448
2. Note from Gustavus (Benedict Arnold) to John Anderson (Andre') on September 18th of 1780 – see *A Hero and A Spy*, by Russell Lea – page 448
3. Description of Joshua Smith's meeting with New York Governor George Clinton – detailed description in *Accomplice to Treason* by Richard Koke – page 70, 71
4. Letter from Beverly Robinson to General Arnold from on board Vulture on September 19th of 1780 – see *A Hero and A Spy*, by Russell Lea – pages 449 & 450
5. Letter from Benedict Arnold to Colonel James Livingston on September 19th of 1780 – see in *A Hero and A Spy*, by Russell Lea – page 450

CHAPTER THIRTY-FIVE
1. Pass from Benedict Arnold for Joshua Smith, Esq. on September 20th of 1780 – see in *A Hero and A Spy*, by Russell Lea – pages 453 & 454
2. Letter from John Lamb at West Point to Colonel Livingston on September 20th of 1780 – see in *A Hero and A Spy*, by Russell Lea – page 453
3. From Major Edward Kierse testimony at Joshua Hett Smith's trial on October

20th of 1780 – see in Joshua H. Smith, *Accomplice to Treason*, by Richard Koke – page 173

4. Letter from John Andre' to Sir Henry Clinton on board the Vulture on September 21st of 1780 – see in *A Hero and A Spy*, by Russell Lea – page 455

CHAPTER THIRTY-SIX

1. Letter from John Andre' to Sir Henry Clinton from on board the Vulture on September 21st of 1780 – see *A Hero and A Spy*, by Russell Lea – page 455

2. Letter from ship Captain A. Sutherland to Major General Arnold from on board the Vulture on September 21st of 1780 – see *A Hero and A Spy*, by Russell Lea – pages 455 & 456

3. Letter from Beverly Robinson to Major General Arnold on September 21st of 1780 – see *A Hero and A Spy*, by Russell Lea – page 456

4. More detailed descriptions of events at ferry crossing on September 20th of 1780 – see in Joshua H. Smith, *Accomplice to Treason*, by Richard Koke – pages 72-74

5. Assumption made by Smith's request to get papers for his defense on the way to trial – see Joshua H. Smith, *Accomplice to Treason*, by R. Koke – page 130

6. Testimony of Cahoon brothers at J.H. Smith trial – see Joshua H. Smith, *Accomplice to Treason*, by R. Koke – pages 141-143

CHAPTER THIRTY-SEVEN

1. Pass from Benedict Arnold for J.H. Smith to travel by water to travel by water to Dobbs Ferry on September 21st of 1780 – see in *A Hero and A Spy*, by Russell Lea – page 459 – also well-described in Joshua H. Smith, *Accomplice to Treason*, by R. Koke – pages 78 & 79

2. Letter from Benedict Arnold to Colonel Beverly Robinson on September 21st of 1780 – see Joshua H. Smith, *Accomplice to Treason*, by R. Koke – page 78

3. Pass from Benedict Arnold to J.H. Smith, Anderson and two servants to pass guards at Kings Ferry on September 20th of 1780 – see in *A Hero and A Spy*, by Russell Lea – pages 453 & 454

4. Better and more detailed description of events from the Vulture to Long Cove – see Joshua H. Smith, *Accomplice to Treason*, by R. Koke – pages 81-86

CHAPTER THIRTY-EIGHT

1. Best description in Joshua H. Smith, *Accomplice to Treason*, by R. Koke – pages 86 & 87

2. Letter from Beverly Robinson to Sir Henry Clinton from the Vulture, off Sing-Sing on September 24th of 1780 – see in *A Hero and A Spy*, by Russell Lea – pages 490-492

CHAPTER THIRTY-NINE

1. Quote from John Andre' on September 29th of 1780 – see a more detailed account in Joshua H. Smith, *Accomplice to Treason*, by R. Koke – page 88 – also view in the New York State Library at Albany, New York

2. Passes written by Benedict Arnold for J.H. Smith to travel by boat with three

hands on September 22nd of 1780 – see in Joshua H. Smith, *Accomplice to Treason*, by R. Koke – page 89

3. Better and more detailed description in "Journey to Westchester" – see Joshua H. Smith, *Accomplice to Treason*, by R. Koke – pages 94-99

4. Description presented by Joshua H. Smith book by Smith – *An Authentic Narrative of the Causes Which Led to the Death of Major Andre', Adjutant General of His Majesty's Forces in North America* – pages 26 & 27

5. More detailed description – see Joshua H. Smith, *Accomplice to Treason*, by R. Koke – page 97

6. Ibid., pages 98 & 99

CHAPTER FORTY

1. Sgt. John Paulding's application to Congress for pension increase in 1817 – many descriptions, particular one in Joshua H. Smith, *Accomplice to Treason*, by R. Koke – page 244

2. Letter from John Jameson to Lieutenant Solomon Allen on September 23rd of 1780 – see in *A Hero and A Spy*, by Russell Lea – page 485

3. Letter from John Jameson to Major General Arnold on September 23rd of 1780 – see in *A Hero and A Spy*, by Russell Lea – page 493

4. Letter from John Jameson to 'His Excellency' George Washington on September 23rd of 1780 – see *A Hero and A Spy*, by Russell Lea – page 484

5. Letter from John Jameson to His Excellency George Washington on September 27th of 1780 – see *A Hero and A Spy*, by Russell Lea – page 515

CHAPTER FORTY-ONE

1. Documents questioned – in Arnold's handwriting – no documents were signed by General Arnold – documents 4 & 5 were examined by R. Joseph Talbert & Associates, Document Examiners, Rome, New York

2. All treason papers can be viewed in New York State Historical Digital Archives in Albany, New York – New York State Historical Museum

3. For easy reference, all treason papers allegedly carried by Andre' at his capture can be viewed in *A Hero and A Spy*, by Russell Lea – pages 462-469

CHAPTER FORTY-TWO

1. Letter from Adjutant General John Andre' to His Excellency George Washington written from Salem on September 24th of 1780 – see in *A Hero and A Spy*, by Russell Lea – pages 488 & 489

2. Descriptions in many books, especially George Washington and Benedict Arnold, *A Tale of Two Patriots* by Dave R. Palmer – pages 364 & 365 – see also *A Hero and A Spy*, by Russell Lea – page 493

3. More detailed account of altercation between J.H. Smith and Arnold's aides – see *Accomplice to Treason*, by R. Koke – pages 100-102

CHAPTER FORTY-THREE

1. Letter from John Jameson to Major General Arnold on September 23rd of 1780

– see in *A Hero and A Spy*, by Russell Lea – page 493

2. Description of events – see Joshua H. Smith, *Accomplice to Treason*, by R. Koke – page 109

3. Description of events – see *A Hero and A Spy*, by Russell Lea – page 495

4. Better description of events – see *A Hero and A Spy*, by Russell Lea – pages 495 & 496

CHAPTER FORTY-FOUR

1. Detailed description of events – see *A Hero and A Spy*, by Russell Lea – pages 493-497

2. Actual letters from George Washington to Col. Nathaniel Wade, Lt. Colonel Ebenezer Gray, Col. John Lamb, Lt. Col. John Lamb, Lt. Col. John Jameson, Maj. Gen. Nathanael Greene, Major Law, William Betts, officer in command the wood cutting party (200 men in charge of cutting wood) – on September 25th of 1780 – see *A Hero and A Spy*, by Russell Lea – pages 501-503

3. Note from George Washington to Col. James Livingston on September 25th of 1780 – see *A Hero and A Spy*, by Russell Lea – page 502

4. Letter from Benedict Arnold to George Washington on September 25th of 1780 – written from Vulture – see *A Hero and A Spy*, by Russell Lea – pages 499 & 450

5. Letter from Beverly Robinson, "Colonel of Loyal Americans" to His Excellency George Washington on September 25th of 1780 – see *A Hero and A Spy*, by Russell Lea – page 500

6. Letter from J.H. Smith to his brother Thomas Smith on September 26th of 1780 – see in Joshua H. Smith, *Accomplice to Treason*, by R. Koke – page 119

7. Letter from George Washington to President of Congress on September 26th of 1780 – see in *A Hero and A Spy*, by Russell Lea – page 508

8. Letter from George Washington to Governor Clinton on September 26th of 1780 – see in *A Hero and A Spy*, by Russell Lea – page 509

9. Letter from Nathanael Greene to his wife on October 2nd of 1780 – see quote in *Benedict Arnold, Revolutionary Hero*, by J.K. Martin – in prologue, page 9

CHAPTER FORTY-FIVE

1. Letter from John Jameson to His Excellency General Washington on September 27th of 1780 – see in *A Hero and A Spy*, by Russell Lea – page 515

2. Letter from Benedict Arnold to His Excellency General Washington
written on board Vulture on September 25th of 1780 – see *A Hero and A Spy*, by Russell Lea – pages 499 & 500

3. Letter from General Washington to John Laurance, Esq. – Judge Advocate on September 26th of 1780 – see *A Hero and A Spy*, by Russell Lea – page 510

4. Letter from George Washington to Major General Nathanael Green on September 27th of 1780 – see *A Hero and A Spy*, by Russell Lea – page 514

5. Good, detailed description of events at the "White House" and ransacking of Joshua Smith's property and papers – see in J.H. Smith, *Accomplice to Treason*, by R. Koke – page 130

CHAPTER FORTY-SIX
1. Detailed descriptions of Andre's and J.H. Smith trials – see J.H. Smith, *Accomplice to Treason*, by R. Koke – pages 133-177
2. Letter from John Andre', Adjutant General to Sir Henry Clinton on September 29th of 1780 – see in *A Hero and A Spy*, by Russell Lea – pages 525 & 526
3. Letter to Board of General Officers at Tappan from George Washington on September 30th of 1780 *A Hero and A Spy*, by Russell Lea – page 526
4. Letter from Benedict Arnold to George Washington on October 1st of 1780 – see *A Hero and A Spy*, by Russell Lea – pages 537 & 538
5. Letter from John Andre', Adjutant General to His Excellency George Washington on October 1st of 1780 – see *A Hero and A Spy*, by Russell Lea – pages 537 & 538
6. Description of Andre's execution – see J.H. Smith, *Accomplice to Treason*, by R. Koke – pages 150 & 151
7. Much more detailed description of J.H. Smith's escape – see J.H. Smith, *Accomplice to Treason*, by R. Koke – see Chapter 16 "Escape"

CHAPTER FORTY-SEVEN
1. Letter from Benedict Arnold to George Washington on October 5th, 1780 – see in *A Hero and A Spy*, by R. Lea – pages 543 & 544
2. Proclamation of the Supreme Executive Council of Pennsylvania on October 27th of 1780 – see in *The Tragedy of Benedict Arnold*, by Joyce Lee Malcolm – pages 329 & 330
3. Letter from Benedict Arnold to Inhabitants of America written on October 7th of 1780 – see in *A Hero and A Spy*, by R. Lea – pages 544-546
4. Proclamation by Brigadier General Arnold – published on October 20th of 1780 – see in *A Hero and A Spy*, by Russell Lea – pages 563-565
5. Letter from George Washington to Major General M. Lafayette on February 20th of 1781 – more detailed description of Virginia Campaign – see *Turncoat*, by Stephen Brumwell – pages 311-316
6. Good description of mutiny attempt – see *Turncoat* by Stephen Brumwell – page 313

CHAPTER FORTY-EIGHT
1. Description of events in Guadeloupe – see *Turncoat*, by Stephen Brumwell – pages 328 & 329
2. Letter from Peggy Arnold to Edward Shippen Arnold on July 1st of 1801 – see descriptions in *Benedict Arnold, Revolutionary Hero*, by J.K. Martin in Epilogue – pages 430 & 432
3. Last Will & Testament of Benedict Arnold, best reference found in *Tragedy of Benedict Arnold*, by Joyce Lee Malcolm – pages 332 & 333

INDEX

Adams, John, 106, 109, 135, 148
Adams, Samuel, 20, 22, 66; Stamp Act and, 20
Adamson, Sydney, 80
Adirondacks, 113
African American slaves, 219
Albany, New York, 95
Albany Post Road, 200
Allen, Ethan, 26, 28, 29, 30–31, 32
Allen, Herman, 26
Allen, Solomon, 205–206, 212
American navy, 92; arrival at Fort Ticonderoga, 93; Benedict Arnold and, 86–93; fleet, 87; gundalows, 87; lack of experience sailors for, 87; row galleys, 87; supplies, 86; in Valcour Bay, 90–92
American Revolution: main groups at war, 13
Andre, John, 151–153, 165, 198–202, 225; adjutant general for British Army, 168; ambush of, 227; capture of, 204–206; code name, 168, 169, 177, 180, 185; dangerous parcel of papers, 206–208; execution of, 221, 228; face-to-face meeting with Benedict Arnold, 192–194; letter from Benedict Arnold, 160, 168; letter to Henry Clinton, 220; negotiation with Benedict Arnold, 161; pass for, 198; September 20th secret meeting, 185–187; trapped behind enemy lines, 196–197; trial at Tappan, New York, 220; uniform, 188, 193, 196, 216; Vertical integration, 185
apothecary, 18
aristocracies, 12
Arnold, Absalom, 16
Arnold, Benedict, 84, 149; American navy and, 86–93; apothecary business in New Haven, 18; arrival at Fort Ticonderoga, 93; assistance to Joseph Warren's family, 146; athletic abilities, 16; Baron von Steuben and, 141; Battle of Cowpens, 230–231; at Battle of Saratoga, 123–131; at Bemis Heights, 123–131; Benjamin Tallmadge and, 236; boarding the Vulture, 212–213; in Boston, Mass., 98; burning of New London, 231; by-passed for promotion, 98; at Cambridge, Mass., 26; Canadian campaign expenses, 157; capture on Guadalupe, 232–233; children of, 21, 157, 231, 233; code name, 192–193; confrontation with James Easton, 32; Constitutional Party and, 145–146; Continental Congress and, 40, 106, 121; council of war and, 55, 90, 117, 173, 177; court martial, 149, 153; at Crown Point, 34; in Danbury, Conn., 103; dangerous parcel of papers, 206–208; David Wooster and, 68–70; death of, 233; debts, 20; detachment of, 60–61; early childhood, 16–17; early contacts, 235; education of, 16, 17; face-to-face meeting with John Andre, 192–194; family, 15–19; fighting for Britain, 229–231; formation of militia, 22; in Fort Stanwix, 119; at Fort Ticonderega, 27–28; at Freeman's Farm, 125–126; George Washington and, 41–44, 47, 96, 99–100, 106, 142–143, 211; Green Mountain Boys and, 29; Guy Carlton and, 61; headquarters at Robinson House, 163; hiding near Lexington, 24; home in New Haven Connecticut, 78; home of, 21; Hon Yost Schuyler and, 118; Horatio Gates and, 122, 128; injuries of, 62, 131, 139–140; James Livingston and, 177, 236–237; John Thomas and, 70–72; Joseph Reed and, 145–146; Joshua Smith and, 165–166, 236–237; letter from Beverly Robinson, 149–150, 181; letter from Elisha Sheldon, 169; letter from George Washington, 96, 169; letter from John Jameson, 169, 205–206; letter to Benjamin Tallmadge, 174; letter to Elisha Sheldon, 169; letter to forces in Montreal, 64; letter to George Washington, 99–100, 145–146, 148, 163, 173, 177, 215; letter to Horatio Gates, 74, 117; letter

272

to John Andre, 160, 168; letter to Peggy Arnold, 148; letter to Philip Schuyler, 66; letter to Silas Deane, 156; in London, 232; march to Boston, 25; Marquis de Lafayette and, 140; marriage to Peggy, 149; martial law in Philadelphia, 144; meeting near Dobbs Ferry, 171–172; as merchant, 19, 232–233; missed meeting, 189; Nathanael Green opinion of, 216; Naval Board and, 156–157; in New Brunswick, 233; in New Haven, Conn., 18–19, 96, 100; in Newburyport, Mass., 45; passes, 192, 198; in Philadelphia, Penn., 102–105, 108–109, 109, 144–148; Philip Schuyler and, 38–39; political problems, 235; promotion to brigadier general, 68; in Providence, Rhode Is., 97, 98–99; public reprimand from George Washington, 157; Quebec campaign, 55–58; recovery from injuries, 139–142, 142; recruitment of American officers and soldiers, 230; reputation of, 95; resignation of commission, 33, 100; in Ridgefield, Conn., 104–105; at Sartigan, 50; sea skills of, 19; Second Continental Congress and, 33; September 20th secret meeting, 185–188; Siege of Yorktown, 231; smuggling of goods, 20, 97; storming of Quebec, 60–64; trial of John Andre, 220–221; uniform, 98; in Valley Forge, 142–143; voyage to Quebec, 45–52; war council and, 90; at West Point, 162–164, 235–236
Arnold, Benedict, Sr., 16
Arnold, Benedict VI, 21
Arnold, Elizabeth, 16
Arnold, Hannah, 15, 16, 18, 39, 95, 100, 233
Arnold, Hannah King, 15–16
Arnold, Henry, 21
Arnold, Margaret (Peggy) Mansfield, 21, 39,
Arnold, Margaret (Peggy) Shippen, 146, 147,148, 152, 157, 171, 173, 212, 214, 218, 231, 232, 233, 235
Arnold, Mary, 16
Arnold, Oliver, 15
Arnold, Richard, 21
Arnold family: partible inheritance, 15; in Rhode Island, 15
Arnold's Point, 89

Babcock, Adam, 19
bateaus, 30, 43, 45, 47, 73, 80, 88, 173
Battle of Brandywine Creek, 152
Battle of Bunker Hill, 36
Battle of Cowpens, 230–231
Battle of Monmouth, 152
Battle of Oriskany, 137
Battle of Quebec, 49
Battle of Washington, 95
Baum, Friedrich, 114
Bauman, Sebastian, 207
Bemis Heights, 123
Bergen County, 208
Berkeley Mansion, 230
 black market, 12
Board of Treasury, 157
Board of War, 108
Boston (ship), 87
Boston, Mass.: Benedict Arnold in, 98; siege of, 25

Boston Massacre, 21
Boston Tea Party, 22
Boyd, Ebenezer, 200
Brandywine Creek, Battle of, 152
Brant, Joseph, 115
Brown, John, 167
  Burgoyne, John, 75, 85, 110; at Freeman's Farm, 126–127; march to Albany, 112–115, 123–124; portrait of, 223; push across the Hudson River, 122; ruthless tactics, 113; surrender of, 131
Burr, Aaron, 43, 57

Cahoon, Samuel, 187, 189, 191; meeting with John Andre, 192–194
Cambridge, Mass., 26
Camden, South Carolina, 168–169
Campo Hill, 105
capital punishment, 46
Carleton, Guy, 31, 54–55, 61–62, 65, 85, 95; Benedict Arnold and, 61
Carroll, Charles, 71, 73–74
Caughnawaga Indians, 72
Chadwick, Charles Wesley, 80
Champlain Valley, 92
Chappel, Alonzo, 79
Charleston, South Carolina, 156, 157; fall of, 161
Chase, Samuel, 71, 73–74
Clinton, George, 179, 182
Clinton, Henry, 14, 143, 152, 156, 189, 195, 197, 199, 213, 220–221, 230
Coercive Acts, 22
Colburn, Reuben, 42–43, 45
  colonists, early American: classed society, 12; daily life of, 10–11; employment, 11; food, 11; house, 11; lighting, 11; prohibition against trace with other nations, 12; prostitution, 13
Compound Road, 200
Concord, 24
Congress (ship), 87
Connecticut (ship), 87
Constitutional Party, 145
  Continental Congress: Benedict Arnold and, 40, 106; George Washington and, 36–37; Horatio Gates and, 120; relocation of capital, 139
Continental currency, 159
Continental Northern Army Department, 33
Conway Cabal, 99
Cornwallis, Charles, 169, 231
council of war, 55, 84, 90, 115, 117, 169, 173, 177, 179, 208
court martial, 149, 153
cowboys, 200
Cowpens, Battle of, 230–231
Crown Point, 29, 32, 34, 70, 84, 133
Culper spy ring, 144, 152
Curtis, Martha Dandridge, 36

cutters, 87

D' Rochambeau, Compte, 179
Danbury, Conn., 103
dangerous parcel of papers, 206–208, 209–210, 214
d'Arsac, Charles Louis, 160–161
Dead River, 47, 51
Deane, Silas, 156
Dearborn, Henry, 43, 131
DeBlois, Elizabeth, 98, 100
debts, 20
Declaration of Independence, 84
Delaplace, William, 29
diphteria, 16–17
Dobbs Ferry, 171–172
dogs as food, 50
Dorcester Heights, 66–67
dragoons, 168, 169, 175, 201, 204, 212, 218, 219

Easton, James, 32
Egg Harbor incident, 147
Elmira, New York, 153
Enos, Roger, 47–48
Enterprise (ship), 30–31, 87
Eustis, William, 180

Finger Lakes, 153, 218
Fink, Denman, 80
First Continental Congress: delegates, 22; George Washington and, 36; upper-class members in, 12
Fishkill, 209–210
Foote, Ebenzer, 201
Forster, George, 72–73
Fort Anne, 72
Fort Dayton, 119
Fort Lee, 95
Fort Stanwix, 115, 116, 119, 135
Fort Ticonderoga, 26, 27, 27–28, 70, 78, 79, 84, 86, 93, 95, 120
France, 142, 144
Franklin, Benjamin, 71, 79, 145
Franks, David S., 180–181, 212
Fraser, Simon, 124, 125
Freeman's Farm, 125–126
French and Indian War, 15
French Catholics, 14
French-Canadian Catholics, 42
frostbite, 61, 67

Gage, Thomas, 22

gangs, 200
Gates, Horatio, 37, 110; in Albany, 83; attempt to replace Washington, 143; at Bemis Heights, 123–124; Benedict Arnold and, 88, 122, 128; in Camden, South Carolina, 168–169, 173; Continental Congress and, 120; defensive battle plans, 86; head of southern command, 157; letter from Benedict Arnold, 74; letter to Benedict Arnold, 117; letter to Congress, 121; Philip Schuyler and, 83; portrait of, 133; smear campaign against Benedict Arnold, 97
George (King of Great Britain), 13
George, King, 232, 233
German Flats, 117
Glover, John, 123
Great Britain: peace offerings, 145; war against France, 144
Great Carrying Place, 47–48, 80
Green Mountain Boys, 26, 28, 29, 114
Greene, Christopher, 43
Greene, Nathanael, 155, 173, 216
Grey, Charles, 152
Grier, Joseph, 50
Guadalupe, 232–233
gundalows, 87

Hale, Nathan, 175, 209
Hancock, John, 19, 22, 106, 110, 146; election as president of Second ContinentaCongress, 28; hiding near Lexington, 24; letter to George Washington, 107
Hanyery, 136
Haverstraw Bay, 171, 219
Hay's Landing, 192, 197
Hendrix, William, 44
Henry, Patrick, 22, 145
Herkimer, Nicholas, 115, 116
Hessians, 114
Hinman, Benjamin, 38
Howe, Richard, 85, 109, 112, 139, 143, 152
Howe, William, 85
Hudson Highlands, 169
Hudson River Valley, 124

Independence Hall, 108, 109
inflation, 159
Iroquois Nation, 84, 115
Isle Au Noix: makeshift hospital on, 74, 75

Jameson, John, 169, 205–206, 217
Jay, Jonathan, 148
Jefferson, Thomas, 66, 145, 230; Monticello farm, 11–12
Jersey (ship), 87
Johnson, William, 115

Kennebec River, 42, 45, 46, 80

Kierse, Edward, 185, 187, 189, 190, 200, 218
King, Absalom, 16
King, Hannah Waterman, 15–16. See Arnold, Hannah King
King's Ferry, 179, 189
Kosciuszko, Thaddeus, 122–123, 163

Lady Agent 355, 175, 218
Lafayette, Marquis de (Gilbert du Motier), 140, 143, 158, 224, 230
Lake Champlain region, 26, 27, 29–30, 54, 84, 95
Lake George, 113
Lake Megantic, 48, 50
Lake Ontario, 70
Lamb, John, 97, 105, 159, 177, 179, 180–181, 186–187, 214
Lancaster, Penn.: relocation of capital to, 139
Lathrop family, 17–18
Laurance, John, 218
Lee (ship), 87
Les Bostannais, 50
Lexington Green, 24
Liberty (ship), 30, 33
Liberty (ship), 87, 91
Lincoln, Benjamin, 99
Little Egg Harbor, 147
Livingston, James, 167, 190, 215; bateaus from Benedict Arnold, 173; Benedict Arnold and,
  236–237; capture of John Andre, 199–200; mission to capture John Andre, 177, 180, 183–184, 186–187; at Peekskill, 169; reward for John Andre's capture, 218
Long Cove, 192
Loyalists, 13, 105; nervousness about Benedict Arnold, 21
Ludington, Sybil, 102–103

Maclean, Allen, 55
Mansfield, Samuel, 39
Mason, George, 145
Massachusetts Committee of Safety, 26, 27–28, 32, 36, 38, 39
McBarron, Hugh Charles, Jr., 134
McCormick, James, 46
McCrea, Jane, 113
Medal of Valor, 217
Meigs, Jonathan, 180
Meigs, Return, 64
middle class, 12
Middlebrook Heights, 109
Midnight Ride, 24
Mifflin, Thomas, 99
militia groups, 12–13, 22, 114–115, 147, 217
Miller Farm, 201
Minisceongo Creek, 190
Mohawk Indians, 46, 51, 84, 115

Mohawk River, 119
Mohawk Valley, 115, 116
Monmouth, Battle of, 152
Montgomery, Richard, 57; letter about Benedict Arnold's detachment, 60–61; storming of Quebec, 60–64
Montreal, 70
Morgan, Daniel, 43, 44, 46, 62–63, 79, 114, 123, 129, 157, 169, 230; colonel's commission, 97; at Saratoga, 134; surrender of, 63, 82
Morristown, New Jersey, 155
Mott, Edward, 26
Mount Defiance, 34, 112
Murphy, Timothy, 130
mutiny, 155

Natanis, 46, 51
Native Americans: assault on Montreal, 70; as couriers for Benedict Arnold, 55; Mohawks, 84; Natanis, 51; Oneidas, 115; Senecas, 84; St. Francis Indians, 42; Tuscaroras, 115
Naval Board, 156–157
New Brunswick, 233
New Haven, Conn.: apothecary business of Benedict Arnold in, 18–19
New Haven (ship), 87
New London, burning of, 231
New York City, 109, 129, 144, 153, 163, 165, 187, 194–195, 209, 213, 220, 222
New York Harbor, 78, 84
New York (ship), 87
Newburyport, Mass., 45
Newfoundland, 60
Norridgewock Falls, 47
Norwalk, Conn.: British detachment in, 102

Oneida Indians, 115, 117, 136
Oriskany, Battle of, 137
Oswald, Eleazer, 30, 44, 47

Parliamentary Peace Commission of 1778, 145, 229
Parsons, Samuel, 25–26
partible inheritance, 15
Patriots, 13
Paulding, John, 204, 217
Peekskill, 107, 161, 169, 179, 190
Peggy (ship), 39, 68, 149
Pennsylvania Council, 158
Pennsylvania State House, 108
Philadelphia (ship), 87
Philadelphia, Penn., 108–109, 143; martial law, 144
Philadelphia II (gunboat), 132
Pickering, Timothy, 164, 173
Pines Bridge, 204

Plains of Abraham, 63
pneumonia, 67
Pointe-Aux-Trembles, 57
port cities, 12
Proclamation of 1763, 12
prostitution, 13
Protestants, 14
Providence (ship), 87
Providence, Rhode Island, 97, 98-99
Provincial Congress, 39-40. See also Massachusetts Committee of Safety
Puritans, 14

Quartering Act, 22
Quebec, 42, 55-58, 81; storming of, 60-64, 81
Quebec Act of 1774, 12

Red Coats, 13, 162
Redding, Conn,: militia groups in, 103
Reed Joseph, 145, 147-148, 158
religious persecution, 14
Revere, Paul, 24, 98
Reynolds, Joshua, 223
Richeliu River, 72
riflemen, 46, 47, 97
Robinson, Beverly, 163, 177; John Andre and, 171; letter from Benedict Arnold, 182; letter to Benedict Arnold, 149-150, 172, 183, 190; letter to George Washington, 215-216; letter to Henry Clinton, 197; meeting with Benedict Arnold, 192; request to meet with Benedict Arnold, 181; on science and technology, 213; September 20th secret meeting, 185, 187
Robinson House, 163, 171, 179, 180, 182, 185, 198, 209, 214, 226
Robinson's Landing, 212
Rochambeau, John Baptiste, 160-161
row galleys, 87
Royal Highland Emigrants, 55, 60
Royal Savage (ship), 87

Saratoga, Battle of, 123-131
Sayer, Robert, 81
Schuyler, Hon Yost, 118
Schuyler, Philip, 33-34, 42, 75-76, 83, 115, 116, 132, 167; Benedict Arnold and, 38-39; Continental Congress and, 121; funds to form a northern army, 121; home of, 10; letter from Benedict Arnold, 66, 74; war council and, 84
Second Continental Congress, 28, 31
2nd Dragoons, 168, 169, 175, 201, 204, 212, 218, 219
Seneca Indians, 84, 115
Senter, Isaac, 44, 48, 50, 51, 63-64
Seven Years War, 21, 70-72
Sharpe, James, 134
Sheldon, Elisha, 168, 169

Siege of March-May 1780, 99
Siege of Yorktown, 231
Silliman, Gold, 103
Skenesboro, 86
skinners, 200, 217
Skowhegan Falls, 47
sloops, 87
smallpox, 67, 84
Smith, Joshua Hett, 172, 177–178, 180, 182–183; acquittal, 222; arrest of, 215–216; Benedict Arnold and, 236–237; escorting John Andre, 198–202; George Washington and, 210; James Livingston and, 167; Livingston, James, 165–166; mansion of, 151, 165, 185, 199, 225; meeting with John Andre, 192–194; midnight meeting with John Andre, 191; at Robinson House, 180; September 20th secret meeting, 185–187; sneaking out of prison, 222; transport to Tappan, New York, 218–219; trial at Tappan, New York, 221–222
Smith, Mark, 44
Smith, William, 165, 204
smuggling, 12, 20, 22, 24, 96
snipers, 61
soldiers: cowhides for, 57–58; provisions for, 50; self-inoculation by, 67; starvation of, 50
Sons of Liberty, 12–13, 20
Soviet Union, 123–131
Spain, 144
Spencer, Joseph, 100
Spitfire (ship), 87, 88
Spring, Samuel, 44
spy ring, 109, 144, 152, 167
St. Clair, Arthur, 99, 112
St. Francis Indians, 42
St. Lawrence River, 41, 42, 51–52, 54–56, 65, 68, 73, 88
St. Leger, Barry, 112, 118–119
Stamp Act, 19; Samuel Adams and, 20
Stark, John, 114, 115
Stephen, Adam, 99
Sterling, William, 99, 162
Stony Point, 153, 162
Success (ship), 87
Sullivan, John, 14, 74, 83, 84; arrival at St. Johns, 75
Supreme Executive Council of Pennsylvania, 229
Sutherland, Andrew, 189–190, 213
Sutherland, Edwin, 193
Sword's Farm, 123

Tallmadge, Benjamin, 174, 175–176, 209–211, 219, 226, 235–236; Benedict Arnold and, 236; capture of John Andre, 204–206, 209–211; letter to George Washington, 209; trial of John Andre, 220–222
Talmadge, Ben, 168
Tappan, New York, 189, 220–222

Tarrytown, 204
Teller's Point, 181, 197
Ternay, Charles Louis, 179
Terrible Carrying Place, 48
Thomas, Jeff, 83
Thomas, John, 70–71
throat distemper, 16–17
Tory, 13
Tracy, Nathaniel, 43
trading business, 19
Trumbull (ship), 87
Trumbull, John, 226
Tryon, William, 103–105
Tuscarora Indians, 115, 117
Tyonajanegen, 136

undeground survivalists, 13
Underhill, Isaac, 202
Underhill, Sarah, 202

Valcour Island, 89
Van Schaick Mansion, 223
Van Schaick's Island, 121
Van Wart, Isaac, 204, 217
Varick, Richard, 180–181, 211
Verplank Point, 180, 181, 190
veterans, 235; assistance for, 146
Village of Gilbert, 51
Villefranche (Jean-Louis-Ambroise de Genton), 207
volunteers, 43–44, 217
von Steuben, Baron Friedrich Wilhelm, 141
Vulture (ship), 171, 174, 181, 182–183, 185, 189–191, 192, 193, 196, 197, 210, 212, 227

Warner, Jemima, 49
Warren, Joseph, 26, 36, 146
warships, British, 55, 57, 68, 72, 84, 88, 92–93, 93, 95. See also Vulture (ship)
Washington (ship), 87
Washington, George, 22, 28, 109, 181, 212–213; accusation of treason against Schuyler, 10; actions of, 238–239; arrival at Cambridge, Mass., 36; Benedict Arnold and, 41–44, 47, 96, 99–100, 106, 142–143, 211, 214–216; capture of Dorcester Heights, 66–67; casualties in defeats, 95; Christmas night raid in 1776, 97; Continental Congress and, 36–37; council of war, 169; distrust of Horatio Gates, 120–121; on Egg Harbor attack, 147; estate in Mount Vernon, 12; headquarters, 96, 106, 161, 224; Joshua Smith and, 165; letter from Benedict Arnold, 99–100, 145–146, 148, 163, 173, 177, 215; letter from Benjamin Tallmadge, 209; letter from Beverly Robinson, 215–216; letter to Benedict Arnold, 96, 169; letter to George Washington, 217; letter to John Hancock, 107; Marquis de Lafayette and, 143; in Morristown, New Jersey, 155; on mutiny, 155; public reprimand of Benedict Arnold, 157; retreats, 95; spy ring, 109, 152; at Valley Forge, 140
Washington, Martha, 36

Wayne, Anthony, 153, 162
West Point, 162–164, 235–236
White House, 151, 165, 185, 199, 225
Wilkinson, James, 127
Williams, Abraham, 204
Williams, David, 217
Women's Hall of Fame, 49
Wool, Isiah, 64
Wooster, David, 83; Benedict Arnold and, 66, 68–70; complaints of high-handedness, 69; in Montreal, 58; in Ridgefield, Conn., 103–104Yale College University, 22
Yale University, 17, 18
Yohn, Frederick C., 81, 137
York, Penn.: relocation of capital to, 139

www.ingramcontent.com/pod-product-compliance
Lightning Source LLC
Chambersburg PA
CBHW021938290426
44108CB00012B/883